BugWater

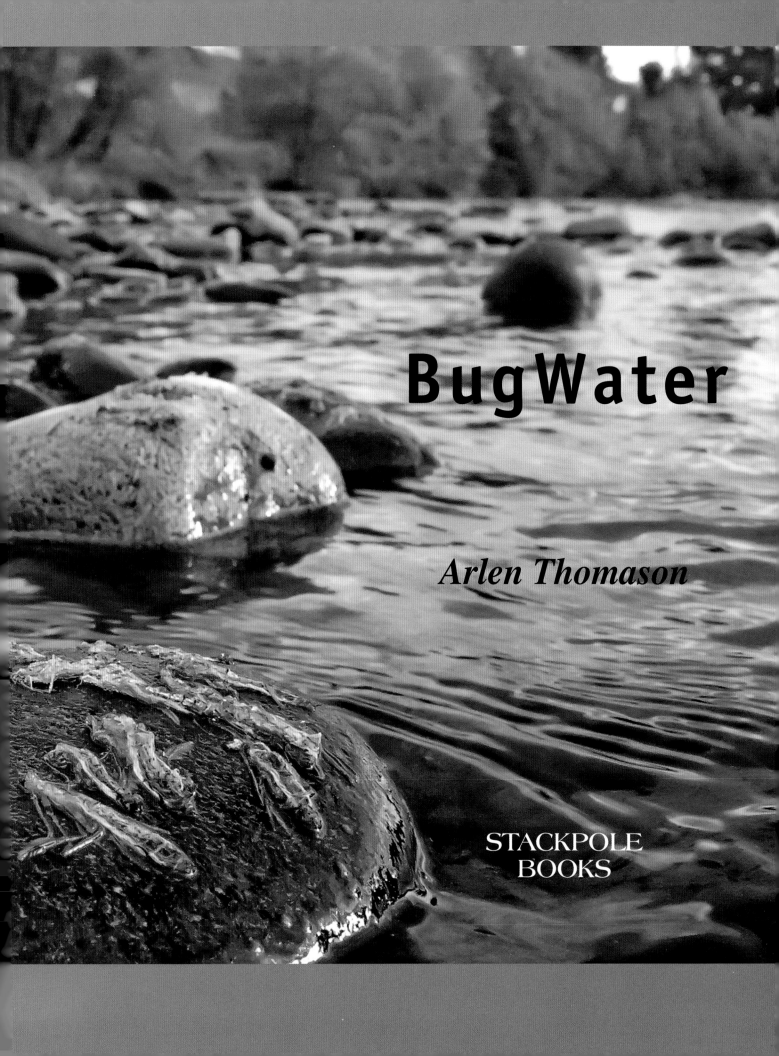

BugWater

Arlen Thomason

STACKPOLE
BOOKS

Published by
STACKPOLE BOOKS
5067 Ritter Road
Mechanicsburg, PA 17055
www.stackpolebooks.com

Printed in China

10 9 8 7 6 5 4 3 2 1

First edition

Photographs by the author except where noted
Drawings by William Marshall

Library of Congress Cataloging-in-Publication Data

Thomason, Arlen Read.
    BugWater / Arlen Thomason. — 1st ed.
        p. cm.
    Includes index.
    ISBN 978-0-8117-0505-9
 1. Fly fishing. I. Title.
    SH456.T495 2010
    799.12'4—dc22
                        2009016078

To Suz,
whose support and patience during the preparation of this book
went far beyond the call of duty;

and

To the members of Westfly.com,
whose encouragement provided motivation to complete the project

Contents

Acknowledgments

The individuals who have influenced this book in ways large and small are many, but some deserve special mention. Bill Marshall has been not only a valued fishing companion, but also contributed his wonderful fly drawings and created all the diagrams. Rick Hafele taught me a lot about aquatic insects in person and in print and provided an expert's opinion whenever it was needed. Monica Mullen, Pete Olson, Brian Marz, Bill Marshall, and Mike Caldwell contributed flies that were both well proven and beautifully crafted. John Hyde of Yamsi Ranch undertook a short-notice collection of *Hexagenia* nymphs from the Williamson River and arranged to quickly transport them 175 miles so they would arrive alive and in good condition. Gene Trump provided not only advice and support, but also acted as a link to editors and publishers. The members of Westfly.com served as a sounding board; their unflagging encouragement and appreciation of my work motivated me to push on. Jay Nichols of Headwater Books noticed my project, championed the idea of getting it published in book form, and provided expert editorial advice. Judith Schnell, Debra Smith, Amy Lerner, Tracy Patterson, and the rest of the crew at Stackpole Books took a manuscript and photographs and masterfully transformed them into a real book. Last, but certainly not least, my wife Margit Susan read every word and provided valuable critical feedback. She also tolerated my strange preoccupation with weird creatures, long hours on the water, and abdication of household duties for many months while I wrote the manuscript.

Bugwater is much more appealing than it sounds.

Introduction

Bugwater is a soggy place inhabited or visited by creepy crawly creatures we collectively, if imprecisely, call bugs. The scientist within me resists this colloquial usage of bug for any ill-defined (small) crawling, hopping, flying, or wriggling member of the animal kingdom, since the word technically and properly denotes only a specific subcategory of the animal class Insecta. Yet in the popular vernacular, no other term quite captures the diverse conceptual collection of diminutive fauna that inhabits our gardens, skies, ponds, and rivers. And if we can use the inexact expression *bug* to describe the critters, then it seems not too far of a stretch to coin the term *bugwater* for the aquatic habitats where many of them can be found. This book then is about bugwater, the bugs living in or falling into such places, and the fish that eat them.

Contrary to the visions it may conjure, bugwater is often both beautiful and healthy. The most pristine streams, rivers, and lakes are usually the ones with the largest and most diverse populations of aquatic insects. In fact, bug populations are a primary measure by which water quality is assessed. Some types of what environmental quality professionals call aquatic macroinvertebrates are quite sensitive to pollution, temperature, and other disturbances. Their absence is often a very bad sign. Water with many different kinds of bugs living in it is healthy water. And because the healthiest waters are usually those least disturbed by the activities of man, they generally rate high on the aesthetics scale, too. I can think of few places I would rather be than on good bugwater.

Some years ago I decided to get serious about fly-fishing entomology. I knew vaguely that the flies at the end of my line were intended to mimic mayflies, caddisflies, stoneflies, or terrestrials. Terms like salmonflies, blue-winged olives, and even *Baetis* were bandied about fly shops and along river banks. Every shop in each area I fished would push a new or different fly; I bought them all. But like many fly fishers, not only was I short on key details, I lacked a general grasp of the big picture—some way to put everything together into coherent concepts.

Which insects were my flies attempting to imitate? By what rationale should I select one fly over another? In any particular stream, river, or lake, which bugs were likely to be there? Where and when should I look for them? How did their behaviors affect optimum fishing strategies? I realized that I was not well grounded in the basics and the particulars of the trout prey that my flies purported to represent.

So I set out to change that. My quest was aided immensely by my retirement from a twenty-five-plus-year career in biomedical research as a molecular biologist, and a move to the banks of Oregon's McKenzie River. At that location I was able to conduct on-the-spot studies of bug behavior. There was nothing quite like having a natural laboratory in my own backyard to speed up the learning process. Moreover, I now had time to consult the accumulated wisdom of the printed page, in the form of both popular writings and the scientific literature.

As I read books on fly-fishing entomology, some of them quite good, I was struck by the general paucity and often poor quality of the bug photographs within many of them. Quite frequently they were small, fuzzy pictures of dead bugs sitting in a lab dish or seining net. I assigned myself the project of changing that. Not only did such illustrations make it difficult to identify a bug from its picture, but these bugs deserved more. Viewed up close, they present striking visages, forms, and colors that should be exhibited in their most favorable light. That's what I've attempted to do in this book.

If there is one thing I've learned that I hope rubs off on the reader, it's that bugs are interesting and fun, in and of themselves—even apart from the role they play in our angling pursuits. Fishing might sometimes be slow, but bug watching never is. There is always something new and fascinating to learn, and I've had some fine adventures during my bug outings. Many of those adventures have been shared via chronicles that I posted on the forums of West fly.com. I've adapted some of those stories for this book, and though I know a lot more about bugs now than when I started, I've tried to preserve the wonder of discovery that

Oregon's Blitzen River offers bugs, water, and trout in a picturesque setting.

I felt when I learned things for the first time. I hope that comes through in my narratives, and that the reader shares some of the amazement that I have experienced.

Over the last twenty years, I've fished across most of the American West, and the information you will find here is representative of much of the region. Furthermore, many of the insects covered have close relatives, or are themselves, found across North America; and the flies that imitate them in one place often work well in another. Nevertheless, my observations are heavily grounded in western Oregon. Having a fine home water within a stone's throw has been a huge benefit, and I've taken advantage of it. The McKenzie River has taught me a lot, without a doubt.

This book is organized loosely around the seasons, starting with spring and progressing to winter. But where I've deemed it logical and appropriate to discuss a bug out of season—i.e., when it's not hatching—I've done so. For example, greater green drake mayflies come up in chapter 8 in a narrative that takes place in early summer, when they are hatching. But I've included the lesser green drakes there too, even though they don't hatch in most places until later in the summer. Both are in the genus *Drunella*, have very similar appearances except for a small difference in size, live in similar places, and are matched by similar flies; so it makes sense to discuss them together.

I've attempted here to span the gap between science and art. I hope I've introduced enough science to spur interest, while employing language that will be accessible to all. At the same time, I've endeavored to show the subjects of the book at their best. It is up to the readers to decide how well I've succeeded.

1

The Morphing Mayfly

The unique ancestry and life history of the mayfly

Two hundred million years ago a Jurassic fish rose to the water surface to gulp down an emerging mayfly. The fish wasn't a trout. It would take millions of years longer for nature to come up with the salmonids, but mayflies were on the piscatorial menu long before trout—or even dinosaurs—were around.

Although the assailant may have had the upper hand for the moment, in a larger sense the mayfly would get the last laugh. This fish and many piscine families of the period would eventually become extinct, but the descendants of the mayfly would survive, little changed, into modern times. Of all the orders of winged insects living today, mayflies are among the oldest. And in some ways, they are among the strangest. Mayflies live in two worlds, water and air, at different stages of their lives and change radically to meet the demands of the two environments.

Their nymphal youth is a time of gills, as well as a time to eat, grow, and avoid being eaten. Mayfly adulthood is a time of breathing air, of winged flight, and of brief but frenzied sex. These traits they share with some other aquatic insects, but one peculiarity is theirs alone: among all living insects, they are the only ones with *two* separate winged-adult stages. Every other living insect ceases molting once it has developed functional wings and is capable of flight, but almost all mayflies molt again into a more mature form. Entomologists refer to the two adult (winged) stages as subimagoes and imagoes, while anglers call them duns and spinners.

Many species of mayflies love the clean, rushing waters of mountain streams.

Mayflies are, without question, the insects most associated with fly fishing, and they will come up many times throughout this book. Anyone who wants to develop a deeper understanding of our sport is well advised to start by learning some things about the mayfly life cycle and life habits. So let's review a few of the basics right now.

AN ABBREVIATED LIFE CYCLE

We'll start with the life cycle. If you think back to your high school biology days, you may dimly remember terms like *complete* and *incomplete* metamorphosis. They refer to the stages that different kinds of insects pass through on their way to adulthood. Many of the more recently evolved and most advanced categories of insects seem to have added a stage of development not found in their more primitive cousins. They are the ones said to have complete metamorphosis, and they embrace all the latest and fanciest steps.

The most famous example of complete metamorphosis is the butterfly. It starts life as an egg, which hatches and turns into a larva (caterpillar), which spins a cocoon and becomes a relatively inactive pupa, which eventually emerges into a startlingly different-looking winged imago (adult). Some aquatic insects (like caddisflies, midges, and crane flies) follow this sequence as well, and we will come to them shortly in subsequent chapters of this book.

Other more primitive types of insects seemingly skip a step during development, apparently preferring a simpler progression: incomplete metamorphosis. Among these are stoneflies and our immediate subject, mayflies. They progress from egg to nymph (larva) to imago, leaving out the pupa stage.

Why should you remember the difference between complete and incomplete metamorphosis, and the types of insects that undergo each scheme of development? Besides the satisfaction of understanding nature a little better, the differences have important ramifications for our fishing strategies. If you know that an insect goes through a pupal stage, and when and where it is likely to be found, you'll be in a much better position to choose flies and techniques that match the prey on which your target fish may be feeding. And if you know that an insect doesn't have a pupal phase (e.g., mayflies), then you won't fish with an imitation of a bug type that doesn't even exist. (See chapter 3 for a full discussion of the two insect developmental pathways.)

For the mayflies, there is only one juvenile, aquatic form to remember, and that is the larva (though for insects undergoing incomplete metamorphosis, the larva is more often called a nymph). But as already mentioned, the winged-terrestrial portion of their lives is unique in that two forms exist, dun and spinner. We'll come back shortly to this very special case and the process involved in the dun-to-spinner transformation.

GROWING UP WET

Mayflies have adapted to a range of water conditions, from fast-flowing rapids and riffles to pools and slower back eddies, and even to still waters. They reach the largest numbers and greatest variety of species in temperate regions, where the water gets neither too hot nor too cold. The environs where a mayfly nymph lives, in terms of both macro- and microhabitats, has a major bearing on its body shape, lifestyle, and feeding habits.

Many mayflies that live in slower water are excellent swimmers, and have evolved a body shape that is streamlined and designed for efficient propulsion through the water, not unlike the bodies of fish. Their tails often sport interlocking hairs that give them a finlike capability. Those in this category are referred to as "swimmer-type" nymphs. Others live in fast-running rapids and riffles, and have developed body shapes and mechanisms to cope with the swift currents and avoid being washed into the drift. They keep a low profile as they cling tightly to the rocks and are called "clinger-type" nymphs. Yet other mayfly nymphs live in a variety of more intermediate currents and make their living crawling about the bottom looking for food; they are in the category of "crawler-type" nymphs. Finally, there are a group of mayfly nymphs that live much of their lives in burrows within the bottom mud, gravel, or silt; appropriately enough these are called "burrower-type" nymphs. We'll talk further about the different categories of mayfly nymphs as we encounter them in ensuing chapters.

Mayfly nymphs are predominantly herbivores, feeding on either living or dead vascular plants or algae. The manner in which they acquire their food places them in the category of either "collector" or "scraper." Collectors scout about the bottom for small plant particles. Scrapers scrape; that is, they use their mouthparts to dislodge the thin layers of algae that grow on the upper surfaces of rocks and sticks in shallow water. Both collectors and scrapers have head shapes and mouthparts adapted for their particular means of making a living.

After a mayfly egg hatches into a nymph, the nymph immediately sets about consuming its favorite food items, and in good times its growth is rapid. Since it wears its skeleton on the outside—an exoskeleton—this soon presents a problem. While the insect inside grows and expands, the exoskeleton does not. Before long the exoskeleton is literally bursting at the seams. The bug then steps out, and soon grows a new, roomier exoskeleton to protect itself. This happens many times during a nymph's life; and each interval between molts is called an *instar*. Mayfly nymphs are the instar champions among aquatic insects. The number varies between species and growth conditions, but some mayfly nymphs may pass through as many as forty-five instars!

Brown dun (*Ameletus*) nymphs exhibit the streamlined shape and paddlelike tails typical of swimmer-type mayflies.

Clinger-type mayfly nymphs like this March brown (*Rhithrogena*) are flattened from top to bottom and cling tightly to rocks, allowing rushing water to flow up and over them.

Strong, robust legs and blocky shapes are frequently observed for crawler-type mayfly nymphs, such as this western green drake (*Drunella grandis*).

Burrower-type mayfly nymphs exhibit modifications of the head to assist with digging, and large gills along the abdomen as an aid to respiration in the oxygen-poor environment of their burrows.

A newly hatched blue-winged olive (*Baetis*) mayfly dun gets its first look at the world above the water surface.

In the later instars, a nymph is not only increasing in size, but is also busy developing some of the structures and organs of the adult it will become. Though many of these organs are concealed from external view, the developing wings become increasingly visible. They are contained within structures called wing pads that become larger and darker as the nymph approaches the moment when the nymphal exoskeleton will split one last time. Instead of a larger nymph, after the final nymphal instar, out pops a winged, air-breathing form—the subimago, or dun.

The emergence, or hatching, of the dun from the nymph is a very big event for a fly fisher. So big, in fact, that I'll devote a considerable amount of time to it in the next chapter. Duns may emerge from the nymph in the water or on its surface; or less frequently, the nymphs may first crawl out upon rocks or sticks protruding from the water, and hatch there. In either case the duns quickly fly to nearby trees or bushes to prepare for the final transformation in their eventful lives.

INIMITABLE ADOLESCENCE

Since duns are young adults that have not quite reached maturity, it is fair to compare them to adolescents. Their bodies have taken on the basic appearance of adults but have still to develop their full capabilities. Once they leave the water and reach the nearby vegetation, mayfly duns sit around in a languid state, doing little. (Not unlike, some cynics might say, many adolescents of all stripes.) This stage doesn't last long—one to several days, depending on the species and temperature. (For the blue-winged olive [*Baetis* sp.] dun shown in the photos, it lasted twenty-three hours, when kept at about 67 degrees F.) Then a most

A blue-winged olive mayfly dun prepares to molt by getting its feet set in a good position.

Next it slowly lowers its wings out to the sides.

A little more effort and the front legs are free, followed by the hind legs and one wing.

With both wings free, a little flapping adds power to the pulling effort.

remarkable thing takes place—the molt to spinner. The accompanying sequence of photographs documents a male blue-winged olive's dun-to-spinner transformation, a signature event that distinguishes mayflies from all other insects.

In the example pictured, the molt took about four minutes from beginning to end. So if you are watching a dun and hoping to see the molt, you have to pay attention or you will miss it. (Trust me; I learned this the hard way.) The ease or difficulty of the molt can be dramatically affected by environmental conditions. In the wrong circumstances, the molt to spinner may not take place at all. That's probably a major part of the reason why mayfly

hatches occur when they do. The dun often needs fairly narrow ranges of air temperature and humidity to get ready for the molt, and is especially sensitive to desiccation.

For example, blue-winged olive duns that emerge in the winter and early spring often do so on humid, even rainy days. The species that hatch in the coastal Northwest usually get a lot of days with those conditions. When outdoor temperatures are in the 40–50 degrees F range, they will molt to spinners in about four days. However, I've found that if the duns are brought inside my house, which is heated to about 67 degrees and has much lower humidity than the outdoors, they molt in twenty-three to twenty-four

3

The top of the dun's thorax splits open and the new spinner thorax emerges, followed by the head. It's amazing to see the covering of the old "eyeballs" left behind during the process.

4

With some steady pulling, most of the emerging spinner becomes visible.

7

The last step, extracting the tails, seems to be the hardest part, and many molted spinners drag around the shed casing on their tails for quite some time. One or more tails are often broken off during the process.

8

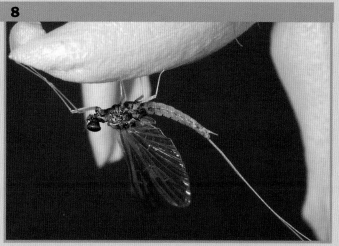

This spinner was successful in completely freeing itself from the shed exoskeleton, and rests for a bit while drying and hardening its wings.

hours. But the indoor duns show a much higher molting failure rate. About two of three will show signs of trying to molt, planting their feet and lowering their wings, but fail to split the exoskeleton of the dorsal thorax. After another day or so, they die without molting. Of the ones that are successful in splitting open the old exoskeleton, a much higher percentage of the indoor, low-humidity duns fail to completely shed the old shuck. When the humidity is too low, mayfly duns are susceptible to drying out, which causes the exoskeleton to become tougher, less pliant, and less well lubricated on its inner surface. As a result, it is more difficult to tear it open and slide out of it.

WIRED FOR SEX

For a mayfly dun lucky enough to make it to a spinner, it's all about sex. Spinners don't stop to eat or drink; in fact, they have lost the nymphal mouthparts and digestive system that would allow them to do so. Reproductive activities are pursued with such vigor that at the end there is nothing left, and the spent spinners drop dead. The whole affair is usually over within a few days; these bugs are not called Ephemeroptera—think ephemeral—for nothing.

Back in the days before dinosaurs, adults of early mayflylike insects were not so single-minded. The fossil record suggests that the primitive ancestors—paleopter-

Cutthroat trout are fervent mayfly fans.

ans—of today's mayflies had functioning mouthparts, and presumably digestive systems. Somewhere along the evolutionary line adult mayflies apparently "decided" that eating was a childish activity. "Better to devote all one's adult mass and energy to the production, fertilization, and deposition of eggs," those ancient mayfly grandparents must have thought.

In the case of mayflies, sex kills. For example, March brown mayflies that hatch in the cool of early spring will mate, lay eggs, and die within two to three days of becoming spinners in the wild. But I've found that if kept in screen cages, where they experience the same environmental conditions as wild bugs, but don't get the chance to mate, the spinners can live about seven to thirteen days.

WHY MAKE THE CHANGE?

So why two distinct winged stages? Entomologists have been deliberating that issue for some time. No one knows for sure, but differences in the structure and function of duns and spinners may provide some clues.

Some of the differences between the two stages are most apparent in the males of many mayfly species. Compared with duns, the forelegs and tails of male spinners are usually much longer and the eyes often much larger, especially in the upper regions. Mayfly mating typically occurs within groups of insects in the air, and males use their longer front legs to reach up and grab females from below. The larger eyes on top of the head are probably useful for spotting females above them, in a throng of males.

Long tails are thought to provide additional stability to spinners in flight, acting as rudders that allow tricky aerial maneuvers. Duns don't fly much after leaving the water, usually undertaking a short flight to the nearest tree or bush and settling in for a long rest. Spinner males, on the other hand, need all the flying help they can get as they often hover in groups waiting for a female to fly through, darting to grab her before another suitor does. It's mostly the conspicuous, amorous males that you see dancing in clouds over or near the water, but after mating in midair they usually fly off to expire on land. The females, when they come back to lay eggs and die, are the ones that most often end up on the surface and are eaten by trout.

Well and good, you may say, but why not just go directly from nymph to spinner? The answer may lie in the requirements for transitioning from water to air. Most mayfly duns emerge from the nymphal exoskeleton in the water. Yet they do not get wet! Water does not adhere to them; they are *hydrofuge*, in science-speak. Being hydrofuge is important to an emerging dun, because a wet mayfly may not fly (sorry, pun intended). Place a spinner, which does get wet, in water and it is usually stuck there for good. Drop in a dun and it will frequently extract itself and fly away. Once a dun pulls itself above the surface film, it floats high and dry (a possible clue for those tying imposters to imitate them).

The key to the dun's relative water resistance is in its outer covering. The wings, body, and legs are covered with tiny hairs, called microtrichia, that repel water and prevent it from accumulating on the surface. While useful for waterproofing, microtrichia are considered to be a liability when it comes to flying. Witness the lumbering flight of most duns compared with the relatively fast and agile aerial moves of a spinner. Hence spinners shed the "wetsuit" of the dun to reveal a slick wing and smooth body more suitable for flying than for exiting the water.

MAKING SENSE OF IT ALL

So now it all begins to make sense. A winged mayfly emerging from water to air needs to stay dry, and we see the necessary equipment in the dun stage. An adult mayfly trying to beat out competing suitors for the most enticing mate needs to be adroit on its wings, in addition to possessing all the tools for interaction with the opposite sex—features of the spinner stage. This explanation may not be exactly correct, but it represents a reasonable scientific hypothesis to fit the evidence. If the evidence changes, so may the explanation. In the meantime, it's all great fun delving into the intricacies of a life form so favored by one of our own favorites—hard-fighting trout.

2
Marching into Spring

March brown mayflies and the anatomy of a hatch

While the signature biological hallmark of the mayfly may be its transformation from one adult winged stage (dun) into a second winged stage (spinner), it is the emergence of the dun from the nymph that is the most glorious of events to a fly fisher. The "hatch" is what nearly every ardent trout angler lives for. The quality of the hatch often goes hand in hand with the quality of the fishing. If we visit a new river, one of the first questions we ask is: "What's hatching?"

And in many parts of North America and Western Europe, after a winter of waiting, the first answer to that question will be: "March browns." Perhaps no other insect is steeped in more fly-fishing lore than this most anticipated of mayflies. Usually arriving with the onset of spring, the hatch signals that good times have returned. The subject of our esteem is a member of the "clinger" clan of mayflies, a subtype with dorsoventrally flattened nymphs adapted for clinging tenaciously to rocks in fast water, and belonging to the family Heptageniidae.

In all locales, the adults are on the medium-large side for a mayfly, usually a number 12–14 hook size, and are of a generally brownish color with pronounced wing venation. But despite having the same common name, March browns are not the same bug the world over. The genus and species going by that name varies from place to place. In Europe, the proper scientific name of the March brown is *Rhithrogena germanica*. In eastern and middle North America, it is *Maccaffertium vicarium* (formerly *Stenonema vicarium*

Cool riffles are ideal bugwater for March brown nymphs.

A March brown (*Rhithrogena morrisoni*) nymph's flattened, shovel-shaped face helps reduce water resistance in swift currents. Body length = 12mm.

and *S. fuscum*, two morphological variations now considered to be the same species), and in the western part of the continent it is primarily *Rhithrogena morrisoni*.

WHAT'S IN A NAME?

Given that there are a variety of mayfly species stretching over two continents that answer to the same common name, you might assume they share this sobriquet because they are all brown and all hatch in March. But you would be just half right—they are all brown, or at least brownish. And the European March brown and the western North American March brown do hatch in a February to April time frame, depending on the latitude, altitude, and weather.

But the U.S. eastern/midwestern March brown doesn't usually start hatching until late May, and even later in some places. So why is it called a March brown, if it doesn't hatch in March, and doesn't even belong to the same genus as the other March browns? And for that matter, are blue-winged olives (chapter 16) the same everywhere, do they belong to the same species, and do they have olive bodies and blue wings? Are all pale morning

duns (chapter 4) of the same species, are they pale, and do they hatch in the morning?

If the common names of insects important to fly fishing have left you scratching your head in bewilderment, you aren't alone. In the beginning I (and doubtless many others) could make no sense of this arcane naming system wherein a March brown may hatch in June; a blue-winged olive may be any of several unrelated species, some of which are neither blue nor olive; and a red quill is not a colored feather, but rather the male of a certain eastern U.S. species of mayfly whose female counterpart goes by the entirely different moniker of Hendrickson. It's as if some club of tweed-wearing insiders got together and decided on a secret, nonsensical naming code that would have meaning only to the initiated.

But take heart, because I'm about to give you the key to the code—even though it may still leave you shaking your head in bemusement, and no more satisfied with the situation. A sort of reverse logic has been selectively applied. To wit: **many insects central to fly fishing are named for artificial flies tied to imitate them, and not the other way around.**

So Blue-Winged Olive was the name of an artificial fly first tied to match a certain mayfly of those colors, and over time the name was transferred to the insect it imitated. The same fly was subsequently used to mimic other mayflies of similar colors, whether or not they were closely related to the original insect; and they eventually took on the name of the artificial fly as well. Just for good measure, the moniker was also transferred to other mayflies that *were* close relatives of the original one, but may have had *different* colors. All very straightforward, no?

And in case you're wondering, a similar naming progression has occurred for pale morning duns. While the original insect imitated by the first Pale Morning Dun fly pattern may have been mutely colored and hatched primarily in the A.M., the name pale morning dun and its acronym PMD are now assigned to a variety of mayflies of varying hues, hatch times, and pedigrees. As a result, you will often hear the term PMD applied indiscriminately to almost any lightly colored, medium-size mayfly whose exact identity is unknown to the observer.

Similarly, Red Quill was first the name of an artificial fly tied to imitate the red-eyed male of the eastern mayfly *Ephemerella subvaria*, and subsequently the appellation was applied to the bug itself. But don't speak of a female

red quill. The opposite sex of this species has a different enough appearance that another fly was developed to represent it, and named Hendrickson in honor of a friend of its inventor. Yes, you guessed it—the female *E. subvaria* is now called Hendrickson by the cognoscenti.

Finally, getting back around again to our March browns—remember the March browns, subject of this chapter?—the name was originally applied to a fly tied at least since the thirteenth century to imitate the mayflies of brownish color found in the British Isles. The first reference to it was in—probably the oldest English-language angling text on record—the *Treatyse of Fysshynge with an Angle*, published in 1496. The flies useful for catching fish there were listed by month. For March, it recommends "The Dun Fly: the body of dun wool and the wings of the partridge." In the late 1600s, the English angler James Chetham developed a variation that he called the March Brown, a fly that has remained essentially unchanged to this day.

A couple of centuries later, fly anglers in the eastern United States discovered that the British March Brown fly worked quite well when presented to trout feeding on a brown and tan mayfly (*M. vicarium*) found in that part of the country. Following convention, the authentic bug took

Keeping a low profile and clinging tightly to their home rocks allow March brown (*R. morrisoni*) nymphs to hold their position in even the fastest flows.

the name of the imposter. As the sport spread westward across America, the same fly proved a good substitute for another similar-appearing mayfly (*R. morrisoni*), and lent its name to yet one more bug.

So there you finally have an explanation for the ambiguities and inconsistencies of the name March brown, and why it is folly to look for too much logic in the common names of insects important to fly fishers. But convoluted as it may seem, this system of nomenclature does have a certain charm. The charm is usually appreciated only after one becomes enthralled with the artistry of fly tying and the history of the sport.

MARCH BROWN NYMPHS

Like all mayflies, March browns spend the overwhelming majority of their lives in the water, as nymphs. The nymphs prefer fast, clean water. And they're built for it. Clinging to rocks with their low profiles, the swift current flows right over the top of them with little resistance.

Members of the genus *Rhithrogena*, including our western March browns, have a further adaptation that allows them to hang onto rocks in faster currents than even other clinger-type mayflies. The series of gills that line the lateral edges of the abdomen in all mayflies are modified in this genus to form a sort of suction cup that helps grip the rocks. This suction cup morphology is achieved by extending and overlapping the first pair of gills underneath the nymph's body, as can be seen in the photograph below. When pressed against a rock—or, as in this case, the glass wall of an aquarium—it forms a tight seal. Anyone who has tried to pull a *Rhithrogena* nymph from its rock knows just how strong this grip can be. What is amazing is that, even while stuck so tightly, these bugs can still scoot with astonishing speed from one side of the rock to the other if disturbed.

Similar to other clinger mayflies (see chapter 6), March brown nymphs have broad heads that are wider than the rest of the body, and big eyes set up on top like those of a flounder. Most *R. morrisoni* nymphs are very dark brown, almost

The presence of enlarged, overlapping gill plates on the first abdominal segment is a key trait for distinguishing *Rhithrogena* nymphs from those of most other clinger mayflies. The gills are semitransparent and usually much harder to see than in the above photo, especially without magnification. So if you don't see them at first, look closer under good lighting before concluding that your nymph is not a March brown.

black. But a substantial subset in some waters has a pronounced reddish cast, especially in the abdominal region.

The nymphs remain hidden from view during bright daylight hours, preferring to hang out in the cracks between rocks or underneath them. In the low-light hours, or sometimes on overcast days, they venture to the top of the rocks where the crops are growing. That is, to the place where the algae and diatom layers are thickest. Clinger mayflies are described as "scrapers," with heads designed for scraping off this thin vegetation. Their mouths are located underneath their shovel-like heads, so they can protect the scraped-off meal from the current long enough to suck it down. This is apparently an excellent system, because many streams support large numbers of clinger mayflies.

During the time of nymphal growth, which takes almost a year, few March brown nymphs fall prey to trout. Hiding under rocks during the day, venturing out by dark while maintaining a firm foothold on their home rock, and ready to scoot at the first sign of danger, they are able to stay out of harm's way. But when the nymphs are mature, sporting large dark wing pads like the ones pictured on page 18, they begin to get restless as thoughts of emergence enter their tiny heads. Many will leave their turbulent homes and migrate to nearby slower water. During the journey, some of them may lose their footholds and get washed into the current. That's when they are at great risk of becoming trout food, and the trout know it. So the days just prior to a hatch are good times to think about fishing a March brown nymph imitation.

DETERMINANTS OF HATCH TIMING

The hatch, of course, is what the trout are really waiting for. Fly fishers wait with no less anticipation. Sometimes we wait, wait, and wait some more, but the hatch doesn't come. Maybe we were on this stream last year at this time and the hatch was prolific, but this year it's weeks late. We go home, and our buddy hits it the next day, returning with tales of an epic hatch. So two days later we go back, sure that this will be the right time. But once again, we are disappointed. What's going on? What determines when these bugs will emerge, and is there any way we can better predict it?

Since this is a question of central and almost overriding importance to me, as well as many fly fishers, I've spent considerable time investigating it. It seems worthwhile to devote some space to what I have learned from my own observations, from perusing fly-fishing publications, and most importantly, from surveying the scientific literature.

Before digging into the details, it's probably useful to comment on some terms and definitions used by fly fishers and the scientists who study insects (entomologists). Fly fishers typically refer to the phenomenon during which an insect transitions from its aquatic phase (nymph or pupa) to its air/land form (usually, adult or imago) as a "hatch," and less often as an "emergence." To an entomologist, hatching refers only to the transition from egg to larva; though emergence is an acceptable scientific description of the water-to-air transfer. Unless specifically noted otherwise, I'll use both hatch and emergence as fly fishers use them—to denote the time when a bug leaves the water.

When we think about hatch timing, I find it helpful to break it down into two conceptual components. Each of these components may involve different processes and have different factors governing it. Let's call the first component of the hatch schedule "long-term timing," and the second component "short-term timing." Long-term timing is concerned with how frequently a hatch occurs (number of hatches per year or years), and in what season. Short-term timing refers to the particular days within the emergence season, and the particular hours within the day during which a given hatch will take place.

Long-term hatch timing is primarily a function of the amount of time required for a newly laid egg to grow and develop into a fully mature larva or preadult, with all the structures of the adult insect and requiring only a molt of the external exoskeleton to complete the transformation. Clearly, if mature wings, genitalia, etc., of the adult have not yet developed, there is no possibility of a hatch occurring anytime soon.

Short-term hatch timing, on the other hand, may be concerned not only with putting the final touches on development of adult structures and physiology; but also, and probably more importantly, on the occurrence of favorable conditions for making the transition from a life in the water to living in air. When a formerly gill-breathing mayfly suddenly pops into the air, think what a shock it must be. I imagine it would be something akin to one of us diving down into the ocean for the first time. Personally, I would want to pick a day and time when the water was warm but not too hot. I would want a strategy for escaping the predators that might await me at water's edge or within the water itself. And if my main purpose in this endeavor were to find a mate (OK, I'm stretching the analogy a bit here), I would want to go when lots of ladies in the same mood were taking the plunge.

LONG-TERM HATCH TIMING

While the picture is far from completely clear, entomologists have strong evidence for the involvement of several factors in the governance of long-term hatch timing in aquatic insects. The most important of these appear to be temperature and photoperiod (daily exposure to light), especially the former. Since rising temperatures and lengthening daylight hours often go hand in hand, it can be difficult to distinguish their effects on growth and development.

It is fairly easy to envision in general terms how water temperature can be important in determining when insect emergence should occur. The pace of growth and development depends on metabolic rate; that is, the rate at which an insect's internal chemical reactions proceed, converting food supplies into body mass and new structures. Those chemical reactions speed up at higher temperatures. Since insects are almost entirely cold-blooded, or unable to regulate body temperature, their metabolic rates are dependent on the surrounding water temperature. So up to a point, rising water temperatures should lead to faster growth and development of mature body parts. A threshold is reached when the deleterious effects of temperatures that are too high counterbalance the beneficial effects of higher metabolic rates.

There is plenty of evidence that our intuitive expectations of the effects of temperature on long-term hatch timing are largely well grounded. For instance, it's well known that spring/summer hatches of particular species start earlier in warmer latitudes, as the water warms there sooner than it does in the more polar regions of a bug's range. Similarly, spring/summer hatches of a species often commence first in the downstream reaches of an individual stream, as the water there tends to warm up before the upstream areas. A warm fall and winter (with warmer average water temperatures) usually leads to earlier than normal spring/summer hatches, whereas the converse is true for a colder than normal autumn/winter.

If it's clear that temperature plays a critical role in aquatic insect growth and development, the ways it exerts its effects are less plain. For instance, does temperature matter only when it is above (or below) a certain threshold? Is the temperature of egg incubation more or less critical than the temperatures experienced by larvae? Are later larval stages more or less sensitive to temperature changes than early stages? If growth and development are retarded during the early stages of egg or larval development by lower than normal temperatures during autumn/early winter; can the larvae catch up, if late winter/early spring temperatures are warmer than normal? Will there be any difference in development rate of larvae that experience a certain average temperature in a relatively constant thermal environment, such as a spring creek, compared with larvae that are subjected to the same average annual temperature but in an environment where temperature varies greatly during the day and from season to season?

In addition, as we ponder these and other questions, we must consider the possible differences among types of insects (such as mayflies, caddisflies, stoneflies, true flies, etc.)—and that even within a type of insect, the differences between genera and species may be large. It thus becomes apparent that scientists and amateur entomologists have an enormously difficult challenge in determining the factors critical to hatch timing for any particular species. Nevertheless, some organizing principles have emerged that help us make sense of many aquatic insect hatches.

One of the most important principles guiding how scientists think about aquatic insect development involves the concept of *thermal summation*, as measured by degree-days. You might think of it loosely as the total amount of heat, above some minimal threshold quantity, to which a developing insect larva has been exposed since it was first deposited in the water as an egg. For the purpose of illustration let's assume that no development toward maturity occurs below 0 degrees C. Then if an egg/larva has been in water with an average temperature of 1 degree for one day, its thermal sum is 1 degree-day. Similarly, if the water has been at 5 degrees for one day, or at 1 degree for five days, then its thermal sum is 5 degree-days.

Entomologists have found that for many aquatic insects, the number of degree-days required for immature stages to reach maturity and undergo emergence is relatively constant. So if the water averages cooler than normal in one year, it will take more days for the insects to hatch; or if warmer, then it will require correspondingly fewer days. For other species, the number of degree-days required to reach maturity may vary with conditions, such as the exact temperature regime, photoperiod, and/or food available. In either case, the thermal sum appears to be an important factor.

Any general model proposed to explain aquatic insect development and emergence must account for the remarkable degree of synchrony in many hatches. In some species, after a year or more of development, the larvae may all emerge into adults over the span of just a few weeks, or even a few days. How is this striking synchronization maintained year after year? Natural differences in development rates of individual larvae, due to variation in nutrition or other factors, would be expected over time to lead to greater and greater disparities in emergence dates, spreading out the hatch. Numerous studies have looked for the cues that signal larvae to terminate development and transform into adults at about the same time.

Several models of synchronization propose that somewhere along the pathway to adulthood, juvenile aquatic insects encounter a developmental roadblock beyond which they cannot pass until they receive an appropriate signal. To help understand how this might serve to synchronize a hatch, let's consider a simplified analogy: a sort of metered off-ramp—instead of on-ramp—for a freeway.

Imagine a group of twenty cars that start at "Eggville" along this freeway and drive, at the same speed, to an exit for "Hatchville." If one car departs Eggville each minute, it will take nineteen minutes for all the cars to get started;

The striking new male dun stands in all its glory for a few more moments on the water surface, resting after its struggle and further drying its wings, before lifting off and heading for the relative safety of the shoreline rocks and bushes.

and assuming there are no obstacles along the way, the last car will arrive at Hatchville nineteen minutes after the first one. Now imagine a second scenario wherein at the exit, there is a very long stoplight—one that lasts thirty minutes, let's say. When the first car reaches the stoplight, the light turns red and the car stops, as eventually do all the rest. We get twenty cars bunched up together at the red light. When the light turns green they all get moving again, with the twentieth car not far behind the first one. And driving at the same speed, they all arrive at the Hatchville destination within a short time span, much less than the nineteen minutes that separated them at the beginning of the journey. The stoplight serves to synchronize the arrival of the cars, even if they started the journey at different times.

In many of the models for aquatic insect development, it is postulated that the synchronization signals (or roadblocks) are primarily thermal. These models propose that there are at least two stages of development, in which the rates are probably different. When an insect larva reaches the end of one stage, it must wait until the water reaches a certain threshold temperature (the green light in our analogy) before it can continue development in the next stage. Both the temperature roadblocks and the differences in development rates between the stages are thought to bring about hatch synchronization.

While growth and development are often linked, and progress simultaneously, they are not the same; and in certain circumstances, one may proceed without the other. Growth is just an increase in body mass, and may occur simply by adding material to existing organs and structures. Development involves building new capabilities and body parts, for example, wings and genitalia, that didn't exist in earlier stages of a juvenile insect.

When a larva reaches one of the developmental road-blocks, it may continue to grow even though further development is temporarily blocked. Thus those larvae, which got a head start (by being laid earlier as eggs, for instance), may keep eating and growing while they wait for the green light allowing further development. They will then be larger than their delayed compatriots when they all get the go-ahead for development of adult organs.

That may be why we see adults of various sizes early in a hatch. As a hatch progresses over a week or two, the average size of emerging adults often tends to get smaller. The larger larvae have quickly matured and hatched, whereas some of their smaller brethren have taken a little longer to fully develop and emerge.

Following a similar logic, colder than normal winters may delay a hatch (by postponing the thermal signals for further development), but when it occurs, the adults often tend to be larger on average. This is because they have had a longer time to grow before final maturation and emergence. The reverse is true for warmer than normal winters.

You may be curious, as I was, about just what happens within an insect larva at the end of these developmental roadblocks that serves to mediate further development. There are good reasons to infer that particular hormones are involved. We are all familiar with how new hormones come into play when humans reach adolescence, with accompanying changes in physiology and behavior. An analogous process occurs when insect larvae transition to advanced juveniles. One or more hormones start being produced, while production of others is turned off, at points along the developmental pathway. In the case of insects, hormonal regulation is often dependent on environmental cues, most notably increases or decreases in temperature of specific magnitudes.

Why do so many aquatic insects go to so much trouble to ensure a relatively synchronous hatch? What are the advantages of hatching over a short time span? We can probably think of quite a few, but here are some that have been postulated by entomologists and for which there is some evidence:

A March brown "cripple" on the water surface, with wings still stuck in the nymphal shuck.

1. To select the optimum time when conditions are most likely to be ideal for the survival and reproduction of the adults. This may include air temperature, humidity, food availability (for those insect types that feed as adults), prevalence and activity of predators, availability of suitable egg deposition sites, etc.
2. To select the optimum time when conditions are most likely to be ideal for the survival and development of eggs and larvae that will shortly follow emergence of the adults. For instance, it may be important to allow enough time for larvae to reach a certain stage before cold weather sets in.
3. To maximize the chances of an adult finding a mate, enabling reproduction of the next generation. This is especially important for insects with short adult lives, most notably mayflies, where there is not much time to wait for the perfect partner to come along.
4. To overwhelm predators with sheer numbers. Hungry mouths may be waiting, but if lots of bugs burst from the water all at once, there is a good chance that enough of them will get through to produce the next generation.

SHORT-TERM HATCH TIMING

So far we have been discussing factors involved in long-term timing of a hatch. Now let's turn our attention to a more microscale, or short-term timing. We may have a fair idea of the approximate time of year that a particular hatch usually occurs, and even whether the hatch is likely to be a few weeks early or late if it has been a warmer or colder winter than normal. But what about the particular days during its season on which a hatch will be prolific or absent? And the exact period of the day that the bugs will choose to emerge?

The conditions in the air and on land may well be more important than conditions in the water as a bug "chooses" when to make the jump. For mayflies, studies have shown that the time spent in the subimago (dun) stage before the insect is able to molt to the imago (spinner) stage is directly related to air temperature. A shorter time as a dun translates into less exposure to predators and other dangers that might cut short a bug's life before it can reproduce. It is probably no accident then that many mayfly hatches occur during the nicest part of the day: midday in winter and spring; but during the hotter days of summer, occurring in the cooler, less desiccating hours of dawn and dusk. Since daily variations in water temperature often lag those of the air, their maxima don't occur at the same times. So an aquatic insect preparing to hatch must have a mechanism for correlating water temperatures with optimum air temperatures.

For some mayflies, it has been concluded that the primary "go" signal is given not on the day of emergence, but on one or two days prior. Emergence of a southeastern U.S. mayfly that hatches at dawn tends to occur when dawn water temperatures—of the preceding day, and to some extent two days before—are above a minimum threshold and exceed the previous day's dawn temperature by at least a certain amount. Thus it seems that these insects somehow monitor the trend in water temperature and not only predict when the optimum for emergence will occur, but commit to it in advance.

You can see how a system like this could go wrong. Just like the weatherman on the evening news, the insects' weather prediction for the coming day (days) may be off. If they have already committed (by, for example, having turned on production of a hormone that irreversibly stimulates molting and emergence), they may have no choice but to carry through with hatching, even in the face of a last-minute change for the worse in the weather. But if the bugs are right most of the time, the strategy will be an overall success.

I think most of us fisher folk look at the weather on the day of the hatch, and try to make conclusions about when hatches of that insect are most likely to occur. If the bugs are emerging today, we note whether it's warm or cool, cloudy or clear, the water temperature, and maybe whether the barometer is steady, rising, or falling. But how many of us have thought to try correlating conditions of the *preceding* hours and days with the occurrence of good hatches?

We don't know how widespread a system like this for governing short-term hatch timing may be, since very few similar analyses have been reported for other aquatic insect species. It would probably be a daunting task for professional entomologists to extend careful, controlled, and costly studies like these to lots of species. It seems to me, however, that there is room for the legions of fly fishers and amateur students of aquatic entomology to add to our knowledge by using a systematic approach and careful observations of our favorite bugs.

Hence I'm trying in my own small ways to make contributions. Living alongside a major western trout stream has assisted those efforts. Besides keeping records of hatch dates, water and air temperatures, and cloudy, rainy, or clear conditions, etc., I've even conducted some limited experiments. For instance, I set up a small aquarium in a shed near the water's edge, and a pump to keep fresh river water flowing through it. Measurements confirmed that the water in the aquarium stays within .5 degrees C of the temperature in the river. One side of the shed is open, but it is under a group of trees, so while the aquarium is lit for the same period as the nearby river, the intensity of the light is considerably reduced. Nevertheless, I have so far found

A March brown (*R. morrisoni*) nymph, viewed from below along with its reflection in the surface film, hangs beneath the surface in preparation for emergence.

Viewed from above, the March brown nymph begins to hatch.

A few seconds more and the folded wings are almost free.

Now the emerging dun's feet grip the surface, and its liberated wings start to expand.

that March brown (*R. morrisoni*) nymphs collected a few days or weeks before their expected hatch time emerge on the same days and times in the aquarium as their counterparts do in the river. More observations and experiments are to come, but at least I know that my basic setup does a pretty good job of replicating natural conditions.

Finally, while we're on the subject of hatches and ways to increase the odds that we anglers will find ourselves on a spot where one is in full swing, don't forget an old standby: birds. In many areas there are birds, which also keep watch for emerging insects, with much sharper eyes than our own and operating from a better vantage point. In the Northwest the dominant watch-bird is the swallow. A group of swallows swarming and dipping repeatedly toward the water surface is an almost sure sign of a hatch in progress. Experienced fly fishers know that watching the birds that watch for the bugs is one of the better ways of locating a hatch in progress.

INSPECTION OF A HATCHING MARCH BROWN

Sometimes a hatch happens so fast, or at such a distance, that it is hard to see exactly what is taking place. I've spent a lot of time studying it, and capturing the steps in photos. Here for your examination is the hatch sequence of a western March brown, *R. morrisoni*, male mayfly.

The first part of the hatching process involves getting from the bottom of the stream or river to the water surface.

3

With the anterior portion of the nymph just breaking the surface, and the rest of its body hanging almost vertically below, the exoskeleton starts to split along the dorsal thorax, and the dun within becomes barely visible.

4

As the split widens, the dun pushes itself farther through the opening.

7

The expanding wings rise to the upright position, and only a last bit of the tails remains to be extracted from the nymphal shuck.

8

Free at last, the remaining task is to fully inflate and harden the wings.

While some authors have reported that western March brown duns often or even usually emerge from the nymph while the latter is still firmly clinging to the rocks on the streambed, others report that the emergence generally occurs at the surface. My own observations, made primarily in western Oregon, support the latter mode. A mature nymph that is ready to undergo emergence, first rises through the water column to just under the surface of the water, aided by gases that build up beneath its exoskeleton.

Sometimes the hatching process begins almost immediately, but often a nymph will hang below the surface for a while, making repeated stabs at breaking the surface tension. It is not unusual for a number of aborted attempts to occur, with a nymph swimming to the surface, hanging for

a few seconds, and then returning to the bottom again. That ritual can be repeated several times before going on to the next step. But finally, everything seems right and the nymph sets up at the surface for the final time.

The whole process in the pictured hatching sequence, from initial splitting of the nymphal exoskeleton to final extraction, took about forty-five seconds.

Note the difference in the eyes of the male and female duns. Those of the male are considerably larger, and often have a red tint. With a little practice it is easy to tell the difference between the male and female March browns by just a glance at their eyes.

The story of the hatching March brown doesn't always have such a happy ending. Many of them encounter trouble

A female March brown dun that had already made it to shore. Body length = 9mm.

March brown spinners of both sexes have elongated tails and forelegs relative to the duns, but in males the lengths are particularly exaggerated. Male eyes are also enlarged in almost all mayfly spinners. Body length = 11mm. Tail length = 25mm.

as the duns try to squirm out of the nymphal exoskeletons, and frequently get stuck. Most often the hang-up comes with those troublesome tails, the last parts to leave the shuck. A dun may struggle for quite some time to free the tails. If it's lucky, one or more of the tails just break off, allowing escape. If not, a dun with a shuck stuck to its tail can't fly off, and that spells disaster. Sometimes the problem is even worse, as for the distressed dun pictured on page 16, which somehow got its tails free but not its wings. A crippled dun like this one is doomed, and will be easy pickings for any nearby trout.

MARCH BROWN SPINNERS

After resting in the bushes and trees for a few days, the March brown duns molt to the sexually mature spinners, with their darker colors; hyaline wings; and, in the case of the males, greatly elongated tails and forelegs.

During the early part of a western March brown emergence, spinners from previous days' hatches often show up over the water as the current day's hatch is coming to a close. Later in the season, the spinner swarms tend to shift more toward the end of the day. Spotting clouds of dancing males is not unusual, and as the spinner ballet progresses, observations of male-female pairs in loving embrace become increasingly common. The spent spinners eventually end up on the water, where trout have been observed to take them occasionally. In my own experience, western March brown spinners don't usually offer as much of a fishing opportunity as the hatching duns do.

FLIES

Catching native rainbow trout that are feeding on hatching March browns can be easy or difficult. I've found that when rising to western March browns (*Rhithrogena*), trout tend to be most cooperative early in the season, and when just moderate numbers of bugs are emerging. At those times I usually start with a size 12 or 14 parachute pattern, in either March brown colors, or very often just a parachute Adams. It's when you see a super hatch in progress and fish rising by the score that things usually get tough. You cast your fly expecting to catch fish right and left, but the trout show their contempt by snatching naturals to the left and right of your fake, rarely touching it. A Comparadun or no-hackle fly will sometimes work better in that situation, but I've had even better luck with emergers.

A cripple/emerger is often a good bet, like the one in the photo tied by my friend and accomplished fly tier, Monica Mullen. With floatant applied to just the deer-hair wing, it floats low in the water like an emerging or crippled dun that has the partially removed nymphal exoskeleton still attached and trailing below. When the fly gets waterlogged, it will sink slightly below the surface, but don't

A **March Brown emerger** with partially released wings and a trailing shuck is a good choice early in the hatch, and for picky trout. Tied by Monica Mullen.

Hook:	TAR 2487, sizes 10–14
Thread:	Dark brown
Tail:	Dark brown poly yarn
Body:	Red peacock herl
Rib:	Fine red wire
Thorax:	Dark brown dubbing
Wing:	Dark deer hair

Underwater view of a Pheasant Tail nymph and its reflection, fished as a dropper from a March Brown dry fly. A PT nymph in this position resembles a nymph trying to penetrate the surface film to hatch.

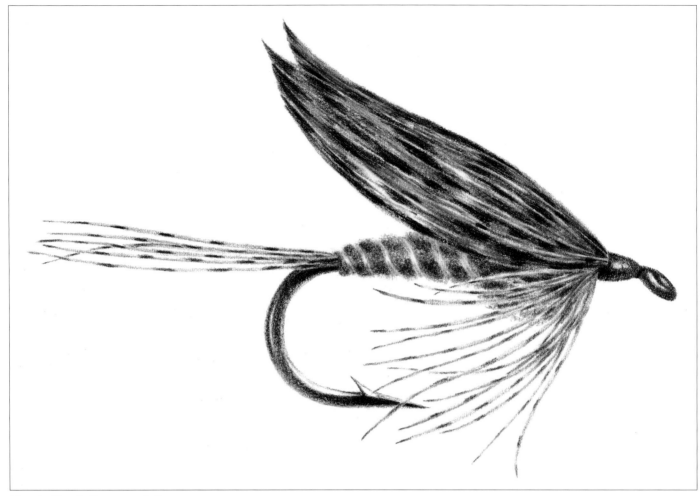

Classic March Brown wet fly.

worry too much about that. Many trout like it even better when it slips underwater.

And when the fish are still uncooperative, I fall back on a technique that occurred to me after watching the behavior of hatching March brown nymphs. As mentioned above, the natural nymphs often spend some time hanging just below the surface film. I've found that a small nymph pattern, like a size 16 Pheasant Tail (PT), suspended from the bend of a dry-fly hook on 6–12 inches of tippet does a good job of mimicking that situation. In a tough hatch I usually catch more fish on the nymph, while still having some chance of catching a fish on the dry fly.

Finally, wet flies that represent half-drowned March brown adults or nymphs that are trying to emerge —like a soft-hackle fly or even the classic March Brown wet pattern developed in England centuries ago—will often take trout when surface flies fail to draw interest. Cast them slightly upstream, mend, and let them drift downstream into the trout water. When the line comes tight and the fly starts to swing in the current, that is the point where most trout will take it. If not, let the fly keep swinging until it is directly downstream, and allow it to hang there for a few seconds before recasting. Some trout just can't resist a fly that seems to be struggling against the current.

3
Grannom Mania

Epic hatches and mating swarms of grannom caddisflies

Bugs by the billions, or so it seemed. I had never seen so many at once. It was one of those days that make you believe insects really do rule the earth.

But for the moment I had no time to contemplate their role in the big scheme of life. I had arrived at the banks of Oregon's McKenzie River late one fine, sunny spring morning to discover a frenzy of writhing bugs and feeding fish already in progress: Grannoms to the left of me, grannoms to the right. Bugs on the water, bugs in flight. Trout slashing here, others slurping there.

With dense clouds of the little caddisflies in the air, an almost solid mat of them covering the water, and new ones constantly popping to the surface, I wondered where to

start. It was an almost overwhelming situation, and my heart was pounding as I raced to choose the right fly and tie it on. Would it be all over before I could swing into action? Should I select a dry fly, an emerger, or a pupa? And how in the world would a fish ever notice my fly among the legions of naturals?

If you've never experienced a grannom hatch, you're missing one of nature's greatest spectacles that a fly fisher can observe. What these little bugs lack in size, they more than make up in numbers and energy; not to mention, ardor. While a mayfly often emerges from the water calmly and with grace, and then rests for a couple of days before seeking a mate, grannoms are more like a mob of frenetic sex

A peek below the water of a foothill stream reveals prime habitat for caddisflies and other aquatic insects.

A rare calm moment for a grannom (*Brachycentrus*) caddisfly on the water surface. Body + wings = 13mm.

Blizzard hatches of grannom caddisflies are typical on the first warm sunny day of early spring.

Sometimes it's hard to see how even one more bug could fit onto a popular grannom gathering spot.

fiends on a mission that can't wait. They arrive in the aerial world with wings flapping, feet tapping, and an eye out for a pretty girl or a handsome fellow. With no apparent shame or regard for proper protocol, masses of mating grannoms soon cover the nearby bushes, shoreline—and anglers.

Grannoms belong to the caddisfly family Brachycentridae—also called humpless case makers (we'll see why in a moment). However, it is important to note that while the same name (grannom) is sometimes applied broadly to all the family's members, it more often refers to the important genus *Brachycentrus*. There are several species that span most of the cooler waters of the North American continent that will answer if you call out the name "grannom." In the East, probably the most important species are *B. numerosus* and *B. appalachia*, also dubbed the apple caddis or light grannom. In the midwestern and western areas of the country, the species *B. americanus* and *B. occidentalis* become predominant. These are often referred to as American grannoms or Mother's Day caddis.

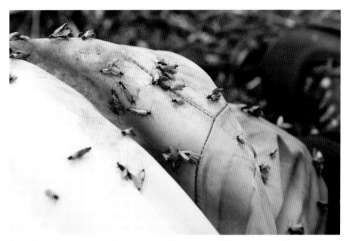

Anglers averse to bugs crawling over them may feel annoyed during a prolific grannom hatch.

PUTTING CADDISFLIES IN THEIR PLACE

Since this is our first close encounter with a caddisfly in this book, let's spend a few moments discussing caddisflies as a group. To set them firmly in their organizational compartment, first recall again from your school days, with fondness, the biology subject of taxonomy. As boring and dry as it seemed back then, now after all these years you will finally see that it does serve some real-life purpose. And that purpose is to put the insects that trout eat, and which our flies imitate, into groups that make sense.

Think of the system as a series of boxes within boxes. A very big box (All Life) is at the top, containing several slightly smaller boxes of kingdoms. Each kingdom box in turn contains a collection of yet smaller boxes of phyla; and so on. The key point is that as you go down the taxonomic scale, individuals within any box become more and more closely related, and share a set of characteristics that distinguishes them from all others. They will tend to more strongly look alike, act alike, and/or function alike.

In the Examples column below, I've marked in bold each box along a specific path—from the largest down to the smallest box, which contains only a single member: a species. This particular species happens to be one of our grannom caddisflies (*Brachycentrus occidentalis*). (Note that by convention, the genus and species are both italicized, but only the genus is capitalized.) The combination of genus name plus species name is unique for any species, so when we write *Brachycentrus occidentalis*, everyone who understands the system will know exactly which species we are talking about. The same cannot be said for common names like grannom, which may apply to several species. Moreover, different common names are often applied in different regions to the same bug.

In this book, we will be focusing primarily on insects (Insecta)—which is a Class category—and the levels

Taxonomic Level	Examples
Kingdom	**Animalia**, Plantae, Fungi
Phylum	**Arthropoda**, Mollusca, Chordata
Class	**Insecta**, Crustacea, Arachnida
Order	**Trichoptera**, Ephemeroptera, Plecoptera
Family	**Brachycentridae**, Hydropsychidae, Limnephilidae
Genus	***Brachycentrus***, *Amiocentrus*, *Micrasema*
Species	***occidentalis***, *americanus*, *appalachia*

below it; so we won't need to think much about categories above that level. Now note that the next formal rank *below* class is order. Insect orders that will be of interest here are Ephemeroptera, or mayflies; Plecoptera, or stoneflies; Diptera, or true flies; Hemiptera, or true bugs; and the subject of this chapter, the order comprising caddisflies, Trichoptera.

Now that wasn't so painful, was it? And from now on, as we discuss the various kinds of insects, we'll be able to organize them in a logical manner that will help us keep our concepts straight. Let's continue then with the caddisflies (Trichoptera), and go over some of their basic, fascinating, and useful traits.

NYMPHS, LARVAE, AND PUPAE: METAMORPHOSIS IN A NUTSHELL

Recall that in chapter 1 on the morphing mayfly, I mentioned that while mayflies pass through a simpler form of development called incomplete metamorphosis, other kinds of insects utilize the alternative complete metamorphosis. Caddisflies fall into the latter category. So in addition to the life stages of egg, nymph, and adult, we have to consider the pupa.

Incomplete Metamorphosis
egg → nymph → adult

Complete Metamorphosis
egg → larva → pupa → adult

Though all aquatic forms of insects are usually called nymphs by fly fishers, the proper term for the analogous stage of insects undergoing complete metamorphosis is *larva*. It is more than a semantic difference: larvae look different and often act quite differently than nymphs. While a nymph closely resembles the adult it is to become, except for wings and a few minor details, you would hardly guess that a larva is at all related to the adult of its species.

To avoid having to repeat the unwieldy phrases "insect that undergoes incomplete metamorphosis" and "insect that undergoes complete metamorphosis," for the remainder of this discussion I will use "nymph" to mean the active juvenile of the former type of insect and "larva" to mean the active juvenile of the latter. Or, when a bit more rigor is

A *Skwala* stonefly nymph is an example of an insect that utilizes incomplete metamorphosis. Nymphs strongly resemble adults without wings.

needed, I'll employ the scientific terms *hemimetabolous* and *holometabolous*, respectively.

So what are some of the visible differences between a nymph and a larva? Nymphs have body shapes and appendages very similar to the adults of their species, with the exception of wings. And there is even a hint of the wings, in structures along a nymph's back called wing pads. The wing pads of an early nymph are small and unnoticeable. But as a nymph grows, the wing pads get longer and wider in proportion to its body, and they darken markedly. Large dark wing pads are a primary indicator that a nymph is nearly mature and almost ready to morph into an adult.

Larvae, on the other hand, have body shapes that vary considerably but are, on the whole, wormlike. Their legs may be scaled down or missing altogether. They may have additional leglike (but nonjointed) appendages along the body called prolegs. The eyes are often markedly reduced in size and complexity compared with those of adults. And most importantly, larvae never have wing pads; the small developing wings are completely internal at this stage. So not only can the status of wing pads not be used to determine larval maturity (and time to emergence), but tied flies that imitate larval insects should not exhibit wing pads, either.

Nymphs that have just hatched from the egg look like tiny, wingless versions of the adults of their species. They grow in size over time, shedding and regenerating their exoskeletons on numerous occasions as they outgrow them; but with the exception of a few minor details (like wing pads), their basic appearance doesn't change until the final molt into an adult.

Newly hatched larvae, on the other hand, resemble their adult parents hardly at all. Their appearance initially changes even less than those of nymphs, as there is no sign of even wing pad development. To our eyes the only real change is in size, and indeed rapid growth is the primary focus of any larva. It puts off most of the development of adult organs and structures, including wings, until a very different stage that comes later: the pupa.

When a larva has finished growing, it enters the pupa stage, turning its full attention to developing the anatomy it will need as an adult. It not only stops eating and growing, it ceases almost all visible activity. The larva seals itself inside a cocoon or shelter and accelerates the development of wings, legs, sex organs, and everything else required by an adult of its species. This process usually takes weeks but can be much longer in some cases. At the end of the pupation period, the adult insect splits open its old pupal exoskeleton and emerges, almost magically transformed from its strikingly different precursor.

A green rock worm (*Rhyacophila*) larva, which undergoes complete metamorphosis, looks almost nothing like the adult caddisfly it will become.

ORIGINS OF THE SCHISM

While not important to your fly-fishing success, you might be wondering how and why this strange developmental division within the insect world came about. My curiosity was certainly piqued, so I went sleuthing through the scientific literature to see what I could find out about the subject.

The first insects appeared on earth at least 400 million years ago in the Devonian period, and they exhibited a form of development in which the youngsters that hatched from their eggs looked very similar to the adults. As time went by and some insects acquired wings, a modified version of this form of development emerged, wherein the last molt to a winged adult was a somewhat more pronounced transition, and became what we now call incomplete metamorphosis (or more formally, hemimetaboly). For a long time the majority of insects utilized it. And many of our oldest living insects still employ it, including the mayflies (order Ephemeroptera), their close relatives the dragonflies and damselflies (order Odonata), and the stoneflies (order Plecoptera).

Then about 290 million years ago, in the Upper Carboniferous period, we see the first indications in the record that hemimetabolous insects have given rise to new forms incorporating a pupal phase and undergoing complete metamorphosis (holometaboly). Paleontological evidence indicates that among still-living (extant) insects that exhibit complete metamorphosis, the order Megaloptera—dobsonflies, fishflies, and alderflies—are among the oldest, and arose in the Permian period about 225–280 million years ago. The new developmental scheme proved wildly successful and spread like wildfire. It has become the dominant strategy of living insects. That includes several groups of primary concern to fly fishers—caddisflies (order Trichoptera); true flies, including midges, crane flies, black flies, mosquitoes, and many others (order Diptera); and beetles (order Coleoptera).

What are the essential differences between incomplete and complete metamorphosis, and why did the new strategy prove so successful? First, let's think about what happens to an insect from the time an egg is fertilized to the moment it becomes a mature adult. As mentioned in chapter 2, two overlapping but conceptually distinct processes are taking place: growth (increase in size of existing organs) and development (the synthesis of *new* types of molecules, tissues, organs, and structures that will eventually lead to the assembly of an adult insect).

While growth and development often proceed more or less simultaneously, they need not be perfectly linked. Early in its life, an organism may concentrate on building most of the organs and structures it will need later on, and then spend the remainder of its life primarily growing larger. Humans are an example of this scheme. At the other extreme, a young animal may grow dramatically in size but remain essentially unchanged in form, delaying the development of adult organs and structures until late in its life. The caterpillar-to-butterfly transition is the most familiar example of this plan. An alternative strategy is to grow and develop more synchronously. Think of a frog, where the tiny tadpole grows larger and at the same time gradually loses its tail, develops legs, and steadily morphs from the form of a tadpole to an adult frog.

It is a change in the timing of development compared with growth that accounts for the essential differences between insects having incomplete or complete metamorphosis. In the former, the nymph develops most of the basic structures of the adult very early, while still in the egg. It is born looking pretty much like a wingless adult. Then as the nymph grows, it also steadily develops most of the remaining organs and structures, notably wings (visible as external wing pads), that it will need as an adult. At the final molt, the new structures are unfolded and unfurled to reveal the adult insect. While there is a final push of development at the end, most of it has occurred simultaneously with the growth of the nymph.

The seminal event in the evolution of complete metamorphosis was most likely a change in the timing of a biochemical signal (or more than one) that trigger development of adult tissues. Lacking the proper development signals early in life, a nymph essentially became a prototypical larva. Over time the larva became specialized in obtaining food and growing in size. The development signal or signals were delayed until an optimum size was achieved, at which time the larva switched over to the development program completely, ceasing all other nonessential activities—such as seeking and eating food. This became the pupal stage (a time of concentrated development of adult organs and structures). The final molt was then a true metamorphosis (a radical change from one body form to another).

WHAT'S SO GREAT ABOUT PUPATION?

So now we may start to comprehend how complete metamorphosis may have come into being, but what about why? The fact that complete metamorphosis has become so prevalent strongly implies that it was a very favorable way of doing business. Why would it be a good thing to delay development of adult structures until near the very end?

The most likely explanation is that it allowed juvenile insects to better exploit habitats for which the adult form was not well suited. The two essential functions of an adult insect are reproduction, and dispersal of the population into a variety of habitats to increase the chances of some of them surviving. To better achieve the latter purpose, most adult insects have developed wings and/or legs, both highly efficient in locomotion.

On the other hand, juvenile insects specialize in another essential process: eating and growing. So the optimum design of a body to achieve juvenile goals may be very different than the one needed to perform the functions of an adult.

When the option of delaying development of an adult body popped up during evolution, it freed the juvenile insect from the compromises imposed by conforming to adult body shapes with burdensome adult body parts. They could, for instance, adopt wormlike shapes—with no wing pads or large legs to get in the way—that would be better suited to penetrating food sources, such as fruit or carrion. Or they could afford to devote energy to making silk glands, which have proven enormously helpful in exploiting a wide variety of new environmental niches, including some aquatic habitats populated by caddisflies.

CADDISFLY DIVERSITY

Above the water, caddisflies may all look pretty much the same to most people, differing somewhat in size and wing patterns, but overall quite similar. Underwater, however, the situation is much different. There is a tremendous variety among the shapes, colors, sizes, habitats, and "housing" of juvenile caddisflies.

Caddisflies can be placed into three broad groups according to where and how they live. The first and probably most primitive category contains the *free-living* caddisflies. Species in this category are the homeless of the caddisfly world, roaming the riverbeds, hiding in rock crannies by day, and often hunting by night. Most of them are predators and virtually all of them live in running water, frequently in the fastest currents. Like all caddisfly larvae, these make silk; and they spin it into threads that they lay down on the rocks as they crawl about. The silk thread serves as a safety line to help the larvae avoid being washed into the currents.

The second category of caddisflies comprises the *net spinners*. Larvae in this group build silken nets in the crevices between rocks, where current will flow through them. Like the free-living caddisflies, the net spinners live in flowing water, where their nets can be effective in filtering food from the currents. The food is often particulate detritus (dead plant or animal matter), but can include small living organisms. Net spinners build crude retreats at one edge of their nets, where they can hide and tend them.

The final, and probably most remarkable, category of caddisflies is made up of *case makers*. The group is very diverse and has spread from cool running waters, where caddisflies are thought to have originated, into many types of aquatic habitats, including slow and even intermittent streams, lakes, and warm ponds. The common trait they share is the construction of portable homes (actually cases), which they carry around with them like turtle shells.

Cases are constructed from a great many materials, although any individual species usually restricts itself to just one or a few types at any particular time. Pebbles, sand, twigs, bark, dead leaves, and living plants may all serve as building blocks for the little cottages. Case designs are as diverse as the materials, with some species building crude and apparently haphazard structures, while others construct intricate and precise homes that would make any human architect proud. The common "thread" in all the case types is the use of silk to bind everything together, and to form a tough but resilient lining inside the case.

THE CASE FOR A CASE

If you're wondering about the function of a caddisfly's case, probably the first potential role that will pop into your mind is protection. And there is ample evidence that cases do afford some defense against predators, although trout are known to consume many types of caddisflies, case and all. A more surprising function is not so obvious, and in fact may seem counterintuitive at first. You might think that a caddisfly's case, often being constructed of stones and other rather impermeable materials, would interfere with water flow over the larva's body, and thus impede respiration. But, in fact, the effect is just the opposite: the case actually improves water flow over the larva's gills and respiratory surfaces.

How can that be? Well, think about how a fish's gills work. The gills are inside what is essentially a tube, open at both ends. The front end is the fish's mouth, and the rear end is the opening under its gill covers. Even when there is no current, a fish provides a constant flow of water over its gills by opening its mouth and expanding its gill covers, sucking water in through the mouth and out the gill opening. It basically pumps water over its gills.

A cased caddisfly larva does effectively the same thing. The case is open at both ends, and the larva rhythmically undulates its body to pump water in through the front and out through the rear. All cased caddisflies—with the exception of the Brachycentridae, including the grannoms—have fleshy "humps" on their first abdominal segment, usually one on the dorsal surface, and one on each side. The humps expand to contact the side of the case, holding the larva firmly in place, yet leaving spaces between the humps so water can flow around them. Fresh, oxygenated water is thus constantly moving over the gills on the larva's abdomen, in some species, or over the oxygen-exchanging abdominal surface in others. This remarkable innovation is so effective that it has allowed many caddisfly species to colonize warmer, oxygen-poor waters that are incapable of supporting organisms with less efficient respiratory mechanisms.

However, the caddisfly family of Brachycentridae, including grannoms—the main subject of this chapter—

Brachycentrus larvae build remarkably engineered cases that they drag around with them while grazing for food. Case length = 12mm.

turns out to be the single exception to having humps on its anterior abdominal region. That is where the family members get one of their common names—humpless case makers—mentioned earlier in this chapter. They seem to get along fine without the humps, so they must have another mechanism for positioning the larva within the case in a way that allows adequate water flow.

Grannoms of the genus *Brachycentrus* build marvelously tapered cases, with a perfectly square cross-section, that resemble skinny log cabins. (The cases of *Amiocentrus* and *Micrasema* species of grannoms are similar, except that they are round instead of square in cross-section.) The building blocks are exactly measured pieces of plant stems or leaves. Of course as the larva inside grows, the case has to get bigger as well. To enlarge the case a grannom larva remains inside and hangs its legs over the anterior (front, nearest the head) edge. It positions its mouth on the rim, and lays down silk from oral glands as it rotates its body to cover the entire circumference of the case. Precisely measured plant fibers are then glued in place along each edge.

How does a caddisfly larva measure its building materials? If you are conjuring images of tiny tape measures and yardsticks, you aren't too far off the mark. The yardstick that a grannom larva uses is the distance between the end of the leg that holds the material to be cut, and its mouth. Think of holding a long stick in your hand by one end, extending your arm as far as possible, and biting off the other end at the point where it reaches your mouth. If repeated, you would get several sticks all the same length. And that's just how a grannom larva does it.

This method of construction also explains how a grannom case comes out so nicely tapered. As the larva inside grows, so do its legs, and the distance between the end of the leg and the mouth gradually gets longer. A longer yardstick is now used to measure them, and that means the building blocks employed in successive sessions of case building also get longer. Since the larva always adds to just one end, that end gets larger and larger in diameter over time, while the other (posterior) end remains unchanged.

YOU ARE WHAT YOU EAT

Eating is the number one job of any young insect. Most fly fishers have probably watched cased caddis larvae graze across the bottom of a stream or pond, pausing only when disturbed. Grazing on algae and detritus is one popular occupation for aquatic insects. But there are other ways in which they can make a living.

Given their small size you might think it shouldn't require much food to support aquatic insects, and that nutrition should rarely be a limiting factor. But in a typical stream or lake, there are an awful lot of mouths to feed, and in the aggregate, insects plus their noninsect competitors can require a surprisingly large stockpile of provisions. Depending on the location and habitat, aquatic insects in streams and rivers may consume 1–1,000 grams of nutrients per square meter of stream bottom per year. That is, in a very productive 100-yard stretch of a river that is 30 yards wide, over a year's time aquatic insects may eat more than 6,000 pounds of food! What kinds of chow are on the bug menu, and where does it come from? What lifestyles have aquatic insects adopted to obtain their fair share of the food supply? And why should you care?

Starting with the last question first, you should care, if you are a fly fisher, because trout tend to congregate around bugs, and you will find bugs where their food is. Moreover, if you are trying to imitate an insect with a particular fly and method of presentation, it is useful to know where that bug is found and how it behaves.

Bug food can come from one of two sources: generated within the water, or entering from its banks. Ultimately this means plants of some sort, since plants are responsible for converting sunlight into chemical energy that can be utilized by animals. Some bodies of water, particularly eutrophic lakes, are capable of internally producing tremendous quantities of vegetation—algae and/or vascular plants—and thus supporting correspondingly large numbers of insects. Other waters, most notably the upper reaches of mountain streams that are largely shaded by hillsides and overhanging trees, depend largely on terrestrial vegetation that enters from the adjacent land as the primary food source.

Large organic materials like leaves and stems obviously can't be consumed whole by small insects, and have to be broken down into smaller pieces. Some insects have evolved to perform this task, and are called "shredders." In the upper regions of a small stream where almost all of the potential food is derived from plants falling into the water, shredders dominate the aquatic insect population. They help break down the available food sources into smaller pieces—known as "coarse particulate organic matter (CPOM)"—that can be utilized, not only by the shredders themselves, but also by other insects that feed on the resulting banquet.

CPOM is small enough to wash downstream where it becomes the primary food source for other insects that can't shred larger items, but have adapted to feed on these coarse particles. Their feeding actions, together with ingestion of the large particles and excretion of the leftovers, generate even smaller particles that are referred to as "fine particulate organic matter (FPOM)." FPOM stays suspended in the water long enough to wash yet farther downstream.

You can probably see the trend here, and can guess what comes next. In the middle to lower reaches of a stream or river, where there is little in the way of large chunks or particles of food, the dominant insects become those that can utilize the really small FPOM. In addition to the small particles that result from the breakdown of terrestrial-derived vegetation, insects that specialize in eating small particles may also consume algae. The middle and lower stretches of a stream are usually more open and less shaded, and the increased sunlight that penetrates the water is often able to support growth of substantial amounts of aquatic algae. Most of this crop is usually attached to the upper surfaces of rocks in shallow water.

All of the insects employing the feeding habits discussed thus far are herbivores (consumers of living plant matter) or detritivores (consumers of decaying plant or animal matter). But just as on land, wherever there are herbivores and detritivores, there will be other animals to eat them: carnivores. Carnivorous aquatic insects can be found in all water types, from upstream to downstream regions of a river, to lakes and ponds. Wherever there is another aquatic insect—or other small animal—to serve as prey, the carnivorous aquatic insects are there to take advantage.

There are insects that are adapted to feeding on each unique food type and size, and others that are opportunists, able to take advantage of several kinds of fodder that might come their way. Entomologists have divided them into four broad categories based on how they obtain their food:

- **Shredders** are herbivores and/or detritivores that specialize in large items, like leaves and stems, which they break into smaller pieces.
- **Collectors** are herbivores and/or detritivores that gather loose food items that have already been broken down into medium or small particles.
- **Scrapers** are herbivores and/or detritivores that eat very small particles, often algae that are attached to surfaces and have to be scraped off.
- **Predators** are carnivores that eat live animals, either by consuming them whole or in part, or by piercing them and sucking out their fluids.

Each type of insect has evolved an anatomy, such as specialized head and mouthparts, which is adapted to its particular feeding mode. And each one lives in a specific habitat where that type of food can be found in sufficient quantity, and has adopted morphologies and behaviors suited for living in that habitat and acquiring the targeted food items.

In most freshwater environments it is the aquatic insects, together with other aquatic macroinvertebrates, that are responsible for converting plant matter into animal protein. In a direct reflection of the amounts of food they consume, it has been estimated that a typical stream or river produces grams to kilograms of aquatic insects per square meter of bottom per year. Without these insects, higher animal life in rivers or lakes would not be possible.

While all of the aquatic insects have roles to play in the nutritional ecology of freshwater environments, it is the caddisflies that have adapted to the greatest variety of niches and food sources. For instance, certain varieties of caddisflies are the predominant insects in the upper reaches of many streams, where there is little particulate organic matter and most of the available nutrients are found in large leaves, needles, and woody material that fall into the water. These large food items can't be processed by many kinds of insects, but caddisflies have filled the gap.

How do grannom caddisflies fit into the feeding-method picture? Those in the genus *Brachycentrus*, at least, are generalists. While they are primarily collectors of small particulate living and dead vegetable matter, they can be omnivorous, and are not above feasting on live animal tissue when they can get it. And they can be surprisingly aggressive. I've watched groups of grannom larvae foraging on underwater plants, moving along the stems. When they encounter one another, they often stop and battle for a

Multiple smaller males often attempt to mate with each larger *Brachycentrus* female immediately after hatching on the water surface, but the party soon shifts to streamside vegetation.

few moments, legs swinging and grappling as if in a wrestling match, before they call it off and move on. And in one scientific study, investigators observed grannom larvae cutting open the sealed cases of some of their brethren, who had already begun pupation, and cannibalizing the pupae inside!

Within their collector repertoire, grannom larvae have two primary feeding behaviors: grazing and filtering. When in grazing mode, they crawl around rocks and water plants hunting for the small organic particles that are their main food source. But larvae of this genus have also developed specific filtering behaviors, not found in other members of their family, for capturing food particles drifting in the currents.

HANGING BY A THREAD

Why crawl about the bottom hunting for your food—when you can wait for it to come to you, and then snatch it out of the current as it passes by? This must have been the question "pondered" by the ancestors of the grannoms. Their evolutionary solution was to enlarge their second and third pairs of legs considerably, and to equip them with sets of

long sticky hairs that can act like filters to strain the water. Whenever there is a substantial concentration of organic particles suspended in the currents, grannom larvae go into filtering mode. Their primary method is to attach one lip of the front of their case (using that versatile silk again, as glue) to a rock, facing upstream; extend their long brush-like legs in front of their heads; and filter the water. As the current passes through the hairs, suspended particles get caught. Every so often the larvae pull in the legs so they can snack on what they've snagged.

But what if some of the richest currents are a bit downstream of your rock, and not directly accessible? No problem, if you are a grannom larva. You just go rappelling! That's right; not unlike a mountain climber descending a cliff, grannom larvae have the ability to let out a rope—really a thread—of silk, and with one end attached to a rock or plant stem, slide down to the other end and hang suspended in the current. In this way they can reach areas they wouldn't otherwise be able to get to. Hanging in the current, swinging to-and-fro; with legs spread and brush filters doing their thing, the larvae are able to fish in the best waters for all those juicy particles rushing by.

Gary LaFontaine wrote in his seminal book *Caddisflies* about caddisfly and black fly larvae dangling in the current on their silk threads. He had learned from some fly fishermen in Maine about a technique wherein a short length of white thread was tied between the tippet and a nymph being fished near the bottom. In certain waters and times of the year, the technique was deadly.

Further investigation by LaFontaine revealed why the technique worked. Large numbers of black fly larvae had a habit of hanging by their own silk threads in the areas of those streams where the method was effective. When viewed underwater, the white threads were extremely visible and likely acted as a magnet to hungry trout. LaFontaine found that certain caddisflies, including grannoms, also frequently hang by similar silk threads.

Ralph Cutter, who runs the California School of Fly-fishing and has spent time underwater observing the behavior of aquatic insects, has watched trout swimming with open mouths through concentrated pods of dangling grannom larvae. Fueled by his observation, Cutter adopted a method first devised by LaFontaine to mimic the larvae dangling in the current by their white silk threads.

The method involves using a white marker—both used the Mean Streak brand—to color a short length of tippet immediately above a fly that imitates a cased grannom larva. Just above the white portion of the tippet, a heavy split shot is attached. When cast into the strong currents where these insects live, the shot sits on the bottom, while the fly dangles in the current on the white tippet and mimics a larva on its silk lifeline. Cutter feels that the exact fly used is not important, but rather that the white thread is the key that draws a trout's interest.

Learning about this bit of aquatic insect and fly-fishing lore was an "Aha!" moment for me. For years I had swung wet flies or nymphs in the current, and at the end the fly was hanging straight downstream. If left there for a few seconds, the result would often be a violent take by a trout. Yet I could think of no natural trout prey that would just hang in the current like that. What were these trout thinking? Were they just striking out of some general impulse rather than mistaking my fly for a real insect? Of course I can never be sure of the answer to that question. But now that I know that at least several types of common aquatic insects exhibit the same sort of hanging-in-the-current behavior, it makes sense that a trout would recognize it as a naturally occurring phenomenon.

GRANNOM PUPATION

As a *B. occidentalis* grannom larva approaches the end of its growth phase, it starts looking for a suitable place to pupate. When it finds a good spot, usually on a rock with just the right current speed, it turns around inside its case and uses silk secretions to glue the narrow posterior end to the rock. It then forms a tough silken membrane over the opening and bites a series of small holes in the middle of the membrane, in a circular pattern. The pattern of holes is remarkably uniform from one pupal case to another. The result resembles the top of a saltshaker, with the number of holes being consistently in the range of eight to eleven in the pupae that I've examined. Then the larva turns around again to face the large end of the case, and repeats the process: glue the rim of that end of the case to the rock, seal it with a membrane across the front, and punch holes in it. Maybe because the front membrane is larger, the larva puts a few more holes in it—about twelve to fifteen of them—than the rear one. The result of all this work is a strong pupal cocoon that resists the incursion of predators, yet still allows fresh water to flow through the case. Stiff bristles on the pupa's mouth and posterior are used to keep the holes on each end of the case clear of debris.

The pupa phase lasts one to two months, depending on water temperature. During that time the developmental program goes into overdrive, and all the adult appendages and body parts are assembled. At the end of the period, a fully formed adult is inside the pupal exoskeleton, just waiting to get out. At this point it is referred to as a pharate (mature, but still inside the pupal skin) adult. The only remaining steps are for the pharate adult caddisfly to cut itself out of the case, swim to the surface, and then emerge from the pupal exoskeleton as a final flying adult. We'll look at a pupa and its emergence into an adult for another caddisfly species, the October caddis (*Dicosmoecus* species), in chapter 15.

ADULTHOOD

The emerging grannom adults that survive the submarine attacks of marauding trout and the air raids of hungry birds flutter to the streamside vegetation by the thousands, with just one thing on their minds—sex. They are neither reticent nor shy. Every female is quickly swarmed by a bevy of male suitors.

It is easy to distinguish male from female grannoms at a glance, because the females are a lot bigger—a full hook size. Males are about a size 18–16, depending on the hook type and how the fly is tied, whereas the females are about a size 16–14. That's a good thing to remember when you're tying a fly to your tippet, especially during the return for egg laying, when only the females will be on the water.

After mating, the females return to the water to lay eggs. The green egg case at their rear end is easy to spot. It's noticeable enough that trout may key on the color, so it's a good idea to carry patterns with some green in the body. You never know when a subtle feature may be the

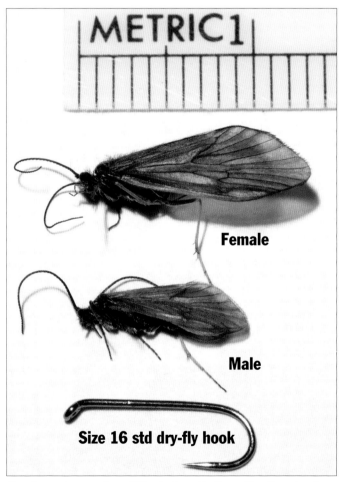

Brachycentrus males differ in length from the females by about one hook size.

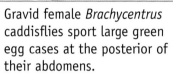
Gravid female *Brachycentrus* caddisflies sport large green egg cases at the posterior of their abdomens.

In the aftermath of grannom egg-laying activities, large numbers of dead or dying caddisflies litter the water surface. Many lie on their sides, but others adopt the classic spent-wing position in the surface film. Selective trout may prefer one profile over another.

difference between catching trout and watching them refuse your offering.

There are reports that some grannom females swim underwater to deposit their eggs on subsurface structure, but in my observations the vast majority appear to lay their eggs on the surface. You can end up with a mass of dead and dying caddisflies floating down the stream, some on their sides and others with wings splayed out in the stereotypical spent position. Bugs in this condition are especially easy prey for trout, and that fact doesn't escape them. So don't forget to try flies imitating these forms.

Of course, it's what the underside of a bug looks like that is more important to a trout. A spent caddisfly adult lying in the surface film should look pretty much the same as it would from above. But what about an adult that has just hatched, and is standing on the water surface? Shouldn't we look at the bug from below to see what our imitating fly should resemble?

Well, yes and no. If a trout is looking straight up above it, an adult grannom standing on the water would look similar to the ventral-view photo. However, a stream-dwelling trout would not usually be looking straight up. It would instead be gazing upstream in anticipation of prey approaching it on the downstream current. When looking at the upstream surface at an angle, the surface presents a mirror to a fish below, and anything above the surface is not visible. We'll discuss this phenomenon in some detail in later chapters. But for now, suffice it to say that in this

situation, a caddisfly standing on the surface would not look as it does in the ventral-view photo. Rather, it would look similar to the photo taken from underwater, but at an angle. Only the parts of the bug's legs and body that contact or break through the surface film are visible.

A FLY IN THE WATER

But on the day of that momentous hatch on the McKenzie River, brought up at the beginning of this chapter, I didn't yet know much about grannom caddisflies or how they might look from a trout's perspective. I just knew that I had to quickly get a fly in the water before the fish had thoroughly stuffed themselves on the smorgasbord of naturals. I decided to go with an old standby dry fly, the Elk Hair Caddis (EHC), in a size 18. It seemed to take forever for my trembling fingers to attach the fly, fumbling with a knot that I had tied thousands of times before. To make matters worse, when I drew the knot tight and pulled hard to test it, it broke. I won't repeat the words I mumbled, but let's just say I berated myself for my haste and retied the knot a bit more deliberately.

When I looked up, the trout were still going at it, and I breathed a sigh of relief. Several fish were working a seam near me and appeared to be sucking down adults from the surface. I had calmed down enough that my first cast was perfect, and with a little mend, the fly came right down the lane without a trace of drag. "This is it," I thought as the fly neared the spot, and I prepared to set the hook. But my

The ventral view of a grannom caddisfly on the surface is what a trout would experience when looking straight up

When looking upstream at a typical angle, a trout can't see the sections of a caddisfly above water. Only the impressions of its feet and body parts touching the surface are visible, surrounded by reflections of the stream bottom.

fly drifted right over the position, perfectly mind you, where the fish should have grabbed it, without even so much as a close look from the trout. As if to show its contempt, two seconds later the fish rose for a real grannom floating just behind my fly.

"Damn, that should have been the ticket," I thought. But several more good drifts yielded the same result. I chalked it up to an obstinate individual and moved on to another group of risers.

After ten minutes of this, I had fooled two small rainbows, but had gotten far more refusals than takes. Time to switch strategies.

By now the initial rush of adrenaline had drained well enough from my system to allow me to think a little more calmly. I pondered the situation. First, I realized that with all these natural grannoms on the water, I needed to do something to make my fly stand out from the crowd. Second, I noted that while some of the bugs on the surface were just resting, many were fluttering to and fro, and it was the active bugs that seemed to most strongly draw the fishes' attention. Finally, I recalled that where there are hatching adult caddisflies on the surface, there will be pupae swimming up from below.

Hmmm. Movement; underwater, but rising; standing out from the crowd. These were the qualities I wanted to try with my next fly choice. I remembered that in previous situations like this where success with dry flies had been less than stellar, swinging a wet fly had sometimes worked.

And it immediately struck me that a soft-hackle wet fly, in a bit larger size to help it stand out, when cast upstream and swung into a trout's feeding lane, would satisfy all those criteria.

So I quickly clipped off the EHC, tied on a size 16 brown soft-hackle, and laid out a cast 25 feet upstream and on the far side of a pod of feeding trout. After stack mending several times to let the fly sink a few feet, I let the current catch the fly and swing it downstream so it would begin to rise just as it came in front of the fish.

Yes! The strike was so vicious that the 4-weight rod was nearly jerked from my hand, but the combination of a soft rod tip and 4X tippet held up to the shock. The loop of line in my hand disappeared and the high-pitched but melodious sound of my classic Orvis CFO click-and-pawl reel told me that this fish was no lightweight. It streaked for the other side of the river, gaining the fast current in the middle to assist its cause. Suddenly it went airborne and it became apparent that not only was this a large fish, but it sported some of the deepest red colors that I had ever seen. I wanted a closer look.

Two long runs and several short ones later, I managed to pull my adversary into some slack side-water. I slipped my little camera from a vest pocket, snapped the fish's picture, and then unhooked it with my homemade fish-release tool. Without having been touched, this spectacular 18-inch native McKenzie redside swam free, and I looked forward to meeting it again.

FLIES

A variety of flies work well at times during grannom hatches. Two that I have found particularly useful for imitating adults on top of the water include the classic Elk Hair Caddis, and the slightly less well-known Peacock Caddis. A favorite for below-the-surface action is a size 16–18 Bird's Nest, which is probably taken for a pupa rising to the surface. The best way to fish the Bird's Nest is as promoted by Gary LaFontaine and Ralph Cutter: coat it in powdered dry-fly floatant (such as Tite Line Dry Fly Powder or Frog's Fanny Powder), which causes air bubbles to stay trapped within it when the fly is submerged. These bubbles are reminiscent of the gases that form underneath the pupal exoskeleton, and exhibit a highly visible sparkling effect when viewed underwater. And finally, the all-purpose soft-hackle wet fly that is effective during hatches of many different kinds of insects often works well when grannoms are on the water.

A Peacock Caddis dry fly and a brown soft-hackle wet fly are good choices during a grannom hatch.

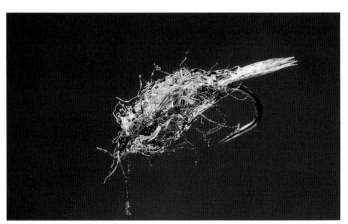

A floatant-coated Bird's Nest fly captures and holds air bubbles underwater, mimicking the shimmering effect of the gases that accumulate under the exoskeleton of the natural pupa.

A Bird's Nest is one of the best patterns when trout are taking rising pupa, particularly if the fly is coated with powdered dry-fly floatant.

The well-known Elk Hair Caddis dry fly is a popular choice for the grannom hatch.

4

PMDs, Perlodids, and the Next Wave

Mid-spring hatches of mayflies, small stoneflies, and caddisflies

Mid-spring is my favorite time of year to be on the river. The bankside vegetation has that almost fluorescent green hue that only fresh foliage backlit by the spring sun can display. Flowers are in bloom. It's a time when a pair of Canada geese takes the family of goslings for a stroll along the bank. And the deer twins cautiously step out from behind a patch of blackberries, as if to get a better look at the newcomer waving a stick over the water.

These are some of the scenes that await fly fishers who ply the right waters in mid-spring. But more to the point, it's the season in many areas of the country when the rivers and lakes come alive with a profusion of hatching insects and fish rising to greet them. Mayflies, caddisflies, stone-

flies, true flies—bugs of all forms and family ties—celebrate the rising temperatures and race to produce the next generation.

PALE MORNING DUNS

While in many places, particularly in the coastal Northwest, March browns may be the first mayfly hatch that gets anglers excited; it is often the pale morning duns (PMDs), which follow them, that provide the most consistent fishing success. The March brown hatch is frequently a hit-or-miss affair as far as trout fishing is concerned. It can be very exciting on occasion, but often the water is still too cold in many streams for trout to pay much attention to what's

An upper McKenzie River riffle is an ideal nursery for aquatic insects.

Western pale morning dun (*Ephemerella*) nymphs are at home among the rocks and sandy bottoms of freestone streams or in well-vegetated spring creeks. Body length = 8mm.

The bright orange eyes of this male pale morning dun are noticeable even from a distance. Body length = 8mm.

Compared with the brighter males, female pale morning duns look, well, pale. Body length = 9mm.

happening on the surface. But by the time the next wave of insects rolls into the picture, most of the fish have warmed up and are actively looking for a good meal.

Juvenile pale morning duns belong to the crawler category of mayflies that were described in chapter 1. They are members of the family Ephemerellidae, and the genus *Ephemerella*. The most predominant species of PMD in the West is *E. excrucians* (formerly called *E. inermis*, a name you will still see in fly-fishing literature). In the East and Midwest, the important *Ephemerella* species are usually called Hendricksons (*E. subvaria*) or sulphurs (*E. invaria* and *E. dorothea*) instead of pale morning duns, but their appearances and behaviors are similar.

In fact, within the last few years, East has met West, figuratively speaking. The sometimes-important species *E. infrequens*, inhabiting primarily western and midwestern streams, has been reclassified as a subspecies of *E. dorothea*—previously thought to be confined to eastern waters. So now we have the situation where a western pale morning dun is a variant of the same species as an eastern sulfur. Maybe we can compromise on a universal common name—say, a pale morning sulfur?

Ephemerella nymphs crawl around the stream bottom in cracks between rocks and in vegetation. Reflecting their preference for flowing but somewhat slower water than the clinger-type nymphs we discussed in chapter 2, PMD nymphs have body shapes that are a little less hydrodynamically sculpted than the clingers. Their generalized form resembles a blocky rectangle. PMDs are the generalists of the mayflies, being at home not only in relatively boisterous freestone streams but also in the more placid waters of spring creeks. In fact, they often reach their highest concentrations in the latter.

Contrary to the implications of their common name, pale morning duns don't necessarily hatch in the morning. I guess that must have been the usual case in the place that the term was first applied, but over their entire range a PMD hatch may occur at just about any time of day, depending on the region, on whether it's early or late in the season, and on air and water temperatures. However, the start time of the emergence will generally be consistent over short periods at any particular place, so if you are visiting an area during a PMD hatch, it's best to inquire of the locals to obtain that information.

PMDs exhibit some of the more conspicuous variations between male and female mayfly appearance, a phenomenon referred to as sexual dimorphism. The most striking difference is undoubtedly in the eyes. Whereas the eyes of females are relatively small and dull, those of the male are larger and bright orange. The bodies of the males also exhibit a light orange tinge, compared with the less vibrant female.

The male eyes almost glow with their bright, saturated color. In fact, once you have observed a number of males and females, it's possible to ascertain the sex of PMDs on the water surface from several feet away, using eye color as the indicator. It was this situation that first led me to realize that male and female PMDs often hatch asynchronously; that is, the males start hatching before the females do.

While fishing one late April day, I saw PMDs starting to pop to the surface. Virtually all of them had big orange eyes. A little while later I noticed that the duller females had joined the party and were now about equally represented. Later, it became hard to spot any males. I've since learned that the earlier hatching of males is common not only in mayflies, but also among many other kinds of aquatic insects.

Thus the overall color of the naturals may gradually change as a hatch progresses, a fact that might become important when you are matching flies to duns over selective fish. Be sure to match the color of the side of the bug that a fish sees—the underside. The ventral color of the duns is lighter than the dorsal surfaces we see from above. So examine the underside of a dun that you pick up from the water surface. Duns darken shortly after emerging, and thus the color of one found at streamside might not be a good indicator of the color of a freshly hatched bug.

PMDs tend to hatch in water with slower currents and a smoother surface than do March browns, a situation that can reach extremes on spring creeks. Under these conditions, a trout can give its prey a leisurely examination. It thus becomes more important to choose a natural-looking fly. The low-riding Compara-dun and no-hackle flies can be good choices where trout are selective.

During a hatch, all mayflies experience difficulties on occasion while trying to escape the nymphal shuck, but for some reason PMDs seem to have more trouble than most. A high percentage of the duns lose legs or tails during the process, or are unable to inflate their folded and crumpled wings. It is very common to see duns struggling on the water surface, having been unable to entirely escape the nymphal exoskeleton, and dragging it around with a leg or wing still trapped inside. Such "cripples" are vulnerable and the trout know it. A smart angler will come prepared with some good cripple patterns when PMDs are hatching, particularly if it's a cool or rainy day, when emergence most frequently goes awry.

If you come across trout quietly sipping something that you can't see from the surface, and it's PMD season, there's a good chance that they are feeding on spinners. Depending on the weather, PMD spinner falls may occur in the morning or the evening. Most spinners, both male and female, take on a deep, dark red color. There are several fly patterns that do a credible job of imitating them,

Pale morning duns experience some of the highest rates of hatching malfunctions among the mayflies. A dun like this one that is unable to get completely free of its shuck makes a very seductive target for lurking trout.

PMD spinners have clear wings and darker, more vibrant colors than the duns. Body length = 8mm.

but a CDC Rusty Spinner, size 16, is what I most frequently use in this situation.

BUG EYES

I don't know about you, but when I see something in nature as striking as the difference between the eyes of male and female PMDs, I become intrigued. I start to wonder about the hows and the whys. For instance, why are the eyes of male mayflies usually bigger—sometimes tremendously so—than those of females? And why are male PMD eyes so brilliantly orange? What purpose does it serve?

If these are not the sorts of things that pique your interest, feel free to skip the rest of this section. Otherwise, read on.

To get some answers, I looked into what entomological researchers had to say on the subject. I learned a lot about how eyes of all kinds work, but more specifically, about what makes those of insects different and special; as well as some reasonable explanations for the peculiarities of mayfly eyes. I'll spare you the long, detailed version and instead will attempt to distill it down to the brass tacks. Let's first get acquainted with how mayfly eyes differ from our own.

Eyes come in two basic varieties. The eyes you are using to read this book are termed *simple eyes*. They work

essentially like a camera, and all higher (vertebrate) animals have this type. A simple eye has a single lens at the front, which focuses light reflected from an object onto a screen (the retina) at the back of the eye to form an image of the object. The screen is made up of millions of tiny light-sensing organs. Thus the defining characteristic of a simple eye is that it uses a single lens to focus light on the entire complement of sensors.

The primary eye of an adult insect, on the other hand, is an example of the other basic type: a *compound eye*. Instead of a single large lens, the outer perimeter of a compound eye consists of up to thousands of tiny facets, each with its own lens. Each lens sits at the outer end of a narrow tube, not unlike the objective lens of a telescope. These telescope-like tubes in the compound eye are called *ommatidia*. And like a telescope, the field of view of each of these tubes is very narrow. A wide field of view is achieved by stacking up to thousands of these minitelescopes side by side, each one aimed at a slightly different area of the visual field. The lens at the outer end of each ommatidium focuses light entering it onto a single light-sensing organ at the inner end of the tube. Thus, the defining characteristic of a compound eye is that it uses separate lenses to focus light on each of its sensor organs.

For both compound and simple eyes, each sensor sends a signal along a nerve connected to the brain. It is the

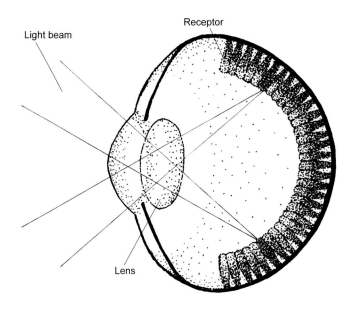

Simple eye. Humans and other vertebrates utilize an eye design in which light enters through a single aperture and is focused by a single lens onto a screen containing many light-sensitive receptor cells.

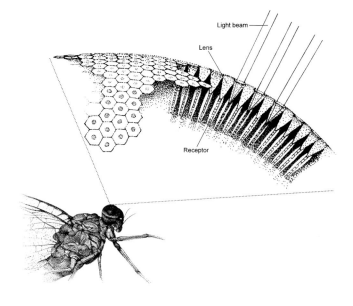

Compound eye. The eye of an insect is divided into many segments, called ommatidia, each of which receives light from just a small portion of the visual field. Every ommatidium contains its own lens that focuses light on a single receptor.

brain's job to take the thousands or millions of signals from the sensing screen and transform them into what we, or insects, perceive as an image of the object from which the light emanated.

Can the compound eyes of insects see color? We know that many of them can, but by somewhat different mechanisms than our eyes use.

Some of the light-sensing receptors (cones) of human eyes are able to differentiate colors by employing pigments (rhodopsins) that absorb light peaking at three different wavelengths: red, green, and blue. Each color receptor responds maximally to only one of the three wavelengths, and by comparing the signals from adjacent receptors of all three types, the brain is able to reconstruct colors intermediate between them.

Insect eyes use variations on the same principles to see color. But their receptors may differ from ours in the way they respond to light of different wavelengths, so the colors they perceive may not be exactly the same. Like we do, most terrestrial insects live in a largely green world, surrounded by vegetation that reflects light of that color. So it should come as no surprise that humans and bugs alike have lots of eye receptors with pigments that respond to green light. But depending on its specific habitat and way of making a living, any particular insect may benefit from being more or less sensitive to other portions of the color

spectrum than we are. As a result, insects vary in the way their photosensitive pigments respond to light of different colors.

Dragonflies spend a lot of time looking up toward the sky, as they watch for the small flying insects that are often their prey. Light from the sky, instead of being predominantly green, is primarily blue and ultraviolet. So as you might guess, the receptors on the part of a dragonfly's eye that looks upward employ pigments sensitive to blue and ultraviolet light.

So now that we understand the basics of insect eye function, let's come around again to the peculiarities of male mayfly eyes, and particularly those of pale morning duns. First, let's consider the question of size.

If we examine them closely, we see that virtually the entire difference in size between the eyes of a male mayfly and those of its sisters is in the dorsal (top) region. The dorsal portion of a male mayfly's eye is greatly enlarged. That segment of the male eye is generally not only taller but also wider, extending into the space on top of the head to an extent that the two eyes often touch, or come very close to it. In addition, the receptors in the ommatidia of the male eye that point upward usually employ pigments sensitive to blue or ultraviolet light, similar to the situation in dragonflies. We can therefore reasonably surmise that the dorsal eye of the male mayfly is also specialized for looking at objects above it.

Now, just what objects in the sky would likely be of such interest to a male mayfly, which would not equally concern a female? The answer is fairly obvious. As for any guy, girl watching is a male spinner's favorite pastime.

Mayflies mate in flight, with the male spinner approaching a female from underneath and reaching up to grab her with those specialized extra-long forelegs. But before that can happen, an amorous male mayfly must first beat out other suitors in the swarm that typically compete for any female visiting the bachelor pad—a spot in the air over or near a suitable body of water. Since normal bug vision is not that great when it comes to resolving small specks in the sky, any advantage that a guy can get in spotting the incoming babes is a welcome development. Bigger really is better, when it comes to mayfly eyes.

And what about the orange hue of male PMD eyes? Is it like the colorful plumage of male birds, designed to impress the ladies? Well, that might be part of it. But in this case it serves a more fundamental function as well. It turns out that when an insect's optical receptors are dedicated to responding to ultraviolet or blue light—like they are in the dorsal portion of a male mayfly's eye—special mechanisms often develop to keep those receptors in the ready state. Those mechanisms involve providing low levels of diffuse, long-wavelength light in addition to the higher levels of direct blue or UV light that the receptor is designed to sense.

How do you get diffuse, long-wavelength light from the sky? The solution employed by many insects, including mayflies, is to line the outer regions of the ommatidia with an orange or red pigment. Such pigments effectively block short-wavelength (blue or UV) light unless its path is directly into a particular ommatidium. Light that comes from an angle hits the walls of the ommatidium, where the red or orange pigment absorbs the short-wavelength components, but transmits some of the long-wavelength light into adjacent ommatidia, and reflects the rest. It's the reflected long-wavelength light that causes the insect's eye to look orange or red to us.

So whenever you see red or orange eyes in an insect—as in many true flies—it's a good bet that those eyes, or portions thereof, are tuned to respond to blue or UV light.

Does the color of a bug's eyes make any difference to a trout? It's hard to say, but we do know that trout can see color, and that at times they can key on particular colors when feeding selectively. You might think that a mayfly's tiny eyes, especially when above water, would not be noticeable to a trout from below. Maybe not, but when a male PMD resting on the surface of the water in a slant tank (discussed in more detail in chapter 17) is photographed from underneath, its orange eyes are very apparent. Who can say whether a little bright orange in a fly just might help when fishing over a PMD hatch?

MAHOGANY DUNS

While we're on the subject of bug eyes, it's a good time to bring up another spring mayfly, the mahogany dun (*Paraleptophlebia*). Male members of the Leptophlebiidae family often have eyes that are even more remarkable than those of the PMDs. They have taken the adaptations for looking up into the sky to yet greater heights. Each male eye is really two in one, with the upper part sitting on the lower one, looking like some sort of headdress. This type of eye is called turbinate, meaning that it is larger on the top than the bottom or is raised on a stalk. Besides Leptophlebiidae, the other family of mayflies in which turbinate eyes are especially well developed is Baetidae. Some Baetidae, including the blue-winged olives, have the most spectacular eyes in the mayfly world; we'll look at them in more detail in chapter 16. The upper part of the turbinate eye is a completely separate section that employs receptors fully specialized for responding to ultraviolet light, and the structure of that region differs markedly from the lower eye.

They may not have the name recognition of a PMD or a March brown, but what the mahogany duns lack in fame they make up in availability even when the glamorous players are scarce. Western species are also large enough to make a decent meal, in contrast to their relatives in the Midwest and East (where they are more often called blue quills), which tend to be on the smaller side. On the other hand, the eastern hatches are often more consistent and prolific. The eastern *P. adoptiva* is an important early season hatch, and the *P. mollis* emergence later in the summer in that region can be locally important but is often overlooked.

In the West, particularly near the northwest coast, several species hatch from spring through fall. Whereas some consider the fall hatches of *Paraleptophlebia* to be the most important, I've found them to be numerous at times during the spring. On occasion a good hatch of mahogany duns even precedes the famed March brown emergence, and while many fly fishers don't pay attention, the fish often will. So it's a good idea to keep an eye out for them at any time of year, and be prepared with some flies that imitate them.

These bugs migrate into quiet water to hatch, and if trout have taken notice, they will usually be sipping them gently, and will be in no hurry. This situation calls for stealth tactics, long leaders, downstream casts, and realistic imitations. I've found a Compara-dun pattern tied in mahogany dun colors to be effective on many occasions. And don't forget to fish subsurface, especially during the hours leading up to the hatch, when the nymphs become

The bright orange eyes of male PMDs are easily visible from underwater, as photographed through a slant tank.

The extraordinary turbinate eye of a *Paraleptophlebia* male spinner has two completely separate sections; the red upper part sees in the ultraviolet, while the lower black section is sensitive to the usual visible range of the light spectrum.

Paraleptophlebia duns have three tails, unmarked gray wings, and reddish brown (mahogany) bodies. Body length = 10mm.

active. *Paraleptophlebia* nymphs are classified as crawlers, but they have a somewhat more streamlined body shape than the typical members of this category. They swim poorly, so when they lose their grip, as they often do near hatch time, they are easy prey for any nearby trout.

Paraleptophlebia spinners usually return to the water in the evenings, sometimes before the duns even get off the water. It can be hard to tell which stage the trout slurping in the side eddies are taking. If your dun imitation is being ignored, try a spinner with a long, thin leader.

LITTLE YELLOW STONEFLIES

Mayflies are not the only aquatic insects taking advantage of the warming spring temperatures to emerge from the water. A profusion of small stonefly nymphs begin to make their way onto land, where they transition to the adult stage. Many of them belong to the group collectively referred to as little yellow stoneflies. Scurrying for cover along the stream margins at the approach of footsteps, the group's smaller members can be easy to miss. But at times, as on the late spring and summer evenings when thousands of some species muster over the water for an egg-laying spree, not even the least observant angler could overlook them. In either case, nearby trout are usually acutely aware of their presence.

Stoneflies of this group are typically quite small—³/₄–1³/₄ inch—compared with their larger and better-known brethren, the salmonflies and golden stones. And they are often hatching at about the same time as more famous aquatic insects. Perhaps those two traits together account for their general lack of renown.

The good thing about little yellow stoneflies is that they occur almost everywhere trout do, from one side of the country to the other. And while there are many species, most of them look quite alike. So if you know the habits of and have flies to imitate the little yellow stoneflies of the West, you will be well prepared when you fish in the East, or vice versa.

What we are calling little yellow stoneflies—also known as yellow sallies, *Skwalas*, and various other local appellations—may not actually be yellow. Most of them tend to be more tan or light brown, and belong to the family Perlodidae. The ones that really do look yellow are in the family Chloroperlidae—the "chloro" part of which means green! (To be fair, there are many members of Chloroperlidae that really are green, or at least chartreuse.)

Since this is the first instance that stoneflies have come up in this book, you might think this would be a good time to talk about stoneflies in general, to put them into their taxonomic pigeonholes, and to go over some of the traits

The wings of *Paraleptophlebia* spinners become completely clear, and the bodies darken in color. As is common in many species of mayflies, part of the abdomen in males also becomes transparent, allowing us to see that there is not much inside other than air. Males retain the big colorful eyes of the duns, but their tails and forelegs lengthen considerably. Body length = 9mm.

A cooperative perlodid (*Isoperla*) little yellow stonefly is content to pose momentarily for the camera. Body length = 12mm.

Perlodid nymphs of the genus *Kogotus* sport alternating light and dark transverse bands on their abdomens. Body length = 14mm.

A chloroperlid of the genus *Sweltsa* begins to take flight. Body length = 10mm.

An *Isoperla* nymph attempts to escape detection by hiding beneath an underwater rock. Dark longitudinal bands are one of the keys to recognizing perlodid nymphs of the genus *Isoperla*. Body length = 10mm.

they have in common; however, chapter 7, the first chapter devoted exclusively to stoneflies, will go into a broad overview of the order Plecoptera.

The little yellow (really, tan) stoneflies of the Perlodidae family are the most numerous and widespread of their clan. In fact, just one genus, *Isoperla*, has nearly sixty species spread across the United States. Isoperlid nymphs lack external gills and are thus easy to distinguish from the nymphs of other stoneflies, like golden stones or perlodids of other genera, with which they might be most easily confused. (Other Perlodidae genera may have gills, but they are always simple and fingerlike, and never have the elaborately branched gills of golden stoneflies.) Instead of gills, isoperlid nymphs absorb oxygen through the thin portions of their exoskeleton, for example around the legs and "neck." This is not a particularly efficient method of respiration, so these nymphs tend to live in the cold, well-oxygenated water of riffles. They hide beneath and between the stones as they search for their small prey, mostly midge larvae, but also any other animal small enough for them to tackle. Their active ways mean that they frequently end up in the stream drift, where trout will notice them. This is especially true in the weeks leading up to emergence, when they migrate from the faster areas of the stream into adjacent slower water, where they can often be found hunting in plant debris.

There are other genera within the Perlodidae family that can be regionally important. Hatches of *Skwala* adults—which are an uncommon case of bugs that have no really common name other than their scientific designation *Skwala*—are a big event on some western rivers, like the Yakima in eastern Washington or the Bitterroot in Montana. Depending on the region and the weather, a *Skwala* hatch may occur in late winter or early spring, but it will be covered as a winter hatch in chapter 16. The majority of the little yellow stoneflies begin hatching about mid-spring, and the various species often continue emergence well into the summer.

Chloroperlid nymphs are smaller and more cylindrical in shape, compared with the perlodids, and have shorter tails. Like the perlodids, they primarily feed on other small insects, and are likely to be found in the leaf packs along stream margins. When it's time to emerge, they don't have far to travel to get to shore.

Little yellow stonefly nymphs in the Chloroperlidae family are small, round, and have short tails. Body length = 7mm.

An adult caddis of the Limnephilidae family.
Body + wings = 17mm.

The nymphs of perlodid and chloroperlid species crawl out on rocks or plant stems near shore, where they get a firm grip before splitting open the dorsal thorax of their exoskeletons. (It has been suggested that some little yellow stoneflies may emerge in open water, but that is very unlikely. Ralph Cutter, in his book *Fish Food*, reported discussions with a stonefly expert who explained why that would be impossible for a stonefly. Cutter has reared these stoneflies in an aquarium and confirmed that they hatched only when given a means to climb out of the water. My own observations with aquarium-reared perlodids are in agreement with Cutter's.) Within a few minutes a winged adult steps out, leaving the discarded nymphal shuck for curious anglers to find. Since adult emergence occurs out of the water, there is no opportunity for trout to go on a feeding spree as they would for a typical mayfly hatch. Instead, the hours of opportunity come when the adults on streamside vegetation fall off into the water, or when they return to lay eggs.

And that egg-laying time can be magical. On warmer late spring or early summer evenings, thousands of them may be in the air at once over a stream or river. I've watched the small, pale yellow chloroperlids of the genus *Sweltsa* seemingly materialize from nowhere over a stream as the light faded. Touching their abdomens to the water repeatedly, the females frequently end up on the surface. Hungry trout snouts usually make sure they don't get airborne again.

Not that it will make a lot of difference to the fish, or the fishing, but if you see some small pale yellow or greenish stoneflies on the water and are not sure whether they are perlodids or chloroperlids, check the length of their tails. Those of perlodids are longer and project rearward past the end of the wings, while the tails of chloroperlids are shorter and usually not visible from above. In addition, the red egg masses within the abdomens of the females are usually discernible through the thin, almost transparent abdominal walls of chloroperlids. They can make the rear ends of the abdomens appear quite red—a characteristic that might be important at times to reflect in your flies.

CADDIS

Let's not forget the multitude of caddisflies that hatch in the spring. The sheer numbers of them can be overwhelming, in species as well as individuals. While the particular species vary from place to place, the well-known families

This member of the Rhyacophilidae family is one of the more striking of the usually dull caddisfly clan. If you've ever used an imitation of a green rock worm larva (chapter 12), this is the adult the larva will become. Body + wings = 14mm.

are represented almost everywhere there are trout. Rather than attempt a comprehensive tally here, I'll just include a few representative examples of the abundant northern case makers of the Limnephilidae family and the free-living caddisflies of the Rhyacophilidae family. Most of these can be imitated as adults by color and size variations on the trusty Elk Hair Caddis fly, or its effective derivative, the X-Caddis. The next chapter will have more details on one of my favorite late-spring caddisflies, the great gray spotted sedge (*Arctopsyche grandis*); or as we call it in my neck of the woods, the McKenzie caddis.

FLIES

Considering the diversity of bugs covered in this chapter, a comprehensive list of useful flies to imitate them could go on for pages. There are plenty of good sources for fly pattern recommendations, so I'll just mention a few that are some of my favorites or that have proven themselves over the years. In general, when there is a hatch going on or adults are visible near the water, I generally start with a dry fly, because that's the type of fishing that I enjoy the most. But I'm always ready to switch to an emerger or a subsurface pattern if the situation calls for it.

The X-Caddis was developed by Craig Matthews to represent a crippled caddisfly that is having trouble emerging from the pupal shuck. Hackle is omitted from the body so that the fly floats low in the water, and trailing fibers are added to represent the shuck. This fly is especially effective on slow, smooth water where trout get the chance to closely examine the fly.

There are a number of flies that do a good job when little yellow stonefly adults are on the water. This pattern developed by Ralph Cutter uses deer hair for the body, rendering it very buoyant, and incorporates yellow and orange to represent body and egg-case colors.

A high proportion of mayfly spinners have dark red or rust-colored bodies and clear wings, including pale morning duns and mahogany duns. The Rusty Spinner does an excellent job of imitating most of them. It can be tied with an Antron wing that is effective, but I prefer a CDC wing. When coated in dry-fly powder, the CDC wings trap air bubbles on the surface, similar to the effect of a natural spinner wing. The CDC also moves enticingly with the slightest microcurrent.

The Hare's Ear nymph is one of the first patterns tied by beginning fly tiers, and it usually remains a go-to fly in the years that follow. Its buggy appearance and ability to represent reasonably well almost any subsurface insect—including mayflies, stoneflies, and caddisflies, when colors and sizes are varied—has made it a perennial favorite.

The Compara-dun dry-fly style is one of my favorites. It often fools trout when standard hackled patterns are being refused, even though it doesn't float as well under choppy conditions. Since it sits low in the water, with the body in the film, it probably looks to fish more like a cripple or an emerger than a healthy dun.

5

McKenzie Green Is the Thing in Late Spring

The big green great gray spotted sedge

"Think Green" has special meaning during late spring in Oregon's southern Willamette Valley. Yes, many here are "thinking green" all year long as it relates to good environmental practices. But by mid-May, not only is the countryside virtually radiating the color; even the underwater world gets in on the act, sprouting vegetation of its own.

Green time is also big-time bug time. The much-loved March brown and blue-winged olive mayfly hatches may be waning, and the grannom caddisfly blizzard may be behind us, but a cornucopia of replacements stands ready. Coming into their own now are the pale morning duns (*Ephem-*

erella), mahogany duns (*Paraleptophlebia*), and the flashy yellow tribe of pale evening duns (*Heptagenia*) that brighten local rivers yet mostly get a Bronx cheer from trout.

But the star of the new show, without doubt, wears a seasonal hue: the big green bug known in my area as the McKenzie caddis or "that big green caddis," but elsewhere in its western range is called the great gray spotted sedge (sedge being another name for caddis). At least, that's what most books say. I have rarely heard anyone refer to it that way in conversation, and suspect it is one of those overly long common names that are not so common. Most likely,

Late spring is a time of green foliage and big green caddisflies on Oregon's McKenzie River.

each region has its own sobriquet for this quite widely distributed insect, which has been reported throughout the western United States, from New Mexico to the Canadian border, and on up into Alberta and British Columbia. But, to be clear as to the object of our adulation, I'll spell out its unambiguous scientific appellation: *Arctopsyche grandis*. You can call it whatever you like, but I'll stick with McKenzie caddis for the rest of this chapter.

LARVAE

We are most concerned in this season with the big fluttering adult bug, but let's start at the beginning (as if a circle has one); not only because it seems most logical, but also because it's a lot easier to distinguish among caddisfly youngsters than it is among their similar-appearing elders. As we learned in chapter 3, caddisflies have four life stages (unlike the three stages of mayflies and stoneflies)—egg, larva, pupa, and adult—that compose the developmental pathway called complete metamorphosis. I'll skip the egg stage (boring and hard to photograph) and get right to the larva.

The one pictured was found in the McKenzie River in mid-April, among the cobble of a riffle, its preferred hangout. It was two years old, minus a few weeks. I know this because *A. grandis* has an unusually long two-year larval stage—it takes a long time to grow so big—and one this size was clearly approaching its second birthday. Note its green color. Its underside is an even brighter shade.

These larvae spend their days in flimsy shelters constructed from their homemade silk, plus nearby bits of what-have-you, attached to a silken "fishing" net that catches whatever drifts by in the current. Like spiders, they emerge occasionally to snack on what they've caught—often other smaller bugs, as well as sundry organic material. Such behavior has led *A. grandis* and its relatives to be called net spinners. The other two categories of caddisflies are case makers, which build solid, mobile homes of pebbles, sand, and/or plant matter; and free-living caddis, which construct neither cases nor nets, but roam about freely on the stream bottom. (See chapter 3 for more details.)

PUPAE

Don't go looking for these larvae now, in late spring. You won't find many, at least not the larger two-year-olds. That's because they've nearly all advanced to the next stage: pupa. A few weeks ago the larvae started adding bits of sticks and stones to their net shelters, then sealed themselves inside and began the remarkable transformation to adult. Shortly after that time, I found one attached to a riffle rock, and broke it free to see what it looked like. The accompanying photos show the (detached) pupal case it built, before and after I cut it open to see what it contained.

You can see the larva/pupa inside, with a bright green abdomen and its dark head at the middle right, all encased in slimy-looking silk. It hasn't progressed very far along the pupal developmental pathway yet, since I found it in mid-April, probably shortly after it sealed itself inside.

When the pupae are ready to hatch—usually in fast choppy runs—they cut themselves free from the encasing shelter and, aided by gas bubbles that have formed under the exoskeleton, swim rapidly to the surface. There the adult splits open the pupal exoskeleton (shuck) and pulls itself above the surface film, leaving the shuck behind.

The presence of these shucks on the surface is a good indication that a hatch is going on. Whenever I see adults flying around, if I'm not positive whether some of them are currently hatching or if they are all returning egg layers, I check the water surface for pupal shucks. If I see them, I know a hatch is in progress. You have to look closely, but you should see something similar to the shuck in the top photo on page 54.

Many times the rising pupae are the primary targets of feeding trout. That's probably why swung soft-hackle and other wet flies often work so well—when cast upstream and allowed to sink, then rising on the swing as the line comes tight. If you see rising trout but they don't seem to be taking adults—or your adult imitation anyway—try swinging a pupa imitation. The fly in the middle photo on page 54 has worked well for me when swung during a McKenzie caddis hatch.

You may be thinking, this fly doesn't match the color of the shuck in the preceding photo. But remember that you're trying to match the pupa with the adult still (at least partially) inside, not the empty shuck. This also includes those unfortunate individuals we insensitively call cripples, which get stuck and are unable to completely free themselves from the pupal shuck. In the bottom picture on page 54, you get a better sense not only of the cripple's helpless (and vulnerable) plight but also of its "greenness."

ADULTS

Although I've come across a few fishing books and articles that claim that the emergence of *A. grandis* adults occurs only at night, that is certainly not the case in western Oregon, at least. Some adults may hatch at any time of day when it is sunny and warm, but more of them generally pop up in the afternoon, with the peak usually 4–7 P.M. Their preferred hatching water temperature seems to be around 52 degrees F. On most days in my region the hatch is not prolific; you'll see one bug hatch here, one there, over a period of hours. Though on the first warm sunny day after an extended cool drizzly period, which frequently occurs during late spring in the Northwest, the hatch can go off with a bang as lots of bugs start popping. (The good

A large McKenzie caddis (*A. grandis*) larva is flushed from its hiding place among the rocks. Body length = 24mm.

A cutaway view of a McKenzie caddis pupal case reveals the young insect inside.

A McKenzie caddis pupal encasement, removed from the rock to which it was attached. Length = 30mm.

The presence of pupal shucks on the water surface is a good indicator of a hatch in progress.

Wet flies like this one are effective imitators of rising pupae. Size 10, 2X heavy.

Crippled emergers unable to get free of their pupal shucks are prime targets for hungry trout.

news is that it doesn't take many of these big insects to get the fish excited.)

While I'm touching the subject of when this *A. grandis* caddisfly emerges, I should mention that despite my coverage of it in the late-spring section of this book, you may find it hatching later in some parts of its range. Though it is a late spring/early summer bug west of the Cascades, at higher elevations and in colder interior regions, the hatch may be delayed into mid-summer or even late summer. So depending on the region in which you are fishing, you may want to look for it hatching a little later in the year.

Now let's finally take a look at one of the large adults about which fish and fishers are so enthused, in the accompanying photos. You can see some of the green peeking through, but to really appreciate where its reputation for the color comes from, we need to flip the bug over and take a look at its underside.

Now you know why some people call this bug a green caddis or something similar. So let's assume that you head out to the river during the McKenzie caddis hatch, that you catch one of the big bugs flying around, and then take a close look—what the...? Where's the green? Maybe you see some tinges, but nothing like the pictures below. You might say to yourself, "That rascal Arlen has been 'Photo-shop-ing' us!"

Before you accuse me of fraud, catch a few more bugs, and at different times of the day. Color varies a lot and depends on several things. One of them might be location;

I need to explore that angle further. But most importantly, the green color is chiefly apparent right at the time of hatching, and fades rapidly thereafter. Furthermore, in my experience, females are a lot greener than males. The undersides of males are more of a yellowish-brown color, like many other caddisflies. (In addition to being greener, females are larger, by a good hook size. Females are a size 8–10, depending on how sparsely you dress your fly, with bodies averaging 12.5mm; males are a size 10–12, with bodies averaging about 9.5mm.)

Now let's say you see some of these big caddis flying around in the vicinity of the river. Are they hatching right now, or are these caddisflies that hatched previously, and are just out taking a spin or returning to lay eggs? And why should you care?

You should care because the fish will. A flying bug is of no interest at all to a trout, except maybe when it is within inches of exiting or entering the water. Hatching caddis-flies are definitely in the fishes' medium, and present feeding opportunities to them as emerging pupae and as adults trying to leave the surface film. Those are opportunities for us, too. Both the fish and we get another chance when the bugs come back to lay eggs. In between those times, thousands of flying bugs or a mob in the bushes doesn't mean much for fishing success.

So the key is to determine if the caddisflies you see are hatching or laying eggs, rather than doing anything else. If you observe them on the water, then voila; you know the

A freshly hatched female McKenzie caddis shows traces of green when viewed from the side. Body + wings = 21mm.

When flipped on its back, the green color—for which the McKenzie caddis is famous—is much more apparent.

answer. Returning egg layers dive into the water quite visibly. A freshly hatched bug usually skitters across the surface a few feet before it gets airborne, and you will often see fish chasing them vigorously during that brief period. However, it might be harder to tell if the nondiving adult in the air has just left the water; and many times you may only see the bugs once they are in the air. Did they just hatch?

Here are three ways to help you identify McKenzie caddis stages in the air: (1) **Flight pattern**. Newly hatched bugs tend to fly in straight lines (but influenced by the wind), are rather slow and lumbering, gain altitude, and head from the water toward the banks. Older caddisflies fly erratically (to avoid predators), faster, more skillfully, and may be headed in any direction, not just toward shore. (2) **Color**. Catch a few bugs, and if a lot of them are very (as opposed to slightly) green on their undersides, they just hatched. (3) **Time of day**. While on some days these insects may hatch at any time, more tend to hatch later in the day. So odds that the bugs you see flying have just hatched are diminished in the morning.

A FISH-EYE VIEW

Take a look at the shot on the next page of a female McKenzie caddis sitting on the water, and photographed from almost directly below. This is approximately what a fish would see if the bug was directly above it, and the fish was holding in the water horizontally, or at least not too close to the bug. (The latter point is important because the way a trout's eyes are situated on its head, it loses sight of anything in the last moment before engulfing it.) The picture was taken with the bug in a "slant tank," with a blue-painted box above it to simulate the sky.

At this point I need to briefly describe a slant tank. It is like a regular rectangular aquarium, except it has a front

A colorful cutthroat trout that fell for a fake McKenzie caddis.

surface that, instead of being vertical, is inclined toward the viewer at a 48.5–degree angle. I could give you a long description of why the tank is constructed like this, the physics of light being bent as it leaves air and enters water (and vice versa), but I'll save that discussion for later. Let it suffice to say now that such a tank allows us to view the water surface from below in the same way a fish would see it. That is, we can see an object above the water surface fairly clearly when it is straight above us, or out in any direction to about 48.5 degrees (in what is referred to as Snell's window); but at any steeper angle, the water surface acts as an opaque mirror, and we can't see through it.

My interest in slant tanks was piqued by the work of Vincent Marinaro, a famous Pennsylvania fly fisher. Marinaro was a pioneer in the use of slant tanks to view insects and flies on the water surface in the same way a fish would see them. His books *A Modern Dry-Fly Code* (1950) and *In the Ring of the Rise* (1976) are classics that I highly recommend. I'll have more to say about slant tanks, and how they can help us visualize surface insects and tied flies in a way that a trout would see them, in chapter 17.

So now let's see what happens when that same McKenzie caddis is viewed on the surface of the water in the slant tank, but with the camera moved from directly below it out to an angle—specifically, to an angle a little greater than 48.5 degrees from vertical. Now, in the photo of the McKenzie caddis in the slant tank, we can see what a fish would see when, instead of looking directly above, it looks at the surface upstream to spot whatever food items the current might be bringing its way. This is what a stream-dwelling trout routinely does. Any bug directly above would already be swept behind it by the time the fish rose to the surface, so it has to look ahead to anticipate the approach of prey, and start rising to intercept it.

The only parts of the bug we can see now are those that break the surface and extend below. Everything around it is just a reflection of the bottom, which in this case is a uniform sand color; we can no longer see the blue "sky" above. A big heavy caddis like this one has a hard time holding itself above water, so some legs, parts of the abdomen, antennae, and wings are variously visible as it struggles on the surface.

Since this picture is what a fish sees when it is deciding whether to rise and intercept our friend the caddis, we might learn something by comparing this view to some of our imitating flies in a similar position. In my experience (and that of Brian Marz of the McKenzie Angler, who called it to my attention) the most successful fly for the McKenzie caddis hatch is a size 10 green-bodied Elk Hair Caddis (EHC) in which the hackle is replaced by cul de canard (CDC)—that is, feathers from a duck's butt. In the several years that I've used it, it has far outfished the standard-hackled version.

A McKenzie caddis on the water surface, viewed from almost directly below, is fully visible.

A green-bodied Elk Hair Caddis with CDC replacing the hackle is an excellent surface pattern when McKenzie caddis are hatching. Size 10.

Only the parts of a McKenzie caddis that break through the surface film can be seen when viewed in a slant tank from below at an angle of slightly more than 48.5 degrees to vertical.

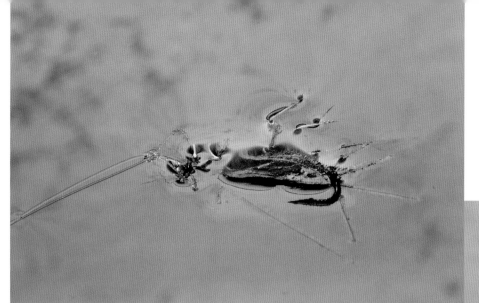

An EHC/CDC fly on the surface of the water, viewed in a slant tank from below at an angle of slightly more than 48.5 degrees to vertical.

A standard EHC *hackled* fly on the surface of the water, viewed from below at an angle of slightly more than 48.5 degrees to vertical.

Now examine the photo above of this fly floating in the slant tank, taken at the same angle as the real bug on page 57. You can also see the 4X tippet that I tied to the fly, to mimic as closely as possible how it would look in a real fishing situation. (The tippet is attached with a nonslip mono-loop knot, which I prefer because it gives the fly more freedom to float naturally and minimizes the influence of the tippet on its position and reaction to microcurrents.)

In this view—let's call it the "fishing situation"—does the EHC/CDC fly look similar to the real McKenzie caddis to you? Apparently it does to a lot of trout. Now for comparison, look at the photo of the analogous standard size 10, green-bodied EHC/*hackled* fly in the same position. Does it look a lot different from the CDC version to you? Again, apparently it does to the trout, because like I said, it catches a lot fewer of them. Still, it does fool some. It hasn't become the standard over the years by not catching any fish.

At the moment, there are still more questions than answers when it comes to what looks good to a trout, and understanding which qualities in artificial flies are most important. My investigations using the slant tank are ongoing. Maybe I'll learn something profound, maybe not. But it does change how I think about what a fish sees and what a fly must do. (See chapter 17 for more about trout vision, slant tanks, and underwater views.)

ON THE RIVER

It is late spring as I write this, and the fishing has been good in western Oregon lately. Rising water temperatures can probably be thanked for a lot of that, but I think old *A. grandis* deserves a big chunk of the credit. It's gotten the trout excited, and looking up even when nothing is hatching. In the last few days, I've fished several sections of the McKenzie River and nearby streams, using mostly imitations of the big caddis. I've caught good numbers of hungry trout, a mix of rainbows, and coastal cutthroats. Check out a picture of one of my favorites on page 56, a respectable cutthroat, still hanging on to an EHC/CDC fly. Not the largest fish, but one of the most handsome.

6
Pale Evening Duns and the Clinger Tribes

Clinger-type mayflies of the family Heptageniidae

Late one afternoon at the end of May, I waded toward a favorite spot on the McKenzie to see if the heavily overcast sky was bringing trout to the surface. But first I stopped at a little side current below a small riffle to check for any emerging insects. A steady dribble of pale morning duns (*Ephemerella*) floated by, accompanied by a few blue-winged olives (*Baetis*). As I was about to move on to the deeper waters, I saw a big yellow bug drifting toward me. It started to lift off, but I netted it for a closer look.

In the next fifteen minutes or so, I saw just four or five more. The water was too shallow where they were emerging for fish to be feeding on them. But they sure grabbed my attention, being bright yellow and big—about a size 12. This was the first time I had seen them, though I had heard tales of a big yellow mayfly making late spring appearances on nearby rivers. Deke Meyer, in his book *River Journal: McKenzie River*, mentioned an "early summer fluorescent yellow mayfly that almost glows." But he didn't name it. My yellow dun fit his description exactly; and since the odds of two such grand mayflies occurring on the same river seemed slim, they no doubt were of the same species. But which one?

No one I asked seemed to know, at least with any certainty. Some opined that it must be a member of the genus

Clinger mayflies thrive in the fastest waters.

Some members of the Heptageniidae family, like this male *Heptagenia solitaria* dun, are among the most brightly colored of the mayflies. At the time of hatching, duns have dark, almost black eyes. Body length = 12mm.

Epeorus, sometimes called yellow quills. Others thought it might be called a sulfur; however, that name is usually applied to eastern mayflies of the genus *Ephemerella*, or sometimes the genus *Epeorus*, and to my knowledge it isn't commonly used for any western mayfly. Because my yellow bug had two tails, and a rather flat head with eyes on the top rather than the sides, there was one thing I was sure of right from the beginning. This mayfly was a "clinger."

CLINGERS

The clinger group of mayflies, unlike the other three types, have been so kind as to restrict themselves to a single family, Heptageniidae; thus providing a tiny bit of relief for the memory department of our overtaxed brains. In a previous chapter we met the March browns (genera *Rhithrogena* and *Maccaffertium*), all of which are proud members of the clinger tribes. We now encounter some of their close relatives.

Like the other three informal categories of mayflies, clingers are defined by the habits and shapes of their aquatic juveniles rather than the terrestrial adults. Clinger nymphs specialize in flowing water environments, so you will never find them in lakes or ponds. In moving water, they are most common in the faster sections. When it comes to current, clingers are uniquely adapted for the turbulent areas, but there is a caveat: while the water nearby may be rushing past, clingers take advantage of a thin layer

of calmer water enveloping the surface of rocks on the stream bottom. This layer is the result of friction, which slows the current in the immediate vicinity of objects within the water column.

Clingers have also adopted hydrodynamic shapes to decrease their exposure to the forces of the currents. Their heads are broad, flat, and shovel-shaped, so that water flows up and over them rather than pushing them downstream. Their legs splay out to the sides in keeping with the low profile. Eyes are on top of the head, since there is no room for them laterally. As we saw in chapter 2, a few clingers have taken an additional step, with gill plates modified into suction cups that permit an even tighter attachment to their favorite rock.

Nevertheless, some types of clinger nymphs do inhabit the moderate or slowly flowing areas, usually adjacent to faster currents. These clingers may be in the process of adapting to a different habitat than the one for which they appear to be best suited. Who knows, maybe sometime in the distant future their descendants might lose the sleek, fast water shape that seems somewhat superfluous in those environments.

Identifying a nymph as a clinger is fairly easy. If it hangs on tenaciously as you lift its rock from flowing water; if it looks like someone squashed it flat with a careless step of a wading boot; if the head is wider than the body, and the eyes are on top, like a flounder's; and if it has three (or occasionally two, as noted below for the genera

Epeorus and *Ironodes*) tails, then your bug is a clinger mayfly nymph.

Why do clinger nymphs go to such trouble to survive in the rather challenging environment of rushing currents, rather than homesteading more placid neighborhoods? Most likely the answer lies in three essential requirements: respiration, nutrition, and protection. Churning water is the place to find more oxygen, a basic necessity for any insect. Rock surfaces in shallow riffles provide foundations for fields of nourishing algae, with little competition from grazers unable to resist the flows. And similarly, most predators are ill suited to ferreting out small bugs from rock crevices in strong currents. A perfect home for those who can take it!

When a clinger nymph grows up, the adult it becomes always has just two tails. This is despite the fact that most of them have three tails as nymphs. So if you spot a mayfly dun or spinner with three tails, you know it's not a clinger type. (In fact, if the adult has three tails, you can surmise that it probably belongs to the crawler group. Other than crawlers, only a few species of adult burrower-type mayflies have three tails.) If it has two tails, it could be a clinger, but you have to look closer to be sure. First, examine the head. Clinger adults retain the flattened, shovel-shaped heads of the nymphs. That will probably be enough for streamside identification, and as far as you can easily go in the field. The final identifying traits for this group require some magnification (reading glass or microscope) and some knowledge of the minute features of mayfly anatomy; namely, the pattern of wing veins (two pairs of cubital-intercalary veins on the trailing edge of the forewing), and the number of segments in the hind "foot" (i.e., five tarsal segments). The specifics of those details are beyond the scope of this book.

Clinger mayflies are widely distributed across North America and beyond. They are at least as significant in the East as they are in the West. The genera important to anglers within the Heptageniidae family are *Rhithrogena*, *Maccaffertium* (eastern and midwestern, formerly classified as *Stenonema*); *Epeorus* (as well as *Ironodes*, formerly *Epeorus*); *Hexagenia* (plus *Ecdyonurus* and *Leucrocuta*, formerly *Hexagenia*); *Stenacron* (eastern and midwestern, formerly *Stenonema*); *Cinygmula* (primarily western); and *Cinygma* (western). We've already seen representatives of *Rhithrogena* in chapter 2, and we'll see examples of most of the others below.

THAT YELLOW MAYFLY AGAIN

So, the striking yellow mayfly with which I began this chapter was definitely a clinger, meeting the criteria just noted. But since that category includes a lot of genera and species, there were a number of possibilities for its exact identity. The leading candidate seemed to be the genus *Epeorus*, known for its yellow mayflies, and even referred to in some circles as yellow quills. I showed its photograph to several people, whose judgments I respect, and the consensus was "yes, most likely *Epeorus*."

But when I compared it with published descriptions, two *Epeorus* characteristics were lacking in my bug: irregular heart-shaped marks on the femurs of the front legs, and eyes that touch on top of the head in males. From published identification keys, I was led to conclude that this yellow mayfly was a member of the genus *Heptagenia*, often called pale evening duns (PEDs). Yet I could find no descriptions of a PED that was as yellow as this one.

Time to enlist the help of an expert. So I sent the bug, in a vial of alcohol, to friend and entomological advisor Rick Hafele. An aquatic entomologist by training and a keen fly fisher by avocation, Rick is a wealth of knowledge on aquatic insects; not to mention one of the nicest guys you could hope to meet. If you ever get the chance to participate in one of his workshops on the subject, you won't regret it. I also highly recommend Rick's books *An Angler's Guide to the Aquatic Insects*; *Nymph-Fishing Rivers and Streams*; and *Western Mayfly Hatches* (with Dave Hughes). Rick's verdict: my yellow mayfly was of the species *Heptagenia solitaria*.

I have subsequently identified *H. solitaria* nymphs from the area and correlated them with the yellow adults. So there is no longer any confusion about this beautiful bug. It's a pale evening dun, and a fine example indeed, at least in the eyes of an admiring fly fisher. Do fish hold it in similar high regard? It has the reputation in my area of being mostly ignored by trout. But I suspect that is because the bug hatches in low numbers here, rather than any purposeful avoidance. For where PEDs are found in abundance, bright yellow or not, trout definitely feed on them; sometimes selectively.

BUG EYES, REVISITED

We first encountered some of the remarkable properties of mayfly eyes in chapter 4, when we performed an up-close-and-personal examination of pale morning duns and mahogany duns. Those extraordinary organs are set to grab our attention once again as we zoom in on members of the Heptageniidae family.

Take another look at the photo (page 60) of the *H. solitaria* male dun netted right after hatching. It has coal-black eyes. Now, look at a photo (page 62) of the male spinner, taken during the daytime. Not only are the eyes of the spinner much larger, there has been a remarkable change in color, from black to greenish yellow.

After I took that photo in midafternoon, I set the bug aside and forgot about it for a while. When I looked at it again a few hours later that evening, I did a double take. Black eyes again? Is this thing a chameleon? Well, over the

Male *H. solitaria* spinners exhibit light yellow-green eyes in the daytime, complementing their golden body color.

At night, a *Heptagenia* mayfly's eyes darken again. Notice the space between the large compound eyes of this male spinner, and the absence of marks on the legs—characteristics useful for identification to the genus level.

next few weeks I conducted my own little research project. Conclusion: the eyes of the males are normally light colored during the day, and slowly change to black as night falls. But if you keep them in the dark during the day or put them in strong light during the night, you can get them to reverse. Why do they do it? For some time I didn't have much of a clue. But as I noticed a similar phenomenon in other members of the Heptageniidae family, I just had to look into it a little deeper.

Finding the answer turned out to be no simple task. I could unearth no published references directly addressing eye color changes in heptagenid mayflies. But after reading a number of articles on insect vision and the mechanisms commonly employed, I think I have the likely explanation. It builds on the principles set out in chapter 4, where we first considered the properties of bug eyes. It has to do with the pigments that insects use in their compound eyes to modify the light entering them.

Colored pigments (like red or yellow) that block short wavelength light but allow some longer wavelengths to pass and reach the visual receptors are useful for insect

eyes specialized for responding to blue or UV light. But the benefits come with a cost. That cost is a higher visual "noise" level, which results in lowered sensitivity. The result is poor vision in low light.

Apparently, whereas many types of mayflies live with poor night vision, a lot of heptagenids have come up with a better idea. They simply change eye pigments at night. Eyes with black-screening pigments enjoy lower noise and higher sensitivity under low-light conditions, even though they aren't as efficient during the bright of the day.

Now I'm left wondering what it is that these chameleon-eyed heptagenids are doing at night—requiring improved vision—that other mayflies are not. But we'll leave that question for another time.

PALE EVENING DUNS

The common name pale evening dun is often applied to a variety of mayflies belonging to several closely related genera, including at least *Heptagenia*, *Ecdyonurus* (formerly *Nixe*, and *Heptagenia* before that), and *Leucrocuta*. Sometimes they are lumped together as the "pale evening

A *Heptagenia* nymph. Notice the small size of its left front leg. Developmental defects resulting in greatly reduced limbs seem to be common among mayfly nymphs, and the abnormalities persist into adulthood. Body length = 8mm.

A female *H. solitaria* dun fully deserves the pale appellation, but in my experience it hatches during the day rather than evening. Body length = 12mm.

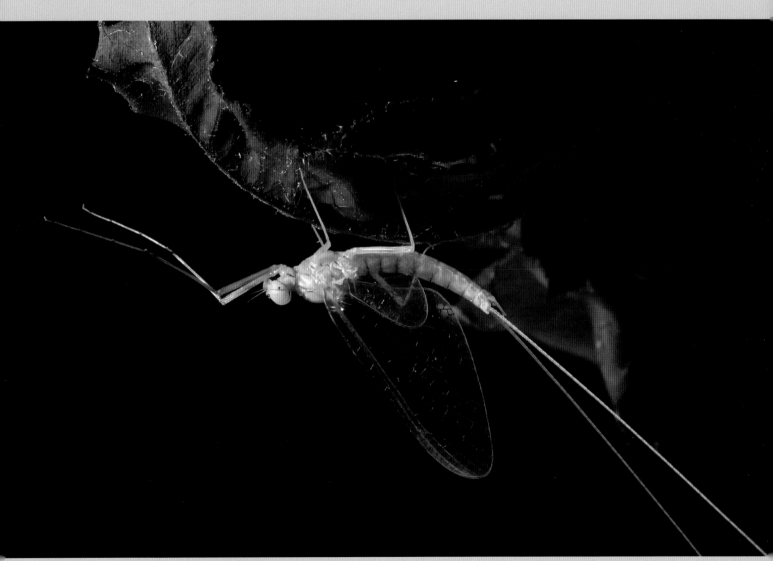

The long forelegs and tails of pale evening dun spinners can more than triple their overall length, making them appear more massive in the air than they really are. Body length = 13mm; front legs = 15mm; tails = 30mm.

dun complex" or the "*Heptagenia* complex." Since *Ecdyonurus* and *Leucrocuta* species are very similar to *Heptagenia*—and were classified within that genus until recently—doing so makes a lot of sense. Only experts can tell many of them apart.

Members of this complex are the clingers that tend to inhabit the moderate or slow currents. They lack the modified "suction-cup" gills of some other heptagenids that specialize in the fastest flows, but the nymphs retain the overall clinger shape. All of them have three tails, like most mayfly nymphs. To distinguish them further, you have to consider things like gill structure and the nature of the claws on their tarsi (feet), which we won't get into here.

Female duns usually look similar to the males, except they have smaller eyes. In fact, eye size, rather than what might first come to mind, is the most obvious way to quickly differentiate the sexes of mayfly duns.

Sexual dimorphism becomes more dramatic in the spinner stage. Not only do the eyes of males get even larger, but forelegs and tails often get ludicrously long. I've found that spinner falls, usually in the evenings, are some of the best opportunities for fishing PED imitations. Big trout don't like to miss an opportunity for sipping helpless bugs at their leisure.

Besides *H. solitaria* , other important species found in the West include *H. elegantula* (which produces probably the most fishable hatches across its range), *E. criddlei*, and *E. simplicoides*. The most notable species in the eastern part of the United States include *L. hebe* and *L. aphrodite*. In different locales they may go by various common names such as gray fox, western ginger quill, little slate-winged dun, little yellow quill, golden dun, and no doubt others. Most of the mayflies in the PED complex can be imitated with a similar collection of brown wet flies in the nymph stage or light-colored dries in the dun and spinner stages.

EPEORUS

The genus *Epeorus* boasts a couple of species in the eastern and midwestern parts of the country—where it is much better known than in the West—that lay claim to some of the most famous names in fly fishing. The quill gordon (*E. pleuralis*) may be the best-known hatch in the East, and its name, derived from the fly that imitates it, is steeped in fly-fishing history. The natural and the artificial take their name from the fly's designer, legendary American angler Theodore Gordon of the nineteenth century. The second most important eastern and midwestern species of *Epeorus* is probably *E. vitreus*, more commonly known as a sulfur (or sulphur). It is said to hatch more sporadically than the quill gordon, but can emerge in good numbers in some locations.

In the West, where dense *Epeorus* hatches are uncommon and are often overshadowed by other better-known insects, the two most important species are *E. longimanus* (slate brown dun) and *E. albertae* (pink lady, pink Albert, or slate cream dun). The infrequency of concentrated hatches doesn't necessarily mean the bugs are scarce or unimportant. They just don't burst upon the surface all at once, stimulating the kind of trout-feeding fracas that raises an angler's heart rate.

Rather, in my experience, the emergence of western *Epeorus* insects is more likely to be what I dub a trickle hatch—a hatch that is diffused over long periods, maybe most of the day. It can add up to a lot of bugs in the aggregate, but neither trout nor we see very many of them at any one time. Some anglers are dismissive of trickle hatches, but under the appropriate circumstances, I like them. When water temperature and weather conditions are right, a trickle hatch can keep fish looking up all day long. You won't see many fish rising as you scan the water, but put the right fly over a good trout lie, and the fish will be primed to respond. And instead of the bite being compressed into a narrow window of time during which you have to compete with lots of naturals, you get each trout's undivided attention as the fun is spread over the day.

Epeorus nymphs are among the clingers that like fast, or at least moderate, currents. The eastern *E. pleuralis* and western *E. longimanus* nymphs both prefer the coldest, fastest streams. And like the *Rhithrogena* March browns, which inhabit similar territories, these two species have developed enlargements in the first and last pairs of their gill plates that effectively turn them into rock-gripping suction cups. Their cousins eastern *E. vitreus* and western *E. albertae*, on the other hand, favor more moderate flows and apparently get along fine in that habitat without suction cups, as their gills are unmodified. If you are interested in identifying the species of any particular *Epeorus* nymph that you find in your local stream, a close examination of the gills should give you a good clue.

Since *Epeorus* nymphs rarely lose their footing and end up in the drift, they aren't usually a big item in a trout's diet except near hatching time. So I usually don't bother fishing an artificial that attempts to mimic them. But if you happen to find a place with so many of them that you can't resist giving it a try, tie something that matches their color and flat contours. Fly-fishing author and friend Jeff Morgan recommends that flies attempting to imitate clinger nymphs be wrapped with an underbody of lead wire, and then flattened with pliers to yield that characteristic pancake shape.

Notice the dark mark in the middle of the nymphs' femurs (the first long segment of the leg, nearest the body). Together with other characteristics (like two tails), this mark is useful in assigning a nymph to the *Epeorus* genus. The mark is sometimes described as heart shaped, but it may require a bit of imagination to make out such an object; somewhat like visualizing a face in the moon.

If you read many fly-fishing books and articles with sections on *Epeorus* hatches, you'll find that nearly all of them assert that members of this genus emerge underwater, and that the dun rises to the surface after gaining its freedom from the shuck. I had no particular reason to doubt that, but I wondered where the information comes from. After all, since these bugs inhabit moving water, often quite choppy, it is not so easy to tell whether a mayfly dun suddenly appearing on the surface emerged there or down below. Have there been studies establishing this phenomenon as fact, or are most fly-fishing authors just repeating what others have said? You know the drill by now—off to the entomological literature I went.

You'll be relieved to hear that there is some direct observational documentation for the claims. But not a whole lot, as far as I can tell. The reference most on point is an article from 1967, in which the author raised *E. pleuralis* nymphs

in laboratory tanks. She found the nymphal shucks of recently hatched duns attached to objects one to two inches below the water surface, and on several occasions also observed nymphs in the process of emerging while attached to the lower surfaces of rocks in a natural setting of a Kentucky creek.

There are a number of references in the literature documenting the underwater emergence of mayflies from other genera, but I could find nothing on other species of *Epeorus*. Ralph Cutter, a noted California guide and angling author who has spent a lot of time watching bugs in their natural environment while snorkeling or scuba diving, also writes of underwater *Epeorus* emergence in his book *Fish Food*. While he doesn't explicitly say it, the section on *Epeorus* hatching behavior seems to be based on his direct underwater observations. If so, then we can extend documented underwater emergence to western *Epeorus*, most likely *E. longimanus*—the species most prevalent in Cutter's Sierra home waters.

What does it matter one way or the other? The biggest implication is for fishing techniques. A dun that emerges

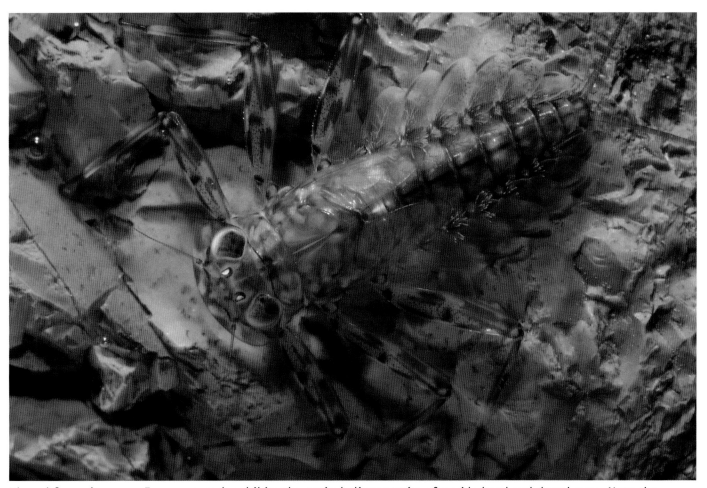

Viewed from above, an *Epeorus* nymph exhibits the typical clinger traits of a wide head and dorsal eyes. Note the presence of two tails—a departure from the usual three, and a relative rarity among mayfly nymphs—as well as dark triangular marks in the middle of the femurs. Body length = 10mm.

A male *Epeorus* dun shortly after hatching.
Body length = 10mm.

An *Epeorus* male spinner in profile displays clear wings
and a clear abdomen. Body length = 9mm.

From the front, the large compound eyes
of an *Epeorus* spinner resemble large
white pillows that almost touch on top
of the flattened clinger head. The three
bubblelike structures—two dark, and one
light in this photo—in front of the
compound eyes are called ocelli. They
are simple eyes that sense light, but are
incapable of forming an image.

underwater looks and acts differently than a nymph rising to the surface. As Cutter says, a freshly emerged dun rising through the water column resembles "nothing less than a dark blob tangled in dangling legs and shimmering wings." He recommends a soft-hackled fly well coated with floatant powder, and with a split shot attached to the tippet a few inches above to take it toward the bottom. At the end of the drift, let the current swing it toward the surface, just like a real dun would do. Another good choice is to swing a classic Quill Gordon wet fly, with or without weight. I've found this works even on my home waters, when the resident "pink ladies" are hatching. While it is not clear that this species (*E. albertae*) exhibits the same underwater hatching behavior as those mentioned above, the local trout sure respond as if it does.

Pink ladies get their nickname from the pinkish color of the duns' bodies in some habitats. I find that their other common name, slate cream dun, is apt for many of the ones I see in my region. But the color can vary depending on how long it has been since the dun hatched, and on the specific locale in which it is found.

Notice the heart-shaped dark blotch in the middle of the femurs. That blotch, which is retained from the nymph stage, helps identify it as belonging to the genus *Epeorus*, rather than one of the other heptagenid genera. Another morphological character helpful in confirming assignment to *Epeorus* is the spacing of the eyes on male spinners. In this genus the eyes should touch on top of the head, or nearly so.

I suspect that two aspects of this spinner will particularly catch your attention. The first is the very light gray, almost white, eyes. Similar to my yellow pale evening dun (*Heptagenia*) that began this chapter, *Epeorus* mayflies, like many other heptagenids, also exhibit those lovely chameleon eyes—a different color, but the same pattern: light during the day, dark at night. The second striking characteristic of this male spinner is its transparent abdomen. You can see right through it, and it's virtually empty! This phenomenon is common in many different types of male spinners. And it really brings home the fact that adult mayflies don't eat—visual confirmation that there are no internal digestive organs to handle any food if they tried. Females use that abdominal space for storing eggs, but in males, there is nothing but air.

Epeorus spinners return to the water in the late afternoon or evenings, to mate and lay eggs. Whereas there are usually few duns on the water at any one time (at least in the West), the spinners that hatched during the day all come back together, so there can be a lot of them. I have enjoyed good fishing over spinner-sipping fish just at dark. You won't be able to easily see the spinners on the water, but if you've seen them in the air, try a Rusty Spinner tied with a lighter body. Since the imitation spinner is often difficult to see in the failing light, I often use a two-fly rig for this situation, with the second fly being something that I can see. I strike whenever there is a rise within the neighborhood of the indicator fly.

CINYGMULA

Mayflies of the genus *Cinygmula*—and those of their similar-sounding sister genus, *Cinygma*—are certainly not the celebrities of the clinger world. In fact, most anglers have never even heard of them. That is probably because their numbers are usually small in the larger, more famous rivers on which the majority of fly fishers most often find themselves. And they are almost absent in the eastern half of the United States, with only one of the ten North American species of *Cinygmula* occurring there. Where anglers know it at all, it might be by the name dark red quill.

While *Cinygmula* may not be of widespread importance, it can generate locally fishable hatches in those places where it thrives. That is usually in higher elevation streams where the water stays cold year-round, with clean gravel bottoms. The nymphs' preferred habitats in those streams are areas of moderate flows, rather than the turbulent riffles and rapids. Good populations of *Cinygmula* nymphs may inhabit such waters over much of the West, from the Pacific Coast to the Rocky Mountains, and from Canada to northern New Mexico. In his book *Nymphs II*, Ernest Schwiebert described having observed large hatches on Clear Creek in Colorado, and that the entomologist George Edmunds had reported similar observations for Oregon's Metolius River in the Cascade Mountains. Rick Hafele and Dave Hughes wrote in *Western Mayfly Hatches* of having fished over emerging *Cinygmula* duns not only on the Metolius River, but also British Columbia's Skagit River and Idaho's South Fork of the Boise. It was Rick who showed me the first *Cinygmula* dun that I ever saw, during one of his aquatic insect workshops, on the lower McKenzie River. Since then I have observed hatches there every year—low in numbers, but sometimes sufficient to bring up a few trout.

In his original scientific description of *Cinygmula ramaleyi* in 1923, G. S. Dodds noted that it was the most abundant of all mayfly nymphs in streams of the South Boulder Valley, Colorado, between altitudes of 8,000 and 11,000 feet. That finding was perhaps prophetic of the type of location where fishing to *Cinygmula* hatches would shine. Jeff Morgan, author of *Small-Stream Fly Fishing* and *Productive Trout Flies for Unorthodox Prey: The Oddballs*, probably has devoted as great a part of his effort as anyone to fishing streams of the high Cascades. Jeff has found that in most of those streams *Cinygmula* nymphs are the most abundant mayfly juveniles in the water. While the hatches are seldom

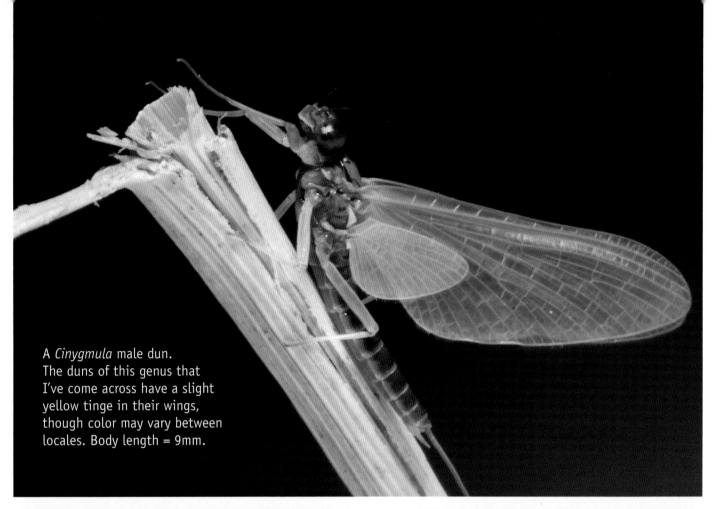

A *Cinygmula* male dun.
The duns of this genus that
I've come across have a slight
yellow tinge in their wings,
though color may vary between
locales. Body length = 9mm.

This male *Cinygmula* spinner retains a bit of the yellowish tint of the dun's wings. It also is experiencing the all-too-common difficulty of freeing its tails from its old exoskeleton after molting from the dun. Body length = 9mm.

dense, trout are used to seeing them more than any other mayfly, so a fly that imitates the dun is a good searching pattern even when there aren't a lot of them in evidence.

I seldom try to imitate *Cinygmula* nymphs specifically, though they have been reported to drift more often than most clingers. A good time to try a nymph pattern might be when the duns are hatching but you are having trouble getting them to accept your dun imitation on the surface. A small size 16–18 dark brown Hare's Ear nymph should be a good choice.

CINYGMA

If anything, *Cinygma* mayflies are still more obscure than their close cousins the *Cinygmula*, even though the former might claim to be the parent of the latter. That's because before 1933 the genus *Cinygmula* had not yet been proposed as a separate taxonomic entity. In that year it was recognized that many of the *Cinygma* species were different enough from the others to deserve their own category, and most of them were transferred into the new genus *Cinygmula*, leaving only three species with their original *Cinygma* designations. They have never gotten over the

slight. I'm sure any *Cinygma* mayfly would tell you, with a sniff, that not one in a hundred fly fishers has heard their name. (If you search the Internet, you may find a few references to their supposed moniker western light cahill, but far more anglers will associate that name with a fly pattern than with an actual *Cinygma* mayfly.)

They deserve better. On appearances alone, admirers of handsome bugs should take note.

And like the *Cinygmula*, *Cinygma* mayflies can also be important if you are in the right place at the right time. Both types inhabit similar cold-water environments, and can hatch in high enough numbers to attract the attention of trout. Ernest Schwiebert wrote in *Nymphs II* that *Cinygma* is quite common in the rivers and streams of the Jackson Hole area in Wyoming, and can be an important hatch to fish there.

Cinygma nymphs are wood lovers. That may be part of the reason they favor the headwater areas of the streams they inhabit, where sticks, limbs, and even whole trees are likely to provide high concentrations of woody debris in the smaller waterways. Several studies have shown the presence of wood fibers in the stomachs of *Cinygma*

A *Cinygma* dun shortly after emergence. Body length = 10mm.

A light-colored *Cinygma* nymph clings to the bottom of a piece of wood stripped of its bark by beavers. Body length = 12mm.

nymphs. The researchers concluded that the wood itself was not the target of their feeding activities, but rather was a by-product of the scraping employed to release what they are really after: algae and, particularly, fungi. Fungal mycelia provide a rich source of nutrition and can be exceptionally abundant on decaying wood surfaces.

This preference of *Cinygma* nymphs for clinging to waterlogged wood was brought home to me one mid-June day while fishing Oregon's lower Middle Fork of the Willamette, a stretch that has lesser quantities of limbs and logs than the upper river. I noticed some light-colored sticks on the bottom that had been stripped of bark by beavers. When I picked one up, several dark nymphs scurried from one side of the stick to the other. I could see immediately that they were three-tailed clingers, but they looked a little different than other clingers I had seen in the area. So I took the time to explore further.

Examination of several other pieces of sunken beaver wood revealed yet more of the mystery nymphs, about fifty of them altogether on ten to twelve sticks. Yet I found only two of them on the nearby submerged rocks, which were inhabited mainly by two-tailed *Epeorus* nymphs. I placed a bunch of the three-tailed beaver-wood nymphs in a con-

tainer of water and brought them back to an aquarium I had set up, with river water running through it to provide a natural habitat. Since they liked beaver wood so much, I provided the aquarium with several pieces to keep the nymphs happy.

With the use of a stereoscopic microscope, I confirmed that all of the mystery nymphs were in fact *Cinygma*. Most of them were dark brown, but a few were a lighter amber color.

I kept tabs on the nymphs in the aquarium over the next few weeks. During that time many of them hatched and I got to observe firsthand how they do it. Emergence occurred in the evenings, from about 5 to 9 P.M. Many times the nymphs would swim to the surface and seek objects floating there, like a piece of wood, and latch on to the bottom of it. They would often crawl partway out of the water before beginning to emerge. If there was nothing at the top of the water to cling to, emergence would occur in the open at the water surface. I noticed that open-water hatching seemed to be a rather difficult affair for them, with a higher failure rate resulting in more crippled emergers.

I suspect that in their preferred habitats, hanging out on the submerged portions of abundant sticks and logs,

Some *Cinygma* nymphs are much darker in color than others. Body length = 9mm.

When the emergence process doesn't go well, a crippled *Cinygma* dun incapable of leaving the water is often the result.

A male *Cinygma* spinner. Body length = 10mm.

Light Cahill dry fly. Originally designed by Daniel Cahill in the 1880s for fishing a *Stenonema* (another clinger genus) hatch in the Catskills, this light-colored pattern has become one of the best-known fly patterns in North America. It is particularly useful in riffled and choppy water where its ample hackles provide excellent floatation.

Quill Gordon wet fly. Theodore Gordon, who lived and fished the U.S. East Coast around the turn of the twentieth century, is often hailed as a pioneer of American fly fishing. Until his time, American fly fishers were devoted to the wet fly. Gordon would take a hand in changing that, but the elegant wet fly that took his name became a classic among subsurface patterns. It's particularly effective during an *Epeorus* hatch, but also works well as a general searching pattern. This example was tied by Brian Marz of the McKenzie Angler, Walterville, Oregon.

Cinygma nymphs often emerge by simply crawling up their home stick to the waterline. They will hatch right there, half in and half out of the water, if they can. Otherwise, if that option is not available, they will hatch in the surface film like many other mayflies.

FLIES

Most of the clinger mayflies, and all of the ones covered in this chapter, are light or pale in coloration. Therefore, lighter versions of mayfly patterns recommended in other chapters, in parachute or compara-dun styles, will serve well for this group. Some favorites in the Catskill style include the classic Light Cahill and Quill Gordon. The Quill Gordon wet fly is a good choice for *Epeorus* species that emerge underwater.

Quill Gordon dry fly. Gordon is best known for turning the fly-fishing tide toward dry flies, by adapting English patterns to fit the insects and less placid waters of the American Catskills. His classic Quill Gordon dry pattern is one of the most famous flies of all time, and it still fools fish from one side of the continent to the other.

7
Getting Stoned

Salmonflies

If your first thought upon seeing the initial image of this chapter is of prehistoric monsters, you aren't too far off the mark. Nearly 250 million years ago this fellow's ancestors, bearing mugs not all that dissimilar, lumbered from the water and onto the land in much the same way as this salmonfly nymph did. The next step was the same, too—splitting open the nymphal encasement to free the winged adult inside. Sorry to say, the emerging adult then or now would be no more likely than this youngster to win a beauty contest. At least not if humans were judging. Fish on the other hand might have a different take on the matter.

STONEFLIES IN A NUTSHELL
Like the mayflies, stoneflies (Plecoptera) are among the oldest of extant insect orders. Stoneflies also share the mayflies' hemimetabolous development scheme—that is, they undergo incomplete metamorphosis. (For more information on incomplete and complete metamorphosis, see chapters 1 and 3.) A hallmark of the hemimetabolous way of life is that nymphal wings develop externally, where they can easily be seen. Large dark wing pads on a stonefly nymph signal that it is reaching maturity and will soon molt into the adult stage.

Although the number of stonefly genera and species across North America rivals that of the mayflies, their diversity of body shapes, habitats, and lifestyles isn't nearly as great. The nymphs are generally flattened from top to bottom, and all possess two long antennae and two tails. Those characteristics are retained in the adults, which look essentially like the nymphs with wings attached. All

With a face only a mother could love, a salmonfly nymph emerges from the water.

Big rivers beget big bugs, as on the Snake River, Idaho.

of the nymphs can be said to be crawlers—no other categories (like the mayfly swimmers or clingers or burrowers) to remember. They are herbivores and detritivores because they eat either algae or *decaying* plant and animal tissues, or carnivores because they also eat other *living* insects. Some start life in the first two categories when small, and then transition to being meat eaters as they grow larger.

Juvenile stoneflies of virtually all types are handicapped by an inefficient respiratory system. When the nymphs have gills, they are usually rudimentary and not very proficient in their job of extracting oxygen from water. Many stonefly nymphs lack even these marginal gills, and instead rely solely on oxygen diffusing through membranous portions of their exoskeletons. As a consequence, the vast majority of stoneflies can exist only in those water types where oxygen is abundant; generally cold, fast-flowing, well-riffled rivers and streams. These types of habitats usually have bottom substrates of clean silt-free stones. No doubt it is this preferred habitat from which stoneflies take their group's common name.

Adult stoneflies generally have two pairs of wings, both of which are large and lay folded flat on top of the body when at rest. The ability to fold their wings against the body when not flying is considered a more advanced trait among insects. The most primitive insect orders, Ephemeroptera (mayflies) and Odonata (dragonflies and damselflies), lack this ability and are constrained to holding their wings above them or out to the sides. All the rest are wing folders (neopterans), and of these, stoneflies are considered the most ancient. (So maybe they are not quite as archaic as the mayflies and dragonflies, but what is a few million years among bug buddies?)

Though the overwhelming majority of stonefly adults have wings that are functional, they are not much more

than that. As a group these bugs are poor fliers. Nearly all of them would rather crawl or hide than fly, and some are so reticent to take to the air that they almost never do it. And a few of the most peculiar have short, almost vestigial wings that prevent anything beyond skittering over the ground or water. (We'll look at one of those, the shortwing stonefly [*Claassenia sabulosa*] in some detail in chapter 13.) Due to their poor flying skills, stoneflies tend to be homebodies and aren't very good at dispersal into new territories. As a consequence, the stoneflies of one body of water can become rather inbred and show differences in details and habits from populations of the same species in a nearby stream or river. In addition, when disaster strikes—like a major scouring flood, a volcanic eruption (think of Mt. St. Helens in Washington), or a pollution event—a stream's depleted stoneflies may take a long time to recover by migration and repopulation from neighboring watersheds.

When a stonefly nymph is ready to hatch into an adult, there is only one fundamental way (in contrast to the situation with mayflies) that it happens. There is no underwater or water surface emergence. Instead, virtually all stonefly nymphs crawl out of the water and molt to the adult on land. (I had to insert the word virtually due to a remarkable, very rare exception. A stonefly species, *Capnia lacustra*, that lives deep in Lake Tahoe—a strange place for a stonefly—not only molts from nymph to adult underwater, but the wingless adult remains underwater as well. There is no terrestrial stage for this species.) The nymph crawls several inches to many feet from the waterline, and only when it has found a suitable spot does molting begin.

Mating may occur immediately, or more typically, up to several days after hatching. Interestingly, many species of stoneflies find members of the opposite sex by a sort of tribal drum signaling. The male usually initiates it by tapping his abdomen against the ground in a certain pattern. Females, having no ears, can't hear the sound but they can feel the vibration. If she is receptive—that is, has not already mated—a female will answer by tapping out a different rhythm of her own. Each stonefly species has its own tapping code, so that no one gets confused and attempts mating with the wrong kind. The tapping goes back and forth until the male finds a female, and then together they pick out a good spot for the nuptials.

Female stoneflies usually deposit their eggs in the water by flying over it and either dropping eggs from the air or dipping their abdomens to the surface, or in some species by crawling underwater. Whatever the method, this is the time when adults are most likely to come into contact with trout. If it isn't eaten, a stonefly adult may live for several days or a few weeks, depending on the species. Unlike mayflies, stonefly adults have functional mouthparts and digestive systems. Not all of them eat while on land, but some of them do, feeding on plant parts or nectar.

The many species of stoneflies can be categorized in various ways, but I think the system suggested by Rick Hafele in *Nymph-Fishing Rivers and Streams* is one of the most useful for fly fishers. Rick divides them into five groups, and within each category, similar flies and techniques will work well for most species.

1. Little brown stones (Nemouridae, Leuctriidae, Capniidae, Taeniopterygidae)
2. Little green stones (Chloroperlidae)
3. Little yellow stones (Perlodidae, Peltoperlidae)
4. Golden stones (Perlidae)
5. Giant stones (Pteronarcyidae)

It is the last category that concerns us now.

GENTLE GIANTS

Stonefly nymphs of the family Pteronarcyidae, genus *Pteronarcys* are among the largest in North America. The major western species, *P. californica*, goes by the common name giant stonefly, or more widely, the salmonfly. The salmonfly emergence on some rivers of the West is among the most famous and most anticipated hatches in the country. Who can resist scads of giant insects falling on the water surface, often greeted by large gaping trout mouths?

You might think that a two-inch nymph with a face like the one pictured at the beginning of this chapter would be among the fiercest predators prowling the river bottoms. But you would be wrong. For all its size and fearsome appearance, a salmonfly nymph is more cud chewer than carnivore. Nothing makes it happier than grazing peacefully on algae and detrital fungi accumulated within the crannies of streambed cobble. Yet it has been reported to feed on juvenile insects on occasion, when opportunity arises and the unfortunate youngster fails to move out of the way.

Salmonfly nymphs generally spend two to three years in the water, depending on temperatures and food supply. Their favorite places are brawling rivers with lots of medium to large rocks, serving not only as debris catchers and hiding places but also to churn lots of oxygen into the water. Stoneflies in the family Pteronarcyidae have the most complex gills of all stoneflies, sporting branched, feathery gills at the base of each leg, as well as on some abdominal segments. The only other stoneflies to have similar branched gills are the golden stoneflies, family Perlidae, though in that family gills are absent from the abdomen. Nevertheless, their gills apparently leave some-

A mature salmonfly nymph on the move.

An adult salmonfly goes out on a limb.

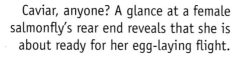

Caviar, anyone? A glance at a female salmonfly's rear end reveals that she is about ready for her egg-laying flight.

thing to be desired when it comes to respiratory efficiency, since both groups prefer fast, well-oxygenated water.

Most cool western streams with good water quality and sufficiently turbulent flow to provide aeration will hold some salmonfly nymphs. But it is the largest such rivers that contain the greatest numbers. A special few of them, like Montana's Madison, Idaho's Henry's Fork, and Oregon's Deschutes, support superhatches that are legendary.

Hatches begin in mid-April among many of the rivers west of the Cascades, and in May to June for most of those in the interior West. A couple of weeks before that, the big nymphs get itchy feet and start migrating toward shore.

Doing so exposes them to perilous currents and they often find themselves swept into the drift. A drifting salmonfly nymph is a sad sight. All it can do is curl into the fetal position and hope to touch down on a rock before it enters a trout's belly. Many don't make it.

The ones that do arrive safely at the shoreline need to choose their exit strategy carefully. Lots of big juicy nymphs emerging from the water are sure to attract attention from above as well as below. It is better to wait until most of the birds go to bed, and sight-hunting trout lose the advantage of good vision. So salmonfly nymphs lumber ashore at dusk and a little after, in the dark. They usually look for something close to climb on. Tall weeds will do, or the

trunks of alders and cottonwoods. If they don't encounter such a perch nearby, they will sometimes crawl quite a distance to find one. Once they've gained some altitude and a vertical position, the molting process begins, and before long another salmonfly adult has entered the world. The morning light often finds it perched on a limb, overseeing its riverside domain, with thoughts of a mate on its mind.

Have you wondered where the name salmonfly comes from? If you look at one from below, the answer becomes apparent. Whereas the top of a *P. californica* adult is mostly brown, the bottom is a striking orange or salmon color. Though I've also read that the origin of the name may lie in the fact that these bugs hatch at the same time as salmon return to the rivers in the Pacific Northwest.

Over the next few days the principal salmonfly business is finding that perfect someone. On prolific bug waters that isn't difficult; there are so many close cohorts of the proper persuasion that bumping into Mr. or Ms. Right is a foregone conclusion. But in most places with average populations, the job requires a little more effort. It is here that the stonefly musical talents come into play. The male starts drumming his beat; a female answers with hers. Love found, they climb the willow altar together. Conjugal bliss is the conclusion, and before long the posterior end of the female's abdomen is flush with a mass of fertilized eggs.

From a trout's perspective, the color of a salmonfly matches the pinkish-orange flesh of the fish for which it is named.

If the weather's right—a warm sunny day, usually in the late afternoon—her wings whir into action and she helicopters out over the water, dropping her eggs as she goes. And so the cycle starts again. Unless, that is, an aeronautical accident—which occurs all too frequently—takes her prematurely onto the water's surface, where a hungry trout engulfs her, eggs and all.

A SALMONFLY SAFARI

Look again at the salmonfly nymph's mug shot that began this chapter. That particular nymph had just crawled out of the water and was starting the transition into a winged adult. If you examine the top of the head, and farther back along the top of the thorax, you can see that the exoskeleton has split and the orange head and body of the adult inside is becoming visible. This one was a denizen of the McKenzie River (as are the others shown below). Although I got a photo of the beginning of the emergence, unfortunately that fellow never progressed any further. I think I may have disturbed him at a critical time. After several such missed chances, I realized that during emergence there is a point when the nymph gets its feet planted in a tight grip on a rock or stick and settles in for the duration; mess with it then and you screw everything up. The

nymphal casing has to be firmly attached to something, or the adult inside can't pull itself out. It's like taking off your pants and shoes—you need to have something holding them down while you pull your legs out.

Thus off I went looking for his buddies—on a photo safari to observe and photograph the remainder of the emergence sequence. If I wanted to find emerging salmonflies, I figured a good place to start would be an area where I found evidence of previous hatches, in the form of discarded exoskeletons.

Unfortunately for photographers, this all takes place in the dark. Right at dusk, the dark brown behemoths trudge out of the water and climb a nearby rock, stick, or weed.

So I set out one evening with flashlight and camera in hand, crawling around the river bank looking for likely suspects. I was glad this was the McKenzie, where rattlesnakes are rare; on some snaky rivers like the Deschutes, I'd be jumping at every movement and sound.

Then I came across my quarry, just deciding whether to leave the water, and as always I was amazed at how large they get—this one was almost $2^{1}/_{2}$ inches long, not counting another $1^{1}/_{4}$ inches of antennae and tails. I brought my camera to bear, aimed, and began firing; capturing the story of the emergence in the accompanying photo sequence.

1

"To climb out on the stick or not?" this nymph seems to be asking itself.

2

Decision made, the nymph starts to climb. After salmonfly nymphs leave the water, they like to find something to climb up on, which most often is nearby vegetation or tree trunks.

5

With good progress made, now we can see major portions of the wings, legs, and antennae but none of those structures are completely free yet.

6

The wings and legs are out now, and it just needs a big backward bend to pull free the ends of its antennae.

9

Now to spend some time inflating those crumpled wings.

10

"This takes a while; don't rush me," I think I heard it say.

3

Following a period of some indecision—going up, then down, then up again—the nymph finally settles on an acceptable spot and plants its legs in preparation for the effort to come.

4

The nymphal exoskeleton splits along the dorsal head and thorax, and the orange (salmon) adult begins to push through the opening.

7

Yes! Got those long appendages free, so it is no longer bound at the head.

8

One last effort, and a new adult salmonfly stands above its old nymphal encasement.

11

"Hold your horses; I'm almost done." (This one is a little sassy.)

12

Ahhh, wings tucked away flat, at last.

Underwater view of a salmonfly struggling at the surface.

And so ended my nocturnal photo safari to the exotic jungles of the river bank. I had bagged my quarry, and now it was back to base camp to savor my success.

The time for the adult to emerge, from the initial splitting of the nymphal exoskeleton until the adult stepped free, was a little more than half an hour. It was about another hour until the adult's wings were fully inflated and laid flat upon its back. This is a lengthy period in which the bug is very vulnerable; much longer than the rapid emergence of most mayflies, for instance. That's probably a major reason that it happens at night, when it's much harder for them to be seen, and there are fewer birds around to take advantage of their helplessness.

FISHING THE SALMONFLY HATCH

My first significant encounter with a salmonfly hatch was in June 1996 on Montana's Madison River. I was spending that summer in Bozeman near Yellowstone Park, and was determined to fish all the famous and not-so-famous rivers in the land of fly-fishing legends. The storied salmonfly hatch was high on my list. Unfortunately, that was a spring with record runoff, and many of the area rivers were blown out well into the summer. The Yellowstone River flooded parts of Livingston and even washed out the renowned spring creeks nearby, which took several years to fully

recover. That river didn't fall back into fishable shape until the end of July.

Though the water was a little higher than I would have liked, by the end of June the Madison was accessible to a careful wader. I had heard that the salmonfly hatch was happening, so I drove over one day to see for myself. And it was spectacular. Every bankside bush was covered with brown and orange bugs as big as 747s. I imagined this was what the biblical locust plagues must have looked like. It was hard to conceive that such large insects could be present in such huge numbers.

But I was puzzled. With so many bugs in the bushes, inevitably quite a few of them were falling into the water. I kept my eye on one after another as it struggled on the surface, expecting a malevolent swirl at any moment. But for the longest time, every drifting bug went unmolested. And my big imitating flies drew the same response.

About five or six P.M. most of the female salmonflies suddenly took to the air—by the thousands, in a cloud headed upstream. As I stood casting in the river, one after another of them flew clumsily into me, crawling up my arms, on my head, and under my shirt collar. There is nothing quite so creepy as a bunch of prickly salmonfly claws rasping down the back of your neck. It makes it difficult to concentrate on your casting, but somehow I managed.

Large trout are drawn to the surface by big bugs.

Of course the number of bugs falling on the water was even greater than had crawled under my shirt, and finally a few fish were taking advantage. A big splash here, another one over there. Still, it was nothing like I expected. With so many steaks on the water, why weren't more fish chowing down? And what's worse, all the rises were to naturals; not a single one came to my flies.

Back at the fly shop, I related my exciting but frustrating experience to some sympathetic ears. "Yep," I was told, "that's nothing out of the ordinary."

It seems that by the time the salmonfly hatch reaches its peak in a particular section of the river, the trout have been gorging themselves on migrating nymphs and returning adults for two to three weeks. They're stuffed, and will only move occasionally to take anything from the surface. The advice: as the hatch moves upstream over a several-week period, try to stay at its leading edge, where fish are just starting to see the activity.

"Go way upstream and try again tomorrow," the locals said—and then further advised, "don't just fish dry flies imitating adults; give some big, heavy dark nymphs a shot."

The next day found me upriver ten to fifteen miles, checking the banks for evidence of salmonflies. Here there were moderate numbers of nymphal shucks, indicating that the hatch had begun in this section, but just a few adults

were evident on the shoreline. I tied on a big Clark's Stonefly and cast it along an undercut bank with overhanging bushes. It was immediately smacked by a nice fish, and several minutes later a pretty 15-inch brown trout was at my feet.

Despite the auspicious beginning, forty-five minutes and several dry-fly changes later; there had been no further action. So I went to Plan B. Off came the dry fly, and on went a heavily weighted Kaufmann's Stonefly nymph. That turned out to be the ticket. In another two hours of fishing, I caught eight or ten trout, up to 21 inches. These trout wanted their steaks all right, but they were more interested in deep dining than having a surface snack. It was important to dead drift the nymph right along the bottom, letting the artificial tumble in the current the same way a hapless natural that had lost its grip on the bottom would do.

That's a lesson that I have never forgotten. Though I've since enjoyed excellent fishing during salmonfly hatches on a number of rivers, including Oregon's Deschutes, dry-fly action can be very fickle. If you head to one of the famous western rivers in search of the celebrated salmonfly hatch, with expectations of stupendous dry-fly action, there is a good chance you will be disappointed. You often have to time it just right for success on the surface. But nymph fishing can be another story. Rick Hafele and Dave Hughes

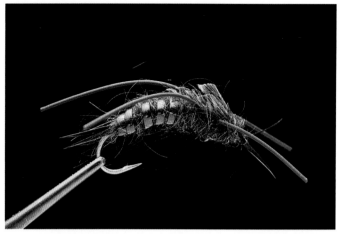

A black Kaufmann Stone in sizes 4–8, with its dark rubber legs, makes a very realistic imposter of a salmonfly nymph that has lost its grip on the bottom as it migrates to shore.

The elk-hair wing and heavy hackling of the Sofa Pillow give an impression of wings and feet in motion when seen from below in rippled water.

wrote in *The Complete Book of Western Hatches* that they would rather be on a good salmonfly stream in the two weeks prior to the hatch than during it. I'm not sure I agree—because fishing the big dry flies is so much fun—but they are probably right that the odds of catching good numbers of big fish are improved.

Lest you get the wrong impression, I hasten to add that there is nothing more exciting than the spectacular mistake of a big fish exploding on a floating salmonfly imitation. There is also nothing tentative about the take, and the sudden shock of the attack has caused many an angler to break off the fish with an overly enthusiastic reaction. (Use strong tippet, at least 3X, to help avoid that; trout eating salmonflies aren't leader shy.) So for many of us it's worth taking the chance of a poor catching day just to have a shot at such an experience. And good days do come along; otherwise, you wouldn't hear all those stories about the fantastic salmonfly hatch. One good day like that can make up for a lot of near misses.

To improve the odds, especially on popular rivers with a heavily fished hatch, look for difficult-to-access places with deeper water right off the bank and an overhanging tree. Big fish lie in such spots waiting for a clumsy salmonfly to lose its grip and tumble in. Cast a big fly—something like a size 4–8 Stimulator, Clark's Stone, or Sofa Pillow is a good choice—right under the tree. This is not like fishing over a mayfly hatch, so you don't need to be very gentle about it when using a relatively light fly like these three. There is nothing delicate or graceful about a salmonfly hitting the water. Once there, it often struggles mightily but uselessly to make headway toward shore. From underwater, the view is of a lot of kicking and commotion.

FLIES

Plenty of patterns have been developed to imitate both the nymphal and adult forms of salmonflies, and most of them work in various situations. Large, heavily weighted nymphs are appropriate for deep or swift water, whereas smaller and lighter patterns are better suited to more moderate flows. I'm fond of the dark Kaufmann Stone tied with black rubber legs, especially when fishing some of the Montana rivers in years with a heavy spring runoff. For dry flies, traditional ties or the newer foam-body stonefly imitations both have their places, depending on water conditions. The popular Improved Sofa Pillow or the similar all-purpose Stimulator tied with an orange body take more than their share of fish when adult salmonflies are on the water.

8
Blood Bonds, Drakes, and a Drenching

Green drakes, lesser green drakes, and a father/son outing

My son Adam was home from college one weekend in June, and despite a somewhat dicey weather forecast we set out for a Father's Day drift in my new raft. The chances to hang out together come too infrequently these days and I had been looking forward to being on the water, engaging in an age-old ritual that fathers and sons have practiced since the days of hunter-gatherers. The sun was shining, even a tad too warmly, as we launched from the McKenzie's Finn Rock landing.

First, let's have some disclaimers. Being that this was only the second time I had floated this stretch, locating the honey holes was a hit-or-miss proposition. And given that I was getting used to rowing the new raft, my attention was more than passingly focused on obstacles to our progress. So when I say that our catch rate did not break any records, you should consider those points. But the search took us floating and wading through scenic waters that averted complaints, and on a day like this any fish caught would be a bonus.

For the first few hours the company was great but the catching wasn't. Then about midafternoon I started noticing western green drakes, one here, another there. It doesn't take too many of these big slow mayflies on the water to get a trout's attention, and as the hatch slowly accelerated, a few fish finally began to notice. I put Adam on the best spots and soon his fishing-muscle memory

Green drakes inhabit waters large and small, but the trout in less pressured streams are likely to exhibit less caution when approaching their imitations.

When fishing with the right people in the right places, catching becomes less important.

kicked in, with the majority of his casts resulting in perfect drifts over good holding water. The hookups started to come, and though none of the fish were record breakers, we were finally tricking enough of the finny little rascals to keep it interesting.

Just as the fishing turned on, the growing cloud cover turned ominous and the wind picked up. The forecast had called for the possibility of thunderstorms, but the sunny day up to that point had allowed us to purge it from our minds. Now the chance to fish over the elusive green drakes tempted us to stay as long as we dared, but a loud crack of thunder and pelting rain sent us scurrying off the water to the relative safety of some low trees. (Not the taller, lightning-prone ones.) Huddled under our raincoats, we enjoyed the light and sound show as we speculated on the nature of lightning strikes and how near one need be to cause harm. A spectacular hit just across the river would provide a good story, we joked, as long as we were still around to tell it.

After about a half hour, we decided that the rain and wind had abated enough, and the thunder seemed far enough away, that we could risk a dash down the river to the take-out point. Despite a few minor misadventures—like getting stuck in shallow water that had been obscured by a low fog layer—we reached the landing relatively unscathed. But Zeus had saved his best thunderbolts for last, and as we pulled the boat out, all hell broke loose. We were hit by torrential sideways rain that soaked around raincoats, into collars, and up sleeves. By the end we were drenched. Later, we would learn that a high-wind storm cell had passed a few miles north of us and torn up a camp-ground.

But we have our story, and it will grow, so there will be future tales of eager fish, monster drakes, storms, lightning, running aground, flooding rain, tornado warnings, and narrow escapes. The cycle repeats, and it is the shared story that counts.

UGLY DUCKLING OR SWAN?

Western green drake nymphs are of the crawler-type, like several other kinds of mayflies that we have already encountered. The large Ephemerellidae family that claims most of the crawlers, including the ubiquitous pale morning duns (chapter 4), extends its umbrella to cover this group, too. In fact, until relatively recently, western green drakes were lumped into the same genus (*Ephemerella*) as the PMDs, and were considered just a subgenus (*Drunella*) of that diverse and important taxon. Then taxonomists, as they are wont to do, threw fly fishers a bit of a curveball and elevated *Drunella* to full generic status. This particular reclassification was less wrenching than some others that have caused a near revolt among anglers determined to hold on to traditional nomenclature, since at least the *Drunella* name had been around for quite a while.

Drunella nymphs have three tails, which are retained in the adults. The nymphs generally prefer moderate to fast water, with clean stones to provide hiding spaces and surfaces for their favorite food (algae) to grow on. Some of them have adapted to living in aquatic vegetation, which can provide the same functions. Like many aquatic insects, *Drunella* nymphs often migrate from faster water to areas of gentler currents in the days or weeks leading up to emergence. That is when they are most available to trout, and of most interest to fly fishers trying to deceive trout.

Drunella mayflies get a lot more notice in the West than in the eastern part of the continent. The most significant eastern/midwestern species is *D. lata*, one of the smaller members that provides fishable hatches in some locales but has not attained the notoriety of its western cousins. *D. lata* benefited from a recent coalescence of several closely related mayflies that were formerly considered separate species; so combined, they provide more widespread and numerous hatches than previously appreciated. Rather than being called green drakes, the eastern species usually go by the most widely employed of all mayfly common names, blue-winged olive, which probably holds the record for being applied to more species of insect than any other appellation. Of course, the western species have borrowed the name "green drake" from another very different eastern mayfly, the burrower *Ephemera guttulata*—a misappellation decried by Ernie Schwiebert in his book *Nymphs*. Maybe the grumbling by those of us who would prefer more rationality in the popular designations of our aquatic insects will eventually encourage more sensible conventions, but I wouldn't hold my breath.

The several *Drunella* species in the West are often split into two groups: the western green drakes and the small or lesser western green drakes. From a fly-fishing standpoint, the main differences between the two groups are size and the timing and duration of the hatches. Insects in the first group are far better known. Big bugs draw attention, not

D. *grandis* nymphs may be less than attractive to human eyes, but all their projections and patterns keep them well camouflaged in their natural environments. The paired vertical spines on the head, dorsal thorax, and abdomen are characteristic of the species. Body length = 12mm (16–19mm when mature).

D. grandis nymphs are usually mild mannered creatures, but in an unusual moment these two began wrestling over some unknowable dispute.

Western green drake (*Drunella*) duns provide one of the most anticipated hatches of the year. Body length = 19mm.

only from fish but probably even more so from anglers. We fly fishers might miss some small bugs floating by, but even the less observant among us are likely to notice something as large as a green drake on the water or in the air. Two widespread species of *Drunella* match that standard: *D. grandis* (whose very name means large) and *D. doddsi.*

D. grandis nymphs are impressive in appearance, but like the salmonfly nymphs in the previous chapter, they would never win a beauty contest. With all their hornlike and prickly projections, you would more likely take them for demonic dragons than mild mayflies. And while I've never seen one breathing fire or menacing fair maidens, I have on occasion observed them engage in a little hand-to-hand combat when contesting a favored resting place. Yet upon hatching, this ugly-duckling nymph morphs into the proverbial swan, one of the most elegant of duns, with a greenish banded body, graceful tails, and gray wings adorned with yellow accents.

Whereas the nymphal visage of *D. grandis* may be fairly described as grotesque, the term comical more readily springs to mind for the countenance of its close cousin *D. doddsi.* This fellow is more at home in the swifter water of the riffle, and is built for it. With rounded contours lacking the spiked armor of *D. grandis*, and sometimes wearing a colorful costume that can differ from one watershed to another, juvenile *D. doddsi* retain the robust build of all *Drunella* nymphs.

Not only do *D. doddsi* nymphs look a lot like clinger nymphs, but to cope with their swift-water habitat, they've also purloined a trick from the clinger playbook. Just as some clingers—most notably those in the genus *Rhithrogena*—have "suction cups" fashioned from modified gill plates, *D. doddsi* nymphs sport their own version of a suction cup constructed from circular rows of small hairs on the bottom of their abdomen. These suction cups help grip the surface of the rocks they call home and further avert their being dislodged by the currents.

Due to their preference for and ability to thrive in swift water, *D. doddsi* nymphs tend to be most abundant in rushing high elevation streams, whereas *D. grandis* nymphs are more likely to be found in larger numbers in the lower valleys where flows have somewhat abated. But the two species overlap considerably and are frequently collected from the same area. Despite the marked differences in the appearances of the nymphs, the adults are virtually indistinguishable to anyone but an expert entomologist with a good microscope and a steady dissecting hand. The dun pictured here could thus belong to either species.

From the front, a *D. doddsi* nymph looks more like a frog than a mayfly.

The strongman build and somewhat obese appearance of a *D. doddsi* nymph is most apparent when viewed from above. Body length = 9mm (13–16mm when mature).

Like the nymphs and the duns, western green drake spinners have bodies that are much stockier than most other mayflies. Body length = 19mm.

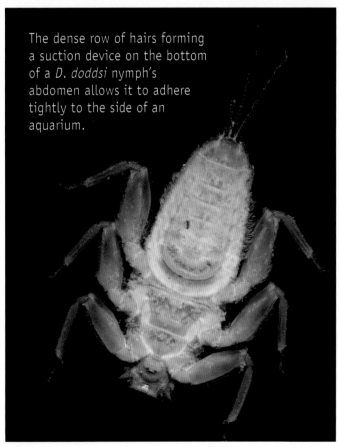

The dense row of hairs forming a suction device on the bottom of a *D. doddsi* nymph's abdomen allows it to adhere tightly to the side of an aquarium.

The exact date of the start of the green drake hatch varies from one river or stream to another, and can be significantly different even between two of them in the same area. The primary key seems to be water temperature, but the variability implies the involvement of other factors as well. On most waters the hatch duration is relatively short, in the range of seven to fourteen days, with possibly just a few of those days producing prolific numbers of bugs. Spring creeks can be notable exceptions. For instance, on Oregon's Metolius River, the hatch often starts in mid-May and continues through the end of June, or sometimes even into the first days of July.

On cool, overcast, and/or especially drizzly days, the emergence may last for several hours, usually in the midafternoon to late afternoon. On a sunny day, it may start earlier, and be compressed into as little as thirty to forty-five minutes. While most duns of the Ephemerellidae family have trouble freeing themselves from the nymphal shuck and getting off the water successfully, *Drunella* duns are noted for being the worst of the lot. They usually split the nymphal exoskeleton on the way up to the surface or just below it, and start wiggling their way out. Some duns get free before they arrive at the surface, but many are still working on it when they get there; quite a few ride the

A lesser green drake nymph, *D. flavilinea* or *D. coloradensis*, lacks the pronounced vertical tubercles (pointed spines) on the head and dorsal abdomen of *D. grandis*, and has a less obese appearance and longer tails than *D. doddsi*. It also has a unique dark band in the middle of its three tails, and short, paired projections on the dorsal abdomen that point toward its posterior; the projections are hard to see without substantial magnification. Body length = 9mm.

currents for a great distance trailing a shuck, or are never able to completely lose it. They provide an easy trout meal. Even the duns that make it successfully onto the surface film spend a lot of time inflating and drying wings, and fluttering their big bodies in aborted attempts to get into the air. It is this tendency for big bugs to foolishly showcase their helplessness that drives big fish to abandon caution at times.

When the duns first hatch, their abdomen often exhibits a distinct greenish hue, from which they take their name. But after a short time the green color fades and becomes browner, with alternating lighter bands on each abdominal segment. It's best to capture a freshly hatched dun on the water you are fishing, and try to match its color with your fly.

After one or two days rest on shoreline vegetation, the duns molt to spinners, with clear hyaline wings and dark bodies. Many authors report that green drake spinners mate in the afternoon but return to the water in the middle of the night to lay their eggs, and are thus not very important to imitate when fishing. But that may not be the case everywhere. John Judy writes in his book *Seasons of the Metolius* about encountering spinner falls in the morning, just as the sun hits the water on that river, and of eager trout waiting to take them.

THE LESSER GREEN DRAKES

Two widespread species, *D. flavilinea* and *D. coloradensis*, constitute this group. Their appearances as nymphs and adults are very similar, so much so that it isn't worthwhile for most of us to attempt differentiating them. Their ranges overlap considerably, with *D. coloradensis* said to prefer slightly colder water. In many places the two are lumped together under the affectionate nickname flavs.

The lesser western green drakes—oh, let's just call them flavs—are distinguished from their larger green drake relatives primarily on size. Whereas the body lengths of the larger green drake duns are about 13–16mm long, the bodies of flavs are in the range of 7–13mm. That translates into a difference of about 1–2 hook sizes. Flavs are still good-size bugs, just not whoppers like the green drakes proper. Though the appearances of the two groups are similar, flavs tend to be a bit less robust in the body, and with less pronounced banding of the abdomens, in my experience. Otherwise they are difficult to tell apart.

What flavs lack in size, they make up in numbers and hatch duration. We're not talking *Baetis*-like abundance here, but substantial enough for trout to be interested whenever they encounter them. In many places, flavs begin to hatch just as the larger green drake emergence is coming

Male lesser green drake duns have large, dark red eyes, moderately sized hind wings, and three tails, similar to the larger green drakes; but with somewhat slimmer abdomens. Body length = 10mm.

Male spinners exhibit clear wings and darker bodies than the lesser green drake duns.

to an end, so the two hatches can seem almost continuous. Lots of anglers might not notice the change in species and just assume that, as with many mayfly hatches, individual size simply gets smaller as the hatch progresses. And that wouldn't be a serious mistake. Since appearances and habits are similar, fishing techniques and flies employed are virtually the same, with just a step down in size. The nice thing about flavs is that not only are they more abundant, but the hatches can continue for some time. On some streams emergence begins in midsummer, and may go on almost into the fall.

A McKenzie rainbow trout that is typical of the colorful strain found in this Oregon river.

FISHING THE GREEN DRAKE HATCH

My first encounter with one of the heralded green drake hatches was on the Metolius River in the early 1990s. It was also my first visit to Oregon. We drove south down Highway 97 along the eastern edge of the Cascades, and the temperature climbed to over 100 degrees as we crossed the Deschutes River at Warm Springs in early July. I wanted to stop and fish there for a while, but my wife and young son looked at me like I was crazy. Fishing in the desert in the summer in the midday heat? No way. So we drove on, hoping to find cooler air in the alpine surroundings of the Metolius.

Unfortunately we had arrived during an atypical heat wave that extended even up into the foothills of the Metolius basin, so the relief we found there was modest. Still, I was excited to learn that though the hatch was petering out, some green drakes were still emerging. I couldn't wait to get on the river and try my luck. The next day found me on the water, eagerly casting the imitations I had bought at the Camp Sherman store.

It was a humbling experience. True to the stories I had heard, whenever one of the few hatching duns would float by, struggling to lift off, a large trout would rise from the clear blue depths of that beautiful stream to suck it down. But when my fly would drift through the same lanes, the fish would calmly rise, give it the once over, and then return to their stations in apparent disgust. This happened time and again. I would like to tell you how I solved it, but the truth is that I didn't. In two afternoons of fishing over those drakes, quite a few trout examined my flies, but not one of them touched a fly.

So when you hear those tales of large trout throwing caution to the winds in their zeal to catch an easy meal, well, yes it can happen that way. But not always. The big drakes hatch in small numbers all over the West, but there are relatively few locales where the hatches are consistently prolific. And only the famous salmonfly hatches rival the international notoriety of a big green drake hatch. The most famous of them all is probably the Henry's Fork of the Snake. Other waters around Yellowstone Park also draw great numbers of anglers in proportion to the productivity of their green drake nurseries. The Metolius, while not as well known as those rivers, still attracts a lot of fly fishers during the famous hatches. And the trout quickly learn to tell the difference between naturals and imitations. Early during the season the catching can sometimes be easy, but don't count on it.

You may be thinking, well, I'll make sure that I get on one of those rivers just when the hatch is starting up. Good luck with that. Green drakes are fickle. The season is usually short, and they seem to hatch when they feel like it. This makes catching a green drake hatch as much a matter of luck as planning, and has frustrated many an angler who traveled miles for the sole purpose of fishing over these big bugs. While I can't fault anyone for reaching for one of those peak experiences in fly fishing, you'll likely leave happier if you plan for success—timing your trip according to best estimates of the peak emergence—but prepare to be satisfied with whatever lady luck hands you once you arrive. Green drakes are great; still, there are more ways than one to catch a fish, most of them fun.

Now with that bit of hard reality out of the way, let's move on to the good news. Sparse green drake hatches on the less famous streams often get fish looking up toward the surface even when no duns are currently in view. The fish on these waters also see a lot fewer fake bugs during the season. Even average fly fishers stand a good chance of having their imitations inhaled by eager fish. A big dry-fly pattern mimicking a green drake dun may be just the ticket in these circumstances. Even better, try a pattern that imitates an emerger or a cripple just below the surface. Since green drakes have so much trouble getting out of their shucks and off the water, a high proportion end up in these very vulnerable states. When a dry isn't working, a wet fly may well be the ticket.

FLIES

The popularity of green drakes, coupled with the wariness of trout on pressured waters, has led to the development of a multitude of patterns designed to give finicky fish a fresh look. Most work at times, so it's a good idea to go armed

Tied in green drake colors, the familiar Quigley Cripple is often the best fly choice during a hatch. Many trout will selectively focus on the high numbers of crippled emergers, rarely bothering to chase a healthy dun.

The **Possie Bugger** doesn't seem to be well known across the country, but in western Oregon it is held in high regard. Few fly fishers who regularly ply the McKenzie River would be without it. It is now sold by Umpqua Feather Merchants, but I haven't been able to determine its origins. Since it's a nonstandard pattern, I'll give the recipe here, as provided by Chris Daughters of the Caddis Fly Shop in Eugene, Oregon.

Hook:	TMC 3761 #8–16
Bead:	Gold tungsten, appropriate to hook size
Weight:	Couple wraps of lead or substitute
Thread:	Black Uni thread
Tail:	Australian possum
Rib:	Pearl Flashabou and copper wire
Hackle:	Brown partridge
Collar:	Black dubbing

The Paradrake pattern was originated by Doug Swisher and Carl Richards, but it was this modified version that was popularized by ace fly fisher Mike Lawson on the Henry's Fork. It remains one of the best patterns for trout selectively feeding on green drake duns.

with multiple arrows in your quiver when fishing over these bugs. The list is too long for me to discuss all of them here, but I am partial to three in particular.

When imitating the nymphs that are crawling around on the bottom, the Possie Bugger in sizes 14–10 is a workhorse in my stable. It's one of the first nymph patterns that I reach for, not only for green drakes, but also when many other kinds of juvenile insects are the target of imitation. But if the hatch has started, an emerger is a good choice, especially with these *Drunella* species that experience so

much trouble making the transition to dun. Here, the Green Drake Quigley Cripple is a good choice. When the fish are clearly targeting duns, classic Catskill-style dries, parachutes, and compara-dun patterns all have their places depending on water conditions. On flat spring creek waters, or popular rivers that receive a lot of pressure, something a little more imitative and realistic may be called for. It was for just such circumstances, on his home waters of the Henry's Fork of the Snake River, that Mike Lawson developed his green Paradrake.

9

Going for the Gold(ens)

Golden stoneflies

As discussed in chapter 7, the pteronarcyids—aka giant stoneflies, aka salmonflies—are known for their bulk and fearsome features, yet gentle natures. The family Perlidae, on the other hand, comprises the wolves of the stonefly clan. Ranking near the top of the carnivorous insect heap in terms of both size and numbers, in many streams the golden stoneflies are responsible for thinning the herds of mayflies, caddisflies, and other insects unlucky enough to cross their paths.

Perlids are the most common and widely distributed of the large stoneflies. Indeed, some books cover the whole group under the heading "Common Stoneflies." Others use the designation "Golden Stoneflies" to mean all the perlids or just certain of the larger members. Some reserve that title for a single species, the very important *Hesperoperla pacifica,* found in the Western United States. But most often the geographically overlapping and very similar species *Calineuria californica* gets lumped in as a golden stonefly. Though it is also called a western stonefly, it frequently hatches on the same river at the same time as *H. pacifica,* and most anglers don't know the difference. Whatever you call them, these two species provide hugely important and well-known hatches on many western rivers.

In the East, the genera *Acroneuria* (which used to include the now-reclassified *H. pacifica* and *C. californica*) and *Perlesta* generate locally important hatches, but are

Besides being a good place to fish, Wyoming's Gros Ventre River is located in one of the most picturesque settings in the world.

Each golden stonefly species has its own characteristic markings, which can be quite intricate and appealing. This one belongs to the species *C. californica*. Body length = 18mm (19–24mm when mature).

not as well known or abundant as the western species. Another large western perlid, *Claassenia sabulosa* or shortwing stonefly, is much less well known but is very important in some rivers. It's a special case because of its morphology, habits, and hatch schedule, so it is discussed separately in chapter 13.

THE NYMPHS

Golden stoneflies begin life as eggs that hatch into tiny nymphs. At first, the newborns are content to forage on whatever small bits of algae and detritus they can find. But as they grow in size, so do their appetites, and only a good helping of raw meat will do. It would be interesting to know how many hapless prey insects are consumed by a typical golden stonefly nymph during its two (sometimes three) years stalking the stream bottom. Ernest Schwiebert noted in *Nymphs II* that studies have shown not only high rates of golden stonefly predation on midge and mayfly larvae, but even a willingness to dig out and attack trout eggs and alevins buried in the gravel.

The extended aquatic phase means that in a stream that supports a golden stonefly population, there are always ample numbers of nymphs in the water, even right after a hatch. In warmer, high-nutrient rivers there will usually be at least two size classes—first-year and second-year nymphs. At higher elevations where the water is colder and often provides less food, development to the adult stage may take three years, thus providing a third size class among the nymphs. Mature golden stonefly nymphs are 25–35mm (about 1–1.5 inches) long, rather flattened from top to bottom, and are usually light to dark brown in color on their dorsal surfaces.

Such long-lived insects go through many instars on their way to maturity, and the transition between each one is marked by a molt. After each molt the new exoskeleton takes a while to harden and darken. If you spend much time poking around the streambed spying on insects, you will frequently come across some pale stonefly nymphs that look like they could use more time in the sun. These are individuals that have recently molted. They are highly visible not only to us, but also to predators.

Other than the pteronarcyids, perlids are the only stonefly nymphs to have complex, branching gills. Both groups have clumps of feathery gills near the base of each leg, but

A light-colored imitation of a pale, recently molted golden stonefly nymph might be just the ticket for fooling trout unable to resist such a vulnerable meal. *C. californica*. Body length = 15mm.

unlike the pteronarcyids, perlids don't have additional gills on the adjacent abdominal segments. Some of them, like *H. pacifica*, do however possess two more gill tufts between their tails.

When fishing some of the famous golden stonefly rivers of the West, where both of the primary species *C. californica* and *H. pacifica* reside, being able to distinguish them won't help you catch fish. But if you are curious, and you want to know which species of nymph you have in your hand, here are the keys to telling them apart. *C. californica* nymphs are a little smaller, about 25–30mm long at maturity, have feathery gills at the base of each leg, and no gills on the abdomen or between the tails. *H. pacifica* nymphs are a little larger, about 28–35mm long, and have two gill tufts between their tails in addition to the ones near the legs. Moreover, *H. pacifica* nymphs have a light-colored, hourglass-shaped mark on the top front of their heads. This mark is helpful in distinguishing *H. pacifica* from another perlid nymph, *Claassenia sabulosa*, to be discussed in chapter 13. *Claassenia sabulosa* nymphs have gills similar to those of *H. pacifica*, including between the tails; but the

mark on their heads is in the shape of the letter M, rather than like an hourglass.

Golden stonefly nymphs hang out in similar habitats as salmonflies. Both like fast, clean, cold water with flows broken by medium-size rocks. And while under the right circumstances salmonflies can be astoundingly abundant, golden stoneflies in the same places will often outnumber them two to one. But whereas salmonfly nymphs might be considered couch potatoes, content to sit in one spot munching their detrital lunches, golden stonefly nymphs are always on the move. A hunter's life is a nomadic one. Darting in and out of rock crevices, they are continually looking for the next victim. Their long antennae and tails are for more than just looks. They are sensitive sense organs used for detecting prey that might be hiding at the back of a stone cranny. There is even evidence that these nymphs can detect small vibrations in the water created by movements of other insects, and use them to locate the prey.

Here is a tip for budding amateur entomologists. If you collect nymphs from your favorite stream with the intention of transporting them alive, perhaps to your home aquarium, be careful about mixing types. I learned that lesson the hard

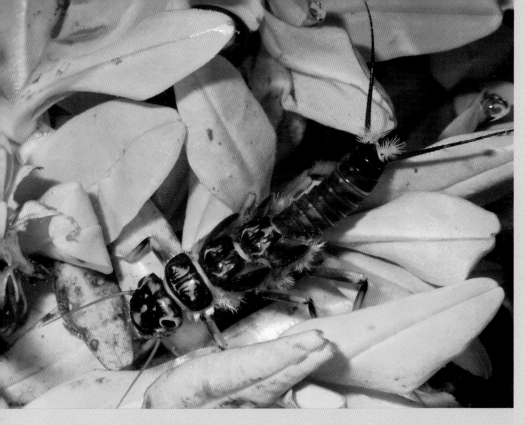

The presence of gill tufts between the tails of *H. pacifica* is a useful marker for those interested in distinguishing the two golden stonefly species, which are often found living together in the same stretch of river.
Body length = 26mm.

If you examine the underside of the golden stonefly nymphs, not only do you get a better look at their feather-duster gills, but you can also see how they get their "golden" moniker. *H. pacifica*.

way on one of my first such expeditions. March brown clinger nymphs were my primary targets that day, and after a careful search I had collected a dozen or so and placed them in plastic containers with a little stream water. Some other bugs I gathered, including golden stonefly nymphs, went into the same containers. But when I got home, I was saddened to find that empty shucks were all that remained of the March browns. The golden stoneflies had eaten them all!

All this roaming about the stream bottom in search of prey has an upside for trout and those who pursue them. Clambering between rocks amid swift currents is risky business, and inevitably some golden stonefly nymphs are swept off their perches. Being poor swimmers, all these nymphs can do is try to latch onto something solid as they tumble downstream. Fish wait at the foot of riffles for just such occasions.

But the risks of everyday hunting activities pale in comparison with the danger a golden stonefly nymph faces when it reaches maturity. For it's then that the mass migration begins, just as for the salmonflies (and most other stoneflies, for that matter), in preparation for emergence. The journey toward shore is bound to attract the attention of all who love a good stonefly snack. So the two weeks or so when this movement is in full surge is a great time for fish and fishermen.

The emergence of golden stoneflies is a close replica of the salmonfly hatch. Nymphs loiter in the shallow water near shore until dusk, and then start crawling out onto land. Sometimes they crawl astonishing distances, 50–100 feet before heading up a tree or other vertical structure. But usually they climb weeds or bushes right at the bank, until finding the perfect spot to transition into adulthood.

Not only do golden stoneflies and salmonflies share the same territories and emergence methods, but their hatches usually overlap. A couple of weeks after the salmonflies start emerging, you may notice a slightly smaller size class of nymphal shucks lining the stream banks. They will grow in number during the coming weeks, as the golden stonefly hatch builds steam. The nice thing about this hatch is that although it may start in late May or June and peak shortly after, good numbers often continue to hatch well into the summer. This keeps them fresh in a trout's mind, and so a golden stonefly dry fly can be a good choice for several months.

THE ADULTS

Adult golden stoneflies have about the same body lengths as mature nymphs, but they look larger. That is because when the wings are unfolded they extend another $1/3$ inch or so rearward beyond the bug's rump, and also expand laterally. The long tails and antennae also make it seem big-

ger than it really is. But even discounting those illusions, an adult golden stonefly is a substantial trout meal.

Like the nymphs, adults of the two western species of golden stoneflies differ somewhat in size and appearance. *H. pacifica* remains a little larger than *C. californica*. Color can vary; nevertheless in my experience, both have light brown wings and mostly brown dorsal surfaces, but the head and ventral surfaces of the former are more orange, compared with a more brownish-yellow color in those regions of the latter species. For a side-by-side visual comparison, I chilled some males and females of each species (to inhibit their tendency to walk off the photo set), and photographed both their dorsal and ventral aspects. (Sorry that they are not lined up in the same order in the two photographs; I must have needed some coffee that morning.)

Adults of both species may be found mingling together in some places, like these were when I collected them. As similar as they appear to us, they seem to be able to recognize members of their own species well enough. Otherwise we would have a bunch of mongrel stoneflies out there.

Just as for salmonflies, the first opportunity for a golden stonefly adult to enter a trout's world is by losing its footing while clambering around overhanging vegetation. And the shorelines of a good golden stonefly river, like the Madison or the Deschutes, provide plenty of opportunity for clumsy stoneflies to fall in the water. The rocks and bushes often seem to be full of them at the peak of the hatch. Look around, and you'll see something like a veritable birds-and-the-bees show-and-tell as the bugs get busy making the next generation.

Fertilized females take to the air late on warm summer afternoons, often in great swarms, with their eggs extruded into small packets at the rear of their abdomens. They fly out over the water, and dip to the surface repeatedly to brush off the eggs. Many of them end up in the drink,

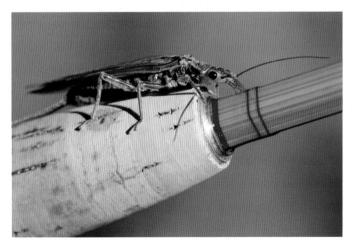

When there are lots of golden stoneflies around, they are apt to crawl almost anywhere. Female *H. pacifica*. Body length = 28mm.

A comparison of golden stonefly adults of both species and genders; ventral view.

H. pacifica female

C. californica female

H. pacifica male

C. californica male

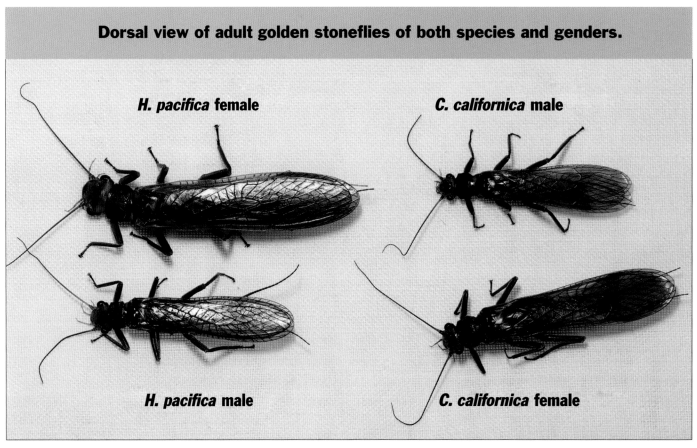

Dorsal view of adult golden stoneflies of both species and genders.

H. pacifica female

C. californica male

H. pacifica male

C. californica female

Species	Gender	Body	Body + Wings
A comparison of golden stonefly adults of both species and genders			
H. pacifica	female	28mm	35mm
H. pacifica	male	19mm	25mm
C. californica	female	24mm	30mm
C. californica	male	19mm	24mm

where they do not cope well. They ride very low, struggling and kicking and making a great fuss, as if oblivious to all the unhealthy attention they are drawing.

A bug in this predicament is very likely to bid farewell to life from the confines of a trout's stomach. If a fish doesn't spot it on the surface, it will soon become waterlogged and sink into the depths, and be picked up by a fish there. The ones that do manage to complete their egg-laying mission successfully and return to base—maybe a streamside willow—live for a few more days before expiring peacefully of old age.

FLY CHOICES AND FISHING STRATEGIES

Despite the greater press coverage of the salmonflies, golden stoneflies are actually more important to fly fishers on many rivers where both types occur. They are often more abundant, and exhibit egg-laying behavior that makes the adults more available to fish. In contrast to salmonflies, which usually drop their eggs from several feet above water, golden stones dip down and touch the water during egg laying. As a consequence, they end up stranded on the surface more often. Maybe that's why trout eat more of them. Or maybe they just taste good.

From below, a trout gets quite a show. Yellow bellies, legs, and even wings are visible as the heavy golden stone sinks into the surface film.

Mating golden stoneflies are a common sight along many western rivers in early summer.

Dave Whitlock's Red Fox Squirrel Nymph can be tied with or without rubber legs. Either way, it's a deadly pattern that has a permanent slot in my fly box. Dave Hughes has written that this is the fly he ties on as a general searching pattern, unless he has good reason to try something else. I prefer it with amber-colored rubber legs, like the one pictured from Umpqua Feather Merchants, which twitch and give additional motion with every change in currents. Larger sizes (hook size 6–8) may be best just before the hatch, but smaller versions (size 10–14) work well year-round.

Lee Clark developed his Clark's Stonefly to match the big salmonflies and golden stoneflies of the Deschutes River, but its fame and usage has spread far beyond. It doesn't weigh much for a big fly and is relatively easy to cast. The gold tinsel body reflects light similar to the refraction of the surface film around a struggling natural's body. The poly yarn underwing and deer-hair wing provide good floatation when coated with dry-fly floatant. Since salmonflies and golden stone hatches often overlap, you can fish this single pattern to imitate both.

Most of the patterns that are useful when fishing the salmonfly hatch will also work when imitating golden stoneflies, but should be tied in lighter colors of brown, yellow, and tan—and, of course, should be smaller. Since nymphs are present in several year and size classes, fly sizes in the 8–6 range are good choices for the oldest and largest of them, but smaller sizes in the 12–10 range should also be carried. The latter are particularly appropriate shortly after the hatch has ended, at which time the larger nymphs will have hatched, leaving mostly smaller individuals still in the water. I particularly like patterns with rubber legs, which provide lots of lifelike movement.

When fishing dry flies, the standard advice is to fish close to shore, next to steep banks and overhanging vegetation. This approach makes a lot of sense because that is where the adults are most likely to fall into the water, and where fish are apt to be waiting for them. I have always found this approach to be effective. However, the tactic is no longer a secret, and such spots on popular rivers often get pounded. You have to find the ones that are very difficult to access, or present challenging casting situations. Ernie Schwiebert noted in *Nymphs II* that on one of his trips to the Madison River, everyone was fishing the banks, and no one was paying attention to the middle of the river. He found some midstream gravel bars that were covered with emerging stoneflies, but everyone was passing right by in their single-minded focus on the shoreline. He soon discovered that the fish around the gravel bar were not only unmolested by other fly fishers, but also willing to take his imitations.

One of my favorite flies for imitating golden stonefly nymphs is a Beadhead Golden Stone with rubber legs. For the adults, a Stimulator or Sofa Pillow or Chernobyl Ant (mentioned in other chapters) are all popular for use during the golden stone hatch as well. But it's hard to beat the dry fly I usually reach for: the highly regarded Clark's Stonefly.

10
Humongous *Hexagenia*

Burrowing mayflies and the Hex hatch

So far we've encountered mayfly nymphs that swim in the water, cling tenaciously to rocks as the currents rip by them, or crawl on the bottom as their predominant lifestyle. Now we come to the last group—those that dig into the bottom and actually live beneath the river or lake, rather than just in it.

THE BURROWING MAYFLIES

Burrower mayflies are so named because of the nymphs' practice of tunneling into bottom sediments. And they come out of their hideaways only at night. As a consequence of these habits, many anglers have never seen a burrower mayfly nymph. But if you are on hand when the adults are around, you cannot fail to be impressed by these albatrosses of the aquatic insect realm. Members of this group are the largest of North American mayflies, with one species, *Litobrancha recurvata*, or dark green drake, holding the record for size at a body length of over 40mm (about 1 2/3 inches).

We haven't had much discussion of colloquial mayfly nomenclature since chapter 2, but the mention of the dark green drake sets my mind running down that path again, so bear with me for a tangential moment. Have you ever wondered what attribute of a mayfly qualifies it to be called a drake, what the term means, and how it came to apply to mayflies? If you browse through a list of mayfly common names, you'll notice that drake is assigned mostly, but not consistently, to the larger species—including the largest of them all, *L. recurvata*. According to the *American Heritage*

Burrower mayflies have an aversion to light, so the late start of the hatch often means fishing into the dark. Big fish are the reward.

Dictionary, a drake is "a male duck" or "a mayfly used as fishing bait" and is derived from the word *dragon* in several languages.

Maybe some fellow in merry old England tied his imitation of a big mayfly using drake feathers, and the name jumped to the natural. Or perhaps after a few too many pints of ale, the same chap described that mayfly as "big as a duck" or even as "big as a dragon." In any event, if today you spot the term drake in a mayfly's name, you will be safe in assuming it is a good-size bug. But the reverse is not true. For instance, burrower mayflies of the species *Hexagenia limbata* are only a shade smaller than *L. recurvata*, yet are seldom called drakes by the typical angler. Rather, they often go by the nonsensical sobriquet "Michigan Caddis" or more frequently, just "Hex."

Getting back on track, there are three mayfly families that are generally consigned to the burrower category: Ephemeridae, Polymitarcyidae, and Potamanthidae. By far the most important to fly fishers is the family Ephemeridae, with the genera *Hexagenia* and *Ephemera* producing widespread and prolific hatches across the North American continent; and the single species within the genus *Litobrancha*, *L. recurvata*, producing fishable hatches in the northeastern United States and eastern Canada. The genus *Ephoron* within the Polymitarcyidae family is responsible for the intense but unevenly distributed emergences of the smaller white miller (or white fly) mayflies, common in some places in the East and Midwest, but found in only a few locales within the West. The single genus *Anthopotamus* within the family Potamanthidae gives rise to hatches of medium-large golden drakes or yellow drakes on some waters in the eastern half of the United States. In all cases, burrower mayfly duns emerge at dusk or later in the evening, with the occasional exception of afternoon hatches on cloudy, dark days. This behavior is consistent with a general characteristic of burrower nymphs: photophobia. They hide underground during the day, and only come out during low light, whether it is to feed or to hatch.

All of the burrower mayflies inhabit waters where sediments of some depth accumulate, whether in slow rivers, slow sections of faster rivers, or in lakes. Such conditions predominate in the Midwest, and thus it is no surprise that burrowers are king in that region. Plenty of waterways in the East and farther south meet the habitat criteria, so most fly fishers in those regions are also quite familiar with these big bugs. Western anglers encounter burrowers much less frequently. The predominance of hills and mountains and freestone streams in most of the West translates into scoured bottoms that are too hard for burrower nymphs to dig into. Most of our western burrower mayfly action is restricted to two species, *H. limbata* (hex), and *E. simulans* (brown drake), in widely separated locations. As a result, my own experience with these behemoths is minimal;

I wish I had been more aware of the opportunities when I lived in Michigan many years ago.

But there is at least one outstanding western venue for fishing the hex hatch, and that is the Williamson River in southern Oregon. The Williamson drains into Klamath Lake, where huge rainbow trout, the size of steelhead, reside. In the summer months they migrate into the lower Williamson to escape rising water temperatures in the lake. That brings them into an area with an excellent hex population, just at the time when the hatch is coming off. It's an excellent opportunity to catch truly large trout on big hex flies. The upper Williamson is smaller and wilder in character, and though it doesn't have the lake-run rainbows, it does have a fine population of nice residents—up to 25–30 inches—and a prolific hex hatch. Access can be tricky due to the predominance of private property, but a couple of ranches in the area provide lodging and the chance to fish the river in an uncrowded setting. The Yamsi Ranch, owned by the Hyde family, is near the headwaters and enjoys an excellent reputation for big bugs, large fish, and congenial hosts.

Since burrower nymphs live most of their lives underground, they have developed anatomies that are specialized for digging their tunnels. The forelegs are very robust, with shapes designed for earth removal. Their heads are shovel-like and sport exaggerated, tusklike mandibles that assist in their ground-boring activities. The exact body design varies from one group to another and is optimized for the type of bottom in which each lives. Some species prefer soft marls and silt, easy to excavate but just firm enough for the tunnels to hold their shape without collapsing. Others prefer harder clays, or mixtures of sand and fine gravel. The soft sediments have to be deep enough, usually at least six to twelve inches, to accommodate the tunnels of the species in question.

All of the burrower mayfly nymphs have long slender bodies with large gills that are usually held in a dorsal position. These gills are the most efficient in the mayfly realm, and allow the nymphs of this group to live in slower, warmer, less oxygenated water than any of their relatives. This is the type of water we would expect trout might avoid, and indeed this is sometimes the case. Such water is often also associated with pollution. But despite their tolerance for low oxygen levels, burrower mayflies are very sensitive to pollution, and will only be found where water quality is good. Where the conditions also permit trout to flourish, we have the ingredients for a fisherman's bonanza: big bugs, big fish.

You might think that in waters where oxygen levels are already low, burrower nymphs are dealing themselves a further handicap by burying into the mud. But in fact, the tunnels that these bugs make are an aid, not a hindrance, to respiration. The explanation follows a rationale similar to

Burrowing *Hexagenia* nymphs have brawny forelegs and a pair of tusks on the front of their heads to aid in digging burrows into the bottom sediments. They are amazingly strong. I've watched them pry even large rocks many times their own weight out of the way. Body length = 28mm.

Long feathery gills wave in the water as a *Hexagenia* nymph stirs up sediment while digging into the bottom.

Using its hair-covered tails and large gill surfaces for propulsion, a hex nymph swims in dolphin fashion with an up-down undulating motion.

Burrower nymphs such as *Hexagenia* construct U-shaped tunnels in the bottom sediment of their natural habitat. When the consistency of the substrate is less than ideal, as in this aquarium, the burrows may collapse. This enterprising individual improvised by tunneling under a rock to construct a stable burrow open to the water on both ends.

the one put forth for the cased caddisflies in chapter 3. Burrower mayfly nymphs construct U-shaped tunnels that open into the water on both ends. Much like the caddisfly larva or pupa in its case, the burrower nymph pumps water gently through its tunnel, providing a constant supply of fresh oxygenated water and carrying away respiratory by-products. It does this by a rhythmic fanning of its large gills, pushing water through the tunnel and over its body from front to back. As was mentioned in the caddisfly discussion, the respiratory principle is essentially the same in fish: water is pumped into one end (the mouth) of a tube, over the gills, and out the other end (the gill covers) of the tube.

Burrower nymphs are good swimmers when they need to be. They can propel themselves surprisingly well with up-down undulations of the body, rather porpoiselike. The large gill surfaces along the abdomen and three tails with fringe hairs at the rear act like fins. But these nymphs don't have to swim very often. During the day, they stay hidden within their tunnels. They come out at night to crawl around the bottom in search of food, often leaving trails that can be seen from above in clear water. Some kinds look for decaying organic matter, usually in no shortage in the type of water these nymphs call home. Others are carnivores, seeking small slow animals like worms and midge larvae for their midnight snacks. Only when pursued by a predator such as a fish, or when rising to the surface to emerge into adults, do these nymphs need to employ their swimming skills.

Though the family Ephemeridae is of most practical interest to fly fishers, the genus *Ephoron* (white miller) within the family Polymitarcyidae exhibits several remarkable characteristics, which are so unlike other mayflies, that they deserve special mention. And it is the females that are so extraordinary. Unlike the males, *Ephoron* female duns have atrophied legs that are incapable of supporting their weight, either on the water surface or on surrounding vegetation. So they fly off the water and into the air quickly, and never land until their egg-laying job is done and they collapse spent to the water. Female duns also have three tails, whereas the males have just two; this is the only case that I know where male and female mayflies show a difference in tail number. And most importantly, *Ephoron* female duns are unique in that they never molt to spinners, although the males do. The male duns hatch first, fly to shore to molt into spinners, and then return to the water to catch female duns that hatch about a half hour later. The male spinners mate with female duns—which then fly upstream to lay eggs and die, without ever molting to spinners. It is a fascinating phenomenon that may provide a clue to the evolutionary history of mayflies.

While on the subject of evolutionary clues, the third family of burrower mayflies, Potamanthidae, may be an intermediary link in the pathway to the other burrower families. These nymphs were originally classified with the other burrowers, until it was discovered that they don't form true burrows. Rather, they make shallow depressions in the bottom substrate. So maybe we can think of them as ditch diggers, rather than tunnel builders. They may thus be the most primitive of this category of mayflies, whose ancestors initiated the practice of digging into the bottom sediments, an activity later extended and refined by the true burrowers.

But it is the family Ephemeridae that is unquestionably the focus of most fly-fishing interest. It gives us the big eastern green drake, yellow drake, and brown drake hatches. And most importantly, it yields the coast-to-coast, often awe-inspiring, flagship-burrower mayfly hatch: the hex.

HEXAGENIA

The first thing to note about *H. limbata* nymphs is their size. At more than $1^1/2$ inches long, excluding tails (which can add another $^1/2$ inch), these things are among the biggest bugs in the neighborhood. But it takes a while to grow that large, from two to four years, depending on water temperature and food availability. Some of the coldest waters in northern Canada have short growing seasons, and it is there where nymphs spend the longest time in the juvenile stage. But everywhere there will be, at any particular time, multiple-size classes of nymphs in the water.

Like all burrower mayflies, hex nymphs need a substantial layer of penetrable sediment on the bottom of the river or lake to dig and hide in. Their specialty is soft mud produced by the settling of fine particles of soil—compacted just enough to avoid collapse of the burrows once they are dug. Even sand is too much work for hex nymphs to tackle. Their kind of bottom substrate is not found in the fast sections of rivers, or even at the margins of wave-swept lakes, because the water action prevents the accumulation of these fine sediments. Yet their close relative, *E. simulans* (brown drake), seems able to dig into somewhat coarser bottoms. The two species *H. limbata* and *E. simulans* are both widespread across North America, both inhabit slow waters with pliant bottom sediments, and yet rarely overlap in any particular habitat. What accounts for the difference?

To address that question, one group of researchers set up an experiment comparing the ability of the two species to burrow into bottom substrates of varying particle size and composition. They found that, whereas hex nymphs could only burrow into firm mud or clay, brown drake nymphs could tunnel into a variety of coarser substrates; though their preferred medium was small gravel. Using oxygen consumption as a gauge, it was found that the brown drake nymphs expended less energy when digging in small gravel than in any other bottom type.

Examination of the two species' forelegs revealed a possible explanation for the difference in substrate preference. The forelegs of hex nymphs are broader, more shovel-like, and seem best suited for scooping out adhesive mud; while the narrower forelegs of brown drake nymphs allow them to move through larger particles more effectively. Thus both species have probably become abundant by avoiding direct competition, via the development of different "digging tools."

Hex nymphs can be found in abundance at depths up to about twenty feet in lakes—with lesser numbers as deep as fifty feet—as well as in shallower water. In some rivers and lakes they will also be found right up to shore, subject only to the absence of wave action that prevents sediment accumulation. Their U-shaped burrows are typically four to six inches deep, but can be even deeper. Some novel studies using X-ray imaging have shed light, so to speak, on what is going on under the surface where observations are normally impossible. The nymphs are much more active than formerly realized. They don't just build a burrow and rest on their laurels. They are constantly digging new tunnels, but they don't come to the top of the mud to start over. Rather, hex nymphs start the new tunnel by digging sideways, and as soon as the new U-shaped home is complete, they seal off the connection to the old one. In this way they are constantly expanding into new territory, probably to find new sources of decaying organic matter as they exhaust the supply in the old burrow. As a side effect—but one that is important to the local ecology—the huge numbers of nymphs in many lakes or rivers provide a sort of tilling action of the bottom sediments.

Most of the time hex nymphs can be found close to home, remaining in their burrows during daylight hours and venturing just short distances during nighttime feeding forays. But they can move greater distances when circumstances call for it. For instance, when water levels in reservoirs are dropped, large areas of the bottom near the shoreline can become exposed to air. Nymphs in that region will undergo mass migrations to reach new habitat. Similarly, if oxygen levels drop or temperatures increase in one region of a lake, the nymphs are quite capable of moving in mass. One study found that mass migrations occurred in some northern lakes at the time of ice-out. Examination of fish stomach contents showed that they had noticed all the activity, as their bellies were full of hex nymphs during these times. Anglers might do well to pay attention to such events as well.

Another better-known migration of hex nymphs often occurs just prior to emergence. As the nymphs sense the time of the hatch approaching they will frequently migrate

Male hex duns exhibit large two-toned compound eyes and three light-sensing ocelli between them. If any bug can be said to have expressive eyes, this would be the one.

Hex duns like this male vary in color from one locale to another, but they are striking creatures in all of their variations. Body length = 28mm.

into shallower water. Then as the big evening arrives, the nymphs get restless, leave their burrows, and start nervously pacing the bottom. At this time, fly fishers using flies that imitate the nymphs do well. (In fact, some experts, like Carl Richards, recommend sticking with nymph imitations throughout the hatch.)

As the sun sets, hex nymphs start bolting for the surface. Swimming with an enticing (to trout) undulating motion, it doesn't take them long to make the journey. If the water is very deep, they might pause to rest on the way up. These big nymphs have no trouble breaking through the surface tension, and it usually doesn't take the duns long to get out of their nymphal skins. Once on the water though, it can require a bit of time for the wings to be inflated, dried, and readied for flight. False starts and crashing back to the surface are common. All that commotion attracts attention, and not of a good kind, if you are a hex dun. There are many stories of the biggest trout of the year being drawn to the surface by these huge bugs. Even larger predators often join the fray: obsessive fly fishers casting into the darkness, guided mostly by the sound of big fish crashing on big bugs. The anglers cast with desperation, because they know that the whole thing is likely to be over within an hour or so, and every cast counts. Duns that escape the onslaught from above and below make their way to the shoreline, where they alight on rocks or vegetation to rest and wait for the next stage of their lives.

Hex hatches are stunning not only for the size of the bugs, but just as much for their sheer numbers. The Great Lakes region has long been famous for the massive emergence of *Hexagenia* mayflies, particularly the relatively shallow Lake Erie. Until the middle of the last century, literally millions of these big bugs would hatch on a single night, and the whole thing might be repeated every day for a week or two. Then in the early 1950s, catastrophe struck. Pollution in the lakes had been building for decades, increasing the pressure on insects and other organisms within the lakes. The last straw was an extended heat wave during the summer of 1953 that was accompanied by two weeks of dead calm, with no wind to help mix oxygen into the water. The resulting oxygen deprivation, coupled with high pollution levels, decimated the *Hexagenia* population. The colossal hex hatches came to a sudden end. Fish and other lake life also decreased drastically.

The calamity was a wake-up call to the region, and efforts were finally initiated to reverse the degradation of water quality in the lakes. During ensuing decades great progress was made in cleaning up the water. Then, in the 1990s, the first *Hexagenia* duns in nearly forty years began popping from the lake. The hex was back. Within a few years the numbers had become so large that great clouds of migrating duns, ten miles wide, could be detected on weather radar screens, and their movement followed as the

Rainbow trout take on colors justifying their name when spawning time approaches.

duns made their way to shore, followed by the reverse migration of the spinners.

It was a tremendous success story for the environment, and demonstrates what can be achieved even in dire situations when there is enough concern and commitment. Today the hex hatches of the Great Lakes seem to be approaching their former glory. Stories that awe the reader, like those of the radar images, are reappearing. Every fly fisher in the Midwest, and many from other regions, has heard of roads and bridges being temporarily closed due to massive spinner falls. News stories show road equipment scraping huge piles of dead mayfly bodies from roadways, where squished bugs make the streets so slippery that they are a road hazard! Such stories boggle the mind.

On a side note—while on the subject of mayflies and roads—it is not unusual for mayfly spinners of many species to be attracted to pavement, and to act as if the road were a river. That's a reproductive dead end for the spinners, so why do they do it? What is it about asphalt roads that mayfly spinners find so enticing?

A group of entomologists who wondered about that same question undertook a study to find the answers. They found the phenomenon to be widespread, and concluded that dry asphalt roads act as mayfly traps: "asphalt roads near ephemeropteran emergence sites (lakes, rivers, and creeks) are a great danger for mayflies, because eggs laid on the asphalt inevitably perish. Asphalt roads can deceive and attract mayflies *en masse* like ancient tar pits." (G. Kriska et al., 1998, *Journal of Experimental Biology*, 201: 2273.)

The primary reason that mayflies mistake roads for rivers lies in the bugs' method for recognizing water surfaces. We perceive polarized light very weakly, requiring the aid of polarized glasses to notice it at all. But mayfly eyes respond to it much more efficiently than ours do. The light reflected from the surface of a river or lake is strongly polarized in a horizontal plane, and the researchers found that feature to be the primary method by which mayflies identify a body of water. Asphalt reflects polarized light in much the same way. The darker and smoother the road surface, the more polarized light it reflects, and the more attractive it looks to a mayfly. Moreover, the long snaking form of a road, and the fact that it is usually free of covering vegetation, enhances its similarity to a waterway. Bottom line: roads are as much a danger to mayflies as they are to people.

I think we can all agree that winding up as a squished greasy spot in the road is an unfitting end for such a graceful creature as a hex spinner.

Hexagenia spinners that somehow manage to escape the dangers of roadways, birds, and fish live on average about three days. They return to the water to mate and lay eggs in the evenings, often mixing in with the duns that are hatching that night. Most of the females deposit their eggs (about 4,000 on average, but up to 8,000) by crashing to the water and extruding all their eggs in one shot. Some of them dip to the water several times, knocking off a part of their egg load each time. And a very few just drop their eggs like bombs from the air.

In the low light when these bugs are active, it can be difficult to determine whether fish are taking spinners, duns, or emerging nymphs. After their first giddy rush at the beginning of the hatch, trout quickly start to fill up, and it's common for them to get very selective. Some authors report that one fish may decide it only wants fluttering bugs, while another opts for just those that are motionless. In the dark, it's hard for an angler to figure out all that. But it sure is fun trying.

WHY FLY?

The astute reader will have noticed by now that all of the insects we are discussing live the vast majority of their lives in the water, then emerge for just a short period in air and on land before dying. *Hexagenia* is one of the more extreme examples, spending two to four years in the water and just three or four days out of it. The paleontological record reveals that winged insects first evolved on land, and later recolonized fresh water. Yet with the exception of a rare stonefly species that lives in Lake Tahoe, none of

With its long tails (22mm) and forelegs, a male hex spinner makes a spectacular and graceful sight—even one that has incurred some damage to its wings.

A hex spinner's wings become clear, but it retains the winning visage of the dun.

them has completely abandoned a winged existence in air. Inquiring minds must wonder, why bother? Wouldn't it be easier to just stay in the water and not hassle with wing development and all that metamorphosis malarkey?

The fact that it hasn't happened (outside of that one exception) strongly implies that there are good reasons for flying and powerful selective pressures to maintain it. The two most commonly given rationales for the importance of insect flight are dispersal of the species into the widest variety of habitats, and assistance with finding a mate. Those explanations are valid for all insects, not only the aquatic sorts. But the dispersal problem is even more acute for creatures that live in rather isolated bodies of water—particularly those that flow—yet don't swim all that well. Insects in streams and rivers are constantly being pushed downstream by the currents. Even the strongest swimmers among them can't maintain any sustained upstream migration. The cumulative result of their riverine existence is a net displacement downstream. Without some mechanism for traveling in the opposite direction, they would eventually all be pushed to sea!

That is why the swarms of adult mayflies, caddisflies, and other insects you encounter on the river are nearly always flying upstream. They're on a mission to regain ground they lost as youngsters, and to seed the next generation in waters where they themselves were born.

In addition, the ability to fly allows aquatic insects the option of moving to new, nearby waters to expand their numbers, or to escape catastrophe when conditions change for the worse in their own neighborhood. Terrestrial insects have similar requirements, and indeed most of them also retain the ability to fly. But the need is not as great, reflected in the fact that some of them no longer develop wings. When you are on land, you can crawl or hop, however slowly, to new territory. In contrast, most bodies of fresh water are comparatively small and isolated. It's pretty hard to swim from one lake to another!

Yes, being a tiny insect in a huge world certainly has its unique problems. One of them is locating a mate. Unless you live in a colony, with many close neighbors, there is a lot of ground to cover. And if you must crawl the whole distance, well, how long does a bug have on this

Burk's Hexagenia Nymph. Many experienced fishers of the hex hatch will stick with a nymph pattern right through the hatch, never switching to a dry. Fish are often less picky with wet than dry patterns. In addition, after the sun goes down, the angler has a better chance of feeling the take with a nymph than hearing it with a dry fly. The keys to a good hex nymph pattern are effective mimicry of the plumose gills, and movement that imitates as closely as possible the undulating swimming motion of a nymph swimming to the surface. Andy Burk designed this nymph for Umpqua Feather Merchants to cover both bases. Gray pheasant filoplume, tied on top of the hook, and an ample marabou tail pulse like the real gills when the rod tip is moved slowly up and down during the retrieve. Size 6.

Hexagenia Paradrake. As effective as a nymph may be, there is nothing quite like the take of a big surface fly by an even larger surface-feeding fish. The extended body Paradrake-style fly was developed by Doug Swisher and Carl Richards. Variations on the basic style have been made by Mike Lawson and others. In a size 6–8 and yellow colors, it is one of the most popular choices for imitating the hex duns.

earth, anyway? There has to be a better alternative, and flying is it.

Speaking of longevity, catastrophe, life, death, and related weighty concepts; why don't the winged stages of aquatic insects last longer? If a short winged phase is good, wouldn't a longer one be better? It seems like it would allow more time to find a new home, or a more appealing consort. Yet all aquatic insects spend the vast majority of their lives in the water, with at most a few weeks in the air; and mayflies take that convention to the extreme. There must be a good reason for it. And if you think about it, there is. The terrestrial environment is a dangerous place for an aquatic insect, with numerous and efficient predators, extremes of heat and cold, and the risk of desiccation. The overriding priority of an adult insect is to breed and lay the seeds for the next generation, and then its job is finished.

Any tarrying or delay in the upper world just increases the chances of fatal disaster and mission failure. Ergo, the bugs' catch phrase might be: "Get it done; pass it on."

FLIES

Hex mayflies are among the largest of their kind. When these big bugs start to hatch, every fish around, including the monsters, get excited. Except for the very occasional emergence on a dark, cloudy afternoon, the hatch usually starts at dusk and often doesn't hit full tilt until it's too dark to see. Then it becomes a game of sound and feel. Since my experience with hex mayflies is minimal, I've looked into the recommendations of experts when it comes to fly choice. The two patterns described above receive uniformly high marks.

11
Where Waters Slow or Don't Flow

Slow and still-water trout prey

I'll confess right up front that I fish fast streams far more often than lakes and slow rivers. Part of the reason is proximity, but personal preferences also have a lot to do with it. Yet some of the biggest trout and the most spectacular of their prey live in still-water homes. This chapter will take a look at some of the prey that are the most important (to trout), and/or the most intriguing (to the author). Let's start with the mayflies.

MAYFLIES

Most mayfly nymphs prefer moving water, and there is a much greater diversity of species in streams and rivers than anywhere else. Yet the few kinds that do live in lakes, ponds, and backwaters are often profusely abundant and major contributors to the food chain. In the West, by far the most important still-water mayflies are in the genus *Callibaetis* (speckled duns). Other groups, of consequence to fly fishers, that are found in some still or very slow waters include the genus *Tricorythodes* (tricos) and its close cousin *Caenis* (white-winged sulphurs; or more cynically, white-winged curses); *Siphlonurus* (gray drakes), which will be covered in chapter 14 along with other large swimmer mayflies; the burrower mayflies *Hexagenia* (hex), *Ephemera* (brown drakes), and *Ephoron* (white drakes), which were the subject of chapter 10; and the *Leptophlebia* (black quills).

Lakes and ponds are frequently the training waters for new generations of anglers.

In a departure from the usual situation, the speckled dun is one of the few widely known mayflies whose scientific name is used by typical fly fishers more often than the supposed common name. *Callibaetis* mayflies, like all members of the family Baetidae, are of the swimmer-type. They have a mostly western distribution, with just a scattered presence in the eastern half of North America. Like the members of its sister genus *Baetis*, *Callibaetis* species thrive in placid, weedy water. But whereas *Baetis* mayflies are mostly present in rivers with just occasional representation in the margins of some lakes, the situation is reversed with *Callibaetis*. *Callibaetis* nymphs are found in western lakes and ponds wherever there is enough vegetation to support them, and in some slow spring creeks and tailwaters with similar habitat. These nymphs spend most of their time resting on plant stems and leaves, but swim from one point to another in short, fast spurts of several inches.

Callibaetis nymphs (and consequently the adults) are a little larger on average than is typical for *Baetis*, with body lengths (excluding tails) of up to about 12mm for the former versus about 9mm for the latter. They have the characteristic streamlined proportions of swimmer mayflies, with a tendency toward being slightly flattened laterally and eyes that are positioned more on the sides of the head than on top. There are three tails with fine interlocking hairs that permit them to function somewhat like a fish's caudal fin. The two antennae are unusually long for a mayfly; at least two times longer than the head is wide. This trait is useful in distinguishing *Callibaetis* from the other swimmer-mayfly nymph with which it is most likely to be confused, *Siphlonurus*, since it sometimes lives in the same habitat and shows considerable resemblance. But the antennae of *Siphlonurus* species are much shorter.

The nymphal stage of *Callibaetis* mayflies is remarkably short, with the time from egg hatching (eclosion) to dun emergence being as little as six weeks. And they hit the water swimming, so to speak, as the eggs hatch almost immediately upon immersion. This means that under appropriate conditions of water temperature and food availability, there may be up to three generations of a *Callibaetis* species in a particular body of water within a single season. (In some exceptional lakes with an unusually long warm period, even four generations have been noted.) Each generation matures faster than the previous one as the water warms from spring through summer. But with less time to eat and grow, each successive brood is also a little smaller than the previous one. So hatching duns may be a size 12 early in the season, but by autumn the average may be down to a size 16. Anglers may well need to downsize their flies in response.

Callibaetis nymphs are found in greatest abundance in heavily vegetated still waters. Body length = 9mm.

The rabbitlike reproductive rate of *Callibaetis* mayflies translates into season-long abundance of the nymphs. Trout are prone to swim through the underwater forest of vegetation, sweeping the plants with their tails as they go. Nymphs are flushed from their resting places and dart for safety, but more often end up in a trout's maw when the movement reveals their positions. Interestingly, in some heavily fished waters trout have learned to let wading anglers perform the prey-flushing chore for them.

Once, while fishing a slow, weedy area of the Colorado River below Glenn Canyon Dam in Arizona, I watched with amazement as half a dozen 12- to 15-inch trout positioned themselves just a couple of feet downstream from me. Every time I took a step, they would rush in to grab the bugs I stirred up, even bumping into my legs! The phenomenon also occurs on other similar waters, and when the bug stirring is done on purpose, it has acquired the derisive appellation "San Juan shuffle." Intentional attraction of trout in this way is considered unsporting by many fly fishers, akin to chumming.

Callibaetis duns usually begin hatching within an hour or so of noon. For a while before the first dun pops above the water, the nymphs exhibit an emblematic restlessness and begin yo-yoing to the surface and back before making a final commitment to switching environments. All that

activity attracts piscine attention, so this is a good time to fish nymph imitations.

Once the hatch gets underway, it may last for several hours if the day is overcast, rainy, and/or windy. In that case the duns often have some trouble getting their wings inflated and ready for flight, and they may spend enough time on the water to make it worthwhile for trout to go after them. But if the day is sunny, not only is the hatch duration often truncated, but the duns seem to get into the air almost as soon as they hatch. In those circumstances, fish may ignore the duns since there are not many of them on the water at any one time, and concentrate instead on all the nymphs that are massing just under the surface film.

After a *Callibaetis* dun leaves the water, it flies to nearby vegetation on shore like most mayflies, and relaxes for a while. By the next day it has molted to a spinner and is ready to mate. Big clouds of male spinners congregate over or near the water and begin their characteristic up-down performance. Females fly into the swarm, pair up with a male, and then after mating return to the bushes and trees. Males also return to land, usually to die there. But the females still have a job to do. Rather than laying eggs right away, they wait up to five days while their fertilized eggs ripen inside them. As a result, when the females return to the water for egg deposition, the eggs are ready to

The white wing pattern on a dark background is what gives *Callibaetis* duns their speckled dun nickname.
Body length = 9mm.

Female *Callibaetis* spinners have wings that are predominantly clear, but retain some of the dark speckling on the leading edge.

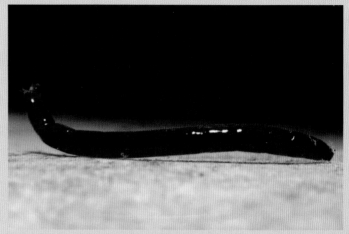

The red color of some chironomid larvae comes from hemoglobin, a more efficient oxygen carrier, within their tissues.

Male *Callibaetis* spinners have clear wings and exhibit the turbinate eyes typical of the Baetidae family. Body length = 9mm.

hatch. All they need is the addition of water to stimulate the youngsters inside to break free and begin their lives as swimming nymphs.

With their missions complete, female spinners expire on the water surface. Spinner falls can thus be a prime opportunity for fish to catch adults without much effort, and many times they will take advantage of the situation. (It's a good idea to keep some spinner dry flies on hand for such occasions, but be sure the imitations match the water-bound female spinners, whose wing patterns are different from the males that are more visible in the air.) Other times, trout inexplicably ignore those spinners, and continue to concentrate on nymphs. But hey, if it were easy and predictable, it wouldn't be much fun, would it?

MIDGES

If there is any bug that fly fishers love to hate, it is the midge. When trout are feeding on things you cannot see, more often than not a tiny midge is the culprit. Someone shows you the fly you are supposed to tie on to match this hatch—sizes 22, 24, or even a 26! And you respond with, "You've got to be kidding." (Not even eagle-eyed youngsters, and certainly not those of us with middle-aged presbyopic vision, have a chance of seeing such microscopic flies on the water; much less threading a tippet through the eye of the hook.)

Luckily, not all midges come in sizes as small as their name implies. Some of them can be imitated with flies as large as a size 10. And there are times when if you want to catch fish, fishing midges is the only game in town. Nevertheless, midge fishing is not for everyone. Sometimes you just have to decide what is important in your version of the sport.

Midges are true flies; that is, they belong to the order Diptera. As such they are in the company of familiar insects like house flies, black flies, horse flies, gnats, mosquitoes, crane flies, and many others. The diversity of the dipterans is astounding: an estimated one million or more species classified into 188 families and over 10,000 genera. Diptera means two wings, which is characteristic of members of this order; whereas most other winged insects have four wings arranged in two pairs. In the Diptera, the hind pair of wings has been reduced to stubby remnants called halteres, which act like gyroscopes to stabilize their remarkable flying maneuvers.

Dipterans are among the most highly evolved of the insects. They undergo complete metamorphosis, a type of development discussed in chapter 3. In that respect they resemble the caddisflies. Both include a pupal phase in their progression from egg to adult.

While the vast majority of true flies are terrestrial, a sizable fraction is aquatic in that the juvenile stages live in water. Because the total number of dipteran species is so great, even this small fraction means there is more diversity among aquatic dipterans than any other insect order, even those that are entirely aquatic. Several of the aquatic dipteran families are important to fly fishers, but none more so than the midges.

True midges are classified into the family Chironomidae. There are more than 200 genera containing over 1,000 species in North America. And they live virtually anywhere there is fresh water, from mighty rivers and lakes to small puddles, from the clearest of mountain lakes to some of the world's most polluted rivers. Many of them live in our trout streams, but it is in lakes and ponds where they really come into their own from a fly fisher's perspective. It is for that reason that I've included them in this chapter.

The chironomid life cycle begins when an egg hatches into a larva. The larvae are typical of dipterans: wormlike or maggotlike. They are vaguely segmented with a well-developed head capsule. They have no true, segmented legs, but the first thoracic segment and the last abdominal segment each have a pair of fleshy, stumplike prolegs that are useful for some crude crawling movements. Coloration may vary, with black, brown, cream, olive, and red being most common. (The red varieties are often free-living, and interestingly, the red color is imparted by hemoglobin within their tissues.) Most chironomid larvae live in the bottom sediments in crude mud cases, and come out only to feed. A few are free-roaming, moving slowly over the bottom and around plants. Trout consume considerable numbers of them, but because of their habits, they are difficult to imitate, and most anglers concentrate on the pupal forms.

Pupation occurs on the lake or river bottom, during which time the larvae develop wing pads and wispy gill-like structures near the head. When it's time to transform into an adult, gases form under the pupal exoskeleton and buoy it slowly to the surface. The pupae have little to no swimming ability, and depend entirely on buoyancy for the ride up. All those gas bubbles under the skin give them a shimmering appearance as they rise. Once at the surface film, the small pupae have difficulty breaking through. They may alternate between hanging vertically, and then assuming a horizontal position at points where they might break through. Emergence generally occurs with the pupa in a horizontal position just under the film.

Emergence is typically quick, and once free of the pupal exoskeleton, the adult usually leaves the water in a hurry. As a result, trout will often ignore the adults and concentrate on the pupae rising slowly through the water column and accumulating under the film. Even when fish break the water surface, they are more often feeding on pupae than emerging adults. The pupae are thus the prime stage that trout consume, and the one that fly fishers most often mimic. Flies for this stage should have very slender bodies, with thoraxes that are about one-fifth of the length.

These pupae also have white, wispy gills near the head, which can be successfully imitated by small amounts of CDC feathers or tiny bead-heads.

Adult midges usually return to the water in huge swarms in the mornings or evenings. In their swirling mating frenzies they can form multibodied clumps that sometimes fall to the water. These balls of amorous midges are often the best chance for imitations of adults to succeed. Probably the best-known adult midge dry fly, the Griffith's Gnat, is designed to imitate these mating midge clusters. Scott Richmond, author and proprietor of Westfly.com, finds that the Griffith's Gnat works better in higher elevation lakes, for unknown reasons. Jeff Morgan, another fly-fishing author, points to three key features of a successful midge imitation: flash (to mimic air bubbles), motion (to make it seem alive), and distinction (to make the imitation stand out from the millions of surrounding naturals). He believes that the Griffith's Gnat owes much of its success to the latter property, as it is larger than most individual naturals. It is also noteworthy that midges on lakes tend to be considerably larger than their relatives residing in rivers, particularly during the early season.

DRAGONS AND DAMSELS

Dragonflies and damselflies belong to the order Odonata. They are the second oldest of the winged insects to have survived into modern times, taking a backseat only to the mayflies in the length of their pedigree. Some of those ancient dragonflies were whoppers, too. According to the fossil record, the all-time champion was *Meganeura monyi*, which lived around 325 million years ago. It had a wingspan of over two and half feet—about the size of a small hawk! As far as is yet known, it was the largest flying insect ever to soar over the earth's surface. Not only did it catch other insects like today's dragonflies do, but it is believed to have fed even on small amphibians. That's a dragonfly that I would love to have seen.

Besides their antiquity, odonatans share with mayflies the inability to overlap their wings and fold them flat over their backs, as other more recently evolved insects do. They are thus easy to recognize and difficult to confuse with other bugs. Dragonflies, which are of the suborder Anisoptera, usually extend their wings horizontally when at rest; whereas resting damselflies, which are of the suborder Zygoptera, hold their wings back above their abdomen, at about a 30-degree angle from the thorax. A mayfly positions its much differently shaped wings almost straight up over its body.

Just about everyone who has been around water is familiar with odonatans, even if they don't know them by that name. There are about 350 species of dragonflies and 130 species of damselflies in North America. Shallow, still waters are home to most of them, but a few live in streams.

While adults are most often found within a stone's throw of the water, it's not unusual for them to travel great distances to dry locales where the smaller insects they prey upon are abundant. Their frequently dazzling color patterns and aerial performances make them favorites of kids and kids-at-heart the world over, even those who shudder at the approach of most other bugs.

As you might expect for such a primordial order of insects, odonatans develop from eggs to adults using the correspondingly old strategy of incomplete metamorphosis. Like the mayflies, there are only three life stages: egg, nymph, and adult. No pupal phase to be concerned with here.

The nymphs have short antennae and large eyes, alerting us to their pronounced orientation toward the visual sense. Keen eyesight, rather than olfactory or tactile sensitivity, is the hallmark of an odonatan. Mature body sizes vary from medium to very large, and body shapes from stout to slender, depending on subfamily and genus. Colors may be brown, black, tan, or shades of green; some even change hue to match the surrounding habitat.

Odonatan nymphs extract oxygen from the water using gills that are, in a switch from the insects we have run into thus far, located rather curiously at their rear ends. In damselflies the gills take the form of three tail-like appendages that extend rearward from the posterior of the abdomen, and do in fact act somewhat like propulsive tails in addition to performing their respiratory function. The gills of dragonfly nymphs, on the other hand, are not so obvious to the observer. Their gills are internal.

A striking feature of all dragonfly and damselfly nymphs is a greatly enlarged, hinged, extensible labium (lower lip). In side view or from underneath, in many species it looks rather like a monstrous growth on their "chin." But if you ever get to see it put to use, you'll be astonished. When another insect gets close enough, the labium unfolds and extends forward in a lightning-quick strike. Faster than the eye can follow, the unlucky victim is snatched up and yanked back to the ravenous mouth of the predator. Odonatan nymphs are carnivores to be feared by those—of a size below an inch—who prowl their neighborhoods.

Development from egg to adult usually takes one to five years, depending on species, water temperatures, and food availability. (Some damselflies develop faster, with two broods per year.) As in mayflies, the appearance of large, dark wing pads signals the approach of metamorphosis to the winged adult stage. All odonatans crawl out of the water, sometimes up plant stalks a few inches above the surface, and other times along the banks and up trees or other vertical structure that can be a fair distance from the water's edge. Emergence of the larger species is usually at night.

Adult odonatans have eyes that are considerably larger than those of the nymphs. In damselflies the eyes are at opposite ends of a wide head, giving them a somewhat hammerhead appearance. Dragonfly eyes are even larger, often coming close to completely covering the top of the head and meeting in the middle. There are no tails, and the two antennae are so short that you have to look closely to even notice them. Wings come in two large pairs, and they are put to excellent use. Each wing can move independently of the others, imparting unmatched maneuvering abilities to the owner, particularly in the case of the dragonfly. While a damselfly is a pretty good flyer, a dragonfly is a superb one. Not only agile, but speedy.

Adults of this group are also long-lived, compared with most aquatic insects. The majority of them spend twenty to sixty days in the terrestrial stage. And unlike the adults of many other aquatic orders, odonatan adults are active eaters. They terrorize the neighborhood, rendering the airways unsafe for any small insect that ventures into their space. Odonatans sweep up mosquitoes, flies, and midges by literally basketfuls. That's because their front legs act like a basket into which they sweep their victim as they fly up from below. Adults may feed for one to two weeks before mating and laying eggs.

Mating behavior of dragonflies and damselflies is quite unusual in more ways than one. Males are often fiercely territorial, claiming their spaces along the margins of a lake or stream and defending them against all interlopers. In places where there are lots of them, the poor males just about exhaust themselves chasing off rivals.

The method of mating is also highly unusual. In addition to the typical sex apparatus on the last abdominal segment, males possess a secondary sex organ on abdominal segment number two. It is a sort of depository for sperm. Prior to mating, the male transfers some sperm from the tip of its abdomen into the secondary organ. When he hooks up with a female, he uses the claspers on the end of his abdomen to seize her from above, just behind her head. Then she bends her abdomen up and forward, so that its tip contacts his auxiliary organ on the second abdominal segment. The resulting union forms a rough circle or oval composed of their two bodies. It's easier to show this than to describe it, so take a look at the accompanying bug porn: a pair of damselflies locked in the mating position.

The male will often maintain his hold on the female even after mating is over. Togetherness is the watchword here: they fly together, land together, do everything together, until she has laid her eggs. This isn't an expression of buggy affection. Rather, he's making sure that she doesn't mate with any other males, whose sperm would then compete with his own to fertilize the eggs that will become the next generation.

After mating and egg laying, the adults of some species soon die. But most others continue living and feeding for

Odonates like this pair of damselflies have a unique mating method. The male (on the left) grabs the female behind the head with claspers on the end of his abdomen, to provide a firm link between them. The female curls her abdomen underneath, forward, and up into the male's secondary sexual organ on his second abdominal segment, into which he has previously transferred sperm. Notice that the female, on the right, is duller in color than her mate. This is typical of odonatans; the males are the gaudy showoffs, while the females are usually a bit more conservative in their dress.

many more weeks before expiring. Thus they are common sights throughout summer in most locales.

Dragonflies

Of course the most noticeable of the adult odonates are the dragonflies. Big and amazingly fast fliers, they also often come in strikingly beautiful patterns and colors. Who could fail to marvel at the bright red Cardinal Meadowhawk, one of the skimmer types?

Most kinds of dragonflies live in still waters, but a few inhabit streams and rivers. Not only are the adults large, but their eyes are huge in comparison with their heads. The second wing pair is wider than the first, and this is a characteristic that helps distinguish dragonflies from damselflies. The different kinds go by names like darners, skimmers, emeralds, and cruisers, based on appearance, behavior, or even on old wives' tales.

Dragonfly nymphs possess a unique respiratory system. Their gills are internal, but are located in a place you would least expect them: their rectums. The nymphs "breathe" by rhythmically "inhaling" water and "exhaling" it again, in a manner very similar to the way our lungs move air. They literally breathe through their butts!

Besides serving to provide a flow of oxygenated water over its gills, a dragonfly nymph can constrict its rectal chamber abruptly, forcing a high-speed burst of water from its rear end. The result is a miniature jet propulsion system, which the nymphs can use to good effect when pursued by a predator. But most of the time they get around in a more pedestrian manner, by crawling.

Dragonflies are sometimes grouped into three informal types based on the habits and shapes of the nymphs: climbers, sprawlers, and burrowers. Climbers are often found prowling along the underwater stems and leaves of aquatic vegetation. Sprawlers spend most of their time on the bottom, blending in with the benthic structure. Burrowers dig down into the sediment.

There is currently some disagreement among experts about how to best classify the families of Anisoptera (dragonflies), but most texts present three families that are of note to fly fishers: Aeshnidae (darners), Libellulidae (skimmers and cruisers), and Gomphidae (clubtails). Clubtails are found primarily in rivers and streams, rather than in still waters. Two other families, Cordulegastridae (spiketails) and Petaluridae (petaltails), are seldom encountered by anglers.

A male Cardinal Meadowhawk dragonfly is hard to miss with its striking red body and orange wing veins. Body length = 37mm.

An aeshnid dragonfly prowls the lake or pond bottom in search of prey. Body length = 32mm.

The Aeshnidae, or darners, fall into the climber group and reach the largest sizes. They are primarily pond and lake dwellers. The nymphs are aggressive hunters, with long (up to 50mm), stout bodies and catlike habits. They slowly stalk their prey among the plants and along the lake bottoms, ready to pounce on anything that moves: insects, tadpoles, and even small fish.

Darner nymphs are more prone to swim than other types, moving between plants with a combination of paddling and jetting. In doing so they risk drawing the attention of other predators, ones large enough to turn the tables on the voracious dragonflies.

These nymphs spend as much time hanging upside down as they do upright. From that position we can get a good look at what appears to be a giant chin; but, in fact, this is a specialized weapon of mass destruction—a killer labium. The labium folds up under the head when it is not in use.

But when an unlucky insect or any other similar-size moving beast is within a couple of centimeters of the dragonfly's head, the labium unfolds and extends with the speed of a snake strike. Two spearlike lobes fold up at the front of the labium when at rest, but during a strike they unfold, then grasp and pierce the victim. The hapless creature is snatched back to the mouth where it is leisurely consumed.

While watching one such dragonfly nymph, a darner, I was lucky enough to see its lancing labium put into action. A *Siphlonurus* mayfly nymph wandered into the vicinity, and I noticed an immediate change in the dragonfly's behavior. It went into a crouch and began creeping slowly down its plant stalk to get a little closer. In the second frame of the accompanying photo sequence, you can see that the mayfly nymph on the bottom has the dragonfly's full attention. In the next instant the labium extended so fast that my eye couldn't follow it, but I saw the mayfly nymph snatched up from the bottom, tails splayed and legs kicking. It was all over but the eating. With its victim firmly in its grasp, the dragonfly settled down for a long period of leisurely mayfly munching. The whole event came as quite a surprise, and I felt fortunate to have witnessed it.

Darner nymphs look like the monstrous murderers that they are, but when they grow up they metamorphose into much more attractive adults, often boasting shades of blue and black arranged into striking patterns. Don't be fooled though. A killer spirit remains beneath that beautiful cloak.

The aeshnid dragonfly nymph has spotted a *Siphlonurus* mayfly nymph (facing away from the viewer, just in front of the dragonfly's head) and is creeping closer.

A close-up view of the extensible labium. The nymph is upside-down, and we are looking up at it. Note the folded, overlapping pointed spears at the thick end near the bottom of the picture.

Darner dragonfly adults are exceptional fliers, and remain on the wing for extended periods of time.

In a strike too quick for the human eye to follow, the dragonfly nymph seizes the mayfly with its labium and yanks it off the bottom.

With the mayfly nymph firmly in its grasp, the dragonfly can take its time in consuming the meal.

The family Libellulidae contains the most common, varied, and numerous dragonflies. These sprawler-type nymphs are also stout in shape but look squat and wide when compared with the more linear aeshnids. The libellulids have more patience than the aeshnids, too. Their strategy is to sit and wait for prey to come to them, then strike out in surprise, rather than actively seeking their victims. The libellulids don't bury themselves, but rather try to blend in with their surroundings. They are more often found in still than in flowing water.

The great diversity of the Libellulidae family has resulted in the creation of several subfamily categories: Macromiinae (cruisers), Corduliidae (emeralds and baskettails), and Libellulinae (skimmers). Some authors elevate two of the subfamilies, Corduliidae and Macromiinae, to full family status; yet others list Macromiinae as a subfamily of Corduliidae. This dispute is of no practical interest to the fly fisher, but I mention it in the event that the reader encounters these confusing taxonomical inconsistencies. This diversity is also reflected in the shapes and habits of the nymphs.

The Libellulinae subfamily contains the most common types of pond dragonflies, the skimmers. Skimmer nymphs resemble the cruisers, but with less exaggerated leg lengths. Their antennae are short and thin. They stay on the bottom most of the time, though they sometimes will crawl about the underwater vegetation. Many skimmer nymphs cover themselves with silt and pond debris, and often wear fine growths of filamentous algae and fungi. Sometimes the camouflage is so complete that it is hard to tell where the scum ends and the nymph begins!

Skimmer adults show a tremendous variety of patterns and hues. They are generally medium to large dragonflies, with eyes so big that they meet on top of the head. Males and females are frequently of different colors and designs.

Larger dragonflies like the darners usually emerge at night, though some smaller species such as skimmers can emerge during the day. It typically takes a long time, up to several hours, for the adults to complete the hatching process—especially for the larger types. During this period the bugs are exposed and unable to escape from predators. That is the most likely reason for the prevalence of nighttime emergence; otherwise birds would have their way with them, decimating the population. Most dragonfly nymphs crawl out of the water and onto vertical surfaces, like plants growing in the water or trees on the banks. The gomphids are an exception. Probably because they are poor climbers, they creep out onto shore and hatch on the horizontal surfaces of rocks.

A few years ago I happened upon a skimmer dragonfly that was in the midst of a daytime emergence. The nymph had crawled out of a pondlike section of a nearby stream, and climbed several inches up the wall of my shop. When I came upon the scene, the adult was just completing its exit from the nymphal exoskeleton, and was still standing on top of the shuck as it began expanding its wings.

The dragonfly at this stage is called a teneral adult. It is very pale, with a yellowish hue and none of the striking colors it will have when the process is complete. Teneral adults are weak and awkward, not yet able to fly and easy pickings for predators. Seeing them in this state helps you understand why most of them prefer emerging at night. If I could spot this one so readily, you know that a bird would have no trouble homing in on this easy meal. The awkwardness of the new adults also means they are subject to losing their grip and falling. Since the objects most often climbed are plants projecting above the water, a tumble there could mean a quick snack for any trout below.

But the dragonfly that climbed out onto my shop wall evaded those dangers. It had started its emergence around noon, and about five hours later it was still standing in the same spot over its nymphal shuck. Some of its adult colors were appearing, but it was still not quite yet ready to take to the air.

Early the next morning I found it still sitting near its shuck, waiting for the sun to warm it enough to fly. It now exhibited fully inflated and outstretched wings, the mature coloration of a female Eight-Spotted Skimmer, and most strikingly—after complete expansion—it was much bigger than the nymphal shuck from which it came. It must have felt really cramped in there!

Once past the teneral stage, dragonflies are not very important to fly fishers other than to keep us entertained. There are occasional reports of big trout taking an adult dragonfly, but for the most part the adults are just too good at flying for a trout to catch them. Dragonflies can fly at up to thirty-five miles per hour, stop on a dime, and even fly backward. Not many trout can match those skills.

However, the nymphs are another story, especially the darners whose active hunting style attracts the attention of prowling trout. As the time approaches for the nymphs to climb out of the water and emerge, they tend to engage in mass migrations toward shallow water. That's the time when trout are most likely to key in on them. And not only trout. Some friends of mine recently caught a bunch of big largemouth bass from central Oregon's Davis Lake—where the bass were illegally introduced into a trophy trout fishery—and found their stomachs engorged with dragonfly nymphs. Imitations of those nymphs proved deadly on

Skimmer dragonfly nymphs of the Libellulinae subfamily have squat bodies and spend most of their time on the bottom, but will sometimes climb vegetation.
Body length = 12mm (25mm when mature).

Adult male skimmer dragonflies, like this Eight-Spotted Skimmer, often perch on the end of sticks where they watch over their territories and drive off any trespassing competitors.

1

A female Eight-Spotted Skimmer teneral adult has just emerged from the nymph.

2

After five hours, the recently emerged skimmer dragonfly has gained color but still hasn't finished inflating its wings.

3

The morning sun of the next day finds the skimmer dragonfly fully colored and inflated and ready to fly away.

the bass, and they work on big trout, too. The trick is to keep the fly crawling slowly across the bottom, with occasional short strips to simulate the jet-propelled escape behavior of a startled dragonfly nymph.

Damselflies

Dragonflies may have the flash, but damselflies have the substance, at least when it comes to fly fishing. What they lack in size and audacity, they more than make up in numbers and availability. Almost any body of still water will hold sizable populations of damselfly nymphs. And their lifestyles bring them into frequent contact with trout. What more could we ask for?

Damselflies are also easier to keep track of in your head. All of the nymphs have a similar appearance, and most of them have similar habits, so you can imitate them with the same flies and techniques. By far, the majority live in still or very slow waters. Even the small number that specialize in streams restrict themselves to habitat common to them all: vegetation, living or dead. Very few dwell in rocky substrates. While the adults vary more in appearance than do the nymphs, the differences are small enough that you can ignore them, unless you take a particular interest in the bugs themselves.

There are just three families of importance to fly fishers: Calopterygidae, or broad-winged damselflies, which are always found in flowing water, but only in the slow weedy sections; Lestidae, or spread-winged damselflies, living mostly in weedy ponds, lakes, and marshes; and the most abundant family, Coenagrionidae, or narrow-winged damselflies, also residing primarily in weedy lakes and ponds, though a few species are found in streams.

Notice the common word in those descriptions? Weeds. Look in the weeds, and you will find damselfly nymphs.

Most mature damselfly nymphs are considerably smaller than the majority of dragonfly juveniles. They also appear to be on a perpetual diet, with svelte, slender bodies that would be the envy of any salad-eating magazine model. Both nymphs and adults have eyes that are large for an insect, but can't compare in size with those of a dragonfly. Damselfly eyes are widely separated on the head. There are three oarlike appendages at the rear of the abdomen that serve both as gills and as a means of propulsion through the water. Colors vary from brown to tan to shades of green, usually matching the vegetation where they live.

Damselfly nymphs aren't jet propelled. Theirs is a slow swimming motion with side-to-side undulations of body and tails. Crawling around plants is the primary mode of locomotion for all of them. Some types swim only rarely, but many swim from plant to plant often enough to become objects of attention for cruising trout.

These slender nymphs need to be imitated by flies that appear similarly anorexic. Jeff Morgan, fly-fishing author and accomplished fly tier, considers three attributes to be important when imitating damselfly nymphs: sparseness, motion, and eyes. Sparseness because the naturals are slim, and many commercial patterns are too chubby. Their enticing swimming action is also a key for fish, so Jeff prefers short bodies and extended marabou tails with lots of motion. And he believes in the theory of eyes as attractors, so uses them on all his damselfly nymph patterns. A fairly fast retrieve, punctuated by short rest periods, simulates the movement of a nymph trying to escape a predator. Since damselflies are primarily associated with plants—and plants usually grow in water depths less than twenty feet—shallow water is the prime area.

The best time to fish a damselfly nymph imitation is in spring and early summer, when there are lots of mature nymphs that are preparing to hatch in the water. The life cycle of most damselflies is one year, though for some there are two broods per year. Most of them hatch in late spring or early summer, so in late summer and early fall there will be few of them left in the water.

When damselfly nymphs get ready to hatch, they move to shallow water where the vegetation grows up to and above the surface. Those are usually the best times to fish the imitations. Nymphs crawl up the stems—usually during the day, in contrast to the typical nighttime dragonfly emergence—then get a firm grip for support in pulling themselves free of the exoskeleton. Emergence is faster for damselflies than it is for dragonflies. But newly hatched adults often fall in the water, so an adult pattern may also work in this situation.

Adult damselflies retain the delicate design of the nymphs. The bodies are slender, much more so than even the most ectomorphic dragonfly, and the relatively narrow wings are usually held above and to the sides of the body, in an almost vertical plane. The forewings and hind wings are more similar in size than in dragonflies. And in most types, there is a marked constriction at the bases of the wings, giving them a yokelike appearance. That characteristic structure gives the suborder Zygoptera it name; it comes from *zygo*, which means yoke. Damselflies fly with agility, but not a lot of speed. They are more like helicopters than jets.

Adult eyes are larger than those of the nymphs, but they are still widely set. A close-up view of a damselfly's face always puts a smile on mine. They look so comical that I can't help but laugh.

When adult damselflies return to the water to lay eggs after mating, it can be a great time to fish adult patterns. Gary Borger relates a story in his book *Naturals* about a fishing expedition he and a friend took to a lake in New Mexico. They encountered lots of egg-laying damselflies that were being blown into the water whenever a gust of wind came up. Trout were gulping them off the surface, and before the day was over both men had caught and

Blue damselflies congregate in great numbers around some lakes.

Damsefly nymphs are slender with three paddlelike tails, and sometimes appear as twins when reflected in the surface film. Family Lestidae. Body length = 19mm.

Damselfly adults have big eyes that are set far apart, similar to the nymphs.

The fierce visage of a predaceous diving beetle larva (family Dytiscidae) scarcely resembles the adult at all. Body length = 48mm.

released numerous large fish. Some anglers are dismissive of adult damselfly patterns, but I always carry a few in my box for times like that.

AQUATIC BEETLES

Beetle or B-grade horror movie? I wouldn't blame you for asking that question upon seeing the picture at the bottom of the preceding page. In fact, the first time I encountered one of these beasts, a brute of nearly two inches, the word "beetle" never entered my mind. While wading in a shallow, weedy lake, I saw something large swimming away from me and captured it with a sweep of my ever-handy bug net. It was not pleased at all to see me, and displayed a disposition as fearsome as its appearance. When I tried to remove it from the net with a pair of forceps, the darned thing seized them so forcibly that I heard the sound of metal clanking! It was so strong that it twisted free of several subsequent attempts to get a grip on it.

I witnessed further aggression while making these photographs. When left alone, the critter would hang quietly just under the surface. But a disturbance anywhere near it would bring on a quick attack of the offending object. These bugs are not to be messed with lightly—they don't call them water tigers for nothing. One thing for sure, no more wet-wading for me in the weedy lakes that these fiends call home.

It turns out that my friend with the attitude is the larva of an aptly named predaceous diving beetle. Both the adults—which actually look like the familiar beetles—and the larvae are voracious predators, but the ferocity of the youngsters is unmatched in the insect domain. Predaceous diving beetles will eat anything that moves—other insects, tadpoles, salamanders, or fish fry. They can even be a problem at times in fish hatcheries, where a sizeable population can take a considerable toll on trout fingerlings.

Predaceous diving beetles belong to the insect family Dytiscidae, just one of a bewildering array of beetle families and species. In fact, beetles as a group are astoundingly successful. The beetle order Coleoptera—meaning sheathed wings, referring to the fact that the front pair of wings is toughened into a sheath covering the rear pair—is represented by 113 families and more than 24,000 species in North America alone. Nearly half of all insect species in the world are beetles. They outnumber all vertebrate species combined by eighteen to one. In fact, beetles represent an astonishing one-fifth of all species on earth.

But I'm going to whittle them down drastically for this discussion. The vast majority of beetles are entirely terrestrial, so I'll sweep those aside for now. About 20 families containing some 1,000 species are at least partly aquatic. Most of those are of little interest to fly fishers, so away they go for consideration in some other book. And while

some aquatic beetles are found in virtually every type of fresh water, they are by far the most abundant in still waters. Finally, the majority of still-water beetles fall into just two families—Dytiscidae, or predaceous diving beetles; and Hydrophilidae, or water scavenger beetles. So I'll restrict the rest of this section to those kinds.

Beetles, including the aquatic types, undergo complete metamorphosis during development. That means they have egg, larva, pupa, and adult stages. It also means that, just as for the caddisflies and midges that we have already encountered, the appearance of juvenile beetles is very different from the adults. That is why most of us don't think "beetle" when we see something that looks like the photo of the predaceous diving beetle larva. You'll find both larval and adult dytiscid and hydrophilid beetles in the water, but not pupae; pupation in these families takes place on land after the larvae crawl out of the water.

Most of the beetles in these families begin life as eggs laid in the spring, which develop into larvae that grow through spring and summer. Toward the end of summer or beginning of fall, larvae leave the water and pupate in damp soil within a few feet of the waterline. After a few weeks, the adults emerge and return to the water completely transformed. Adults spend the winter in the water, then mate and lay eggs in the spring to start the cycle all over again. Dytiscid and hydrophilid beetle adults are very long-lived for aquatic insects. For some of the larger species, the adults can live for two to three years.

Dytiscid larvae can swim quite well using their legs to propel them, but most of the time they crawl on vegetation looking for quarry. Those sharp, sickle-shaped jaws are used to seize and puncture prey, after which a fluid flows through channels in them to kill and digest the unlucky individual. Then the larvae suck the digested fluids from the victim back through the same channels. It sounds like a gruesome bite; I'm happy to have avoided testing that out so far.

Nearly all predaceous diving beetle larvae extract oxygen from air rather than water. To accomplish this feat, they have two spiracles—small tubes—at the rear of their abdomen. The larvae usually rest with their tails arched upward, breaking the surface tension and making contact with the air above.

Adult predaceous diving beetles carry their air supply with them when they go underwater. They capture air under their tough front wings, in a space between the wings and the abdomen. Like the larvae, the adults breathe through two spiracles, but theirs are located high on the midabdomen to contact the transported air bubble. This allows them to spend the majority of their time swimming and hunting below the surface, usually in association with living or dead vegetation.

Occasionally an adult predaceous diving beetle climbs out of the water for a look around. They are also capable of flying and will sometimes migrate to other bodies of water. Body length = 6mm.

Dytiscid adults have the typical beetle coffee bean shape. They are excellent swimmers, kicking their hair-covered rear legs in unison like oars. Catching most of the smaller insects they feed upon is no problem. Whereas the larvae are piercer-suckers, adult predaceous diving beetles are munchers: they hold their prey with their feet while tearing it apart with a chewing motion.

When adult dytiscids come up to refresh their air bubble, they always break the surface—rear end first. Most of the time the beetle will quickly swim back down toward the bottom. But occasionally, they will crawl out on the surface vegetation—for a quick look around, I suppose.

Water scavenger beetles (family Hydrophilidae) are about as numerous as the dytiscids, but don't get as big. They are also slower, both as larvae and as adults. These beetles are scavengers as well as predators, often seen feasting on dead fish or other animals. The larvae have smaller versions of those sickle jaws, and feed in the same way as larval dytiscids. But they rarely swim, preferring to hang onto vegetation and wait for prey to come to them.

Respiration in the water scavenger beetles is similar to that of the predaceous diving beetles. Larvae breathe by pushing their spiracle-containing rear ends through the surface film. Adults carry an air bubble under their wings. But in addition, the adults hold some air underneath them, held in place by fine hairs. The ventral bubble is shiny and reflects nearby objects like a mirror. Another difference from predaceous diving beetles is in the manner in which the adults surface to renew their air supply. Adult water scavenger beetles come up headfirst, usually with just one of their antennae breaking the surface. Air flows down the antenna to the space under the wing cover.

WATER BOATMEN AND BACKSWIMMERS

We finally come to some bugs with an undisputed right to use that appellation—the backswimmers and water boatmen. No apologies necessary to entomologists who reserve the term *bug* strictly for the order Hemiptera, suborder Heteroptera—or true bugs—because these insects are bona fide members of that group.

Hemipterans are mostly terrestrial, including those bearing common names like bed bugs, stink bugs, assassin bugs, cicadas, and aphids. But a number of them are aquatic. True bugs are characterized by piercing-sucking mouthparts that originate at the front middle of the head, as well as forewings that are toughened or hardened on their front half while retaining a soft, membranous rear half. The aquatic members generally fall into two groups: surface or underwater dwellers. Water striders are an example of surface dwellers. Those that spend most of their time underwater include giant water bugs, creeping water bugs, water scorpions, water boatmen, and backswimmers. The latter two kinds are the only ones of real importance to fly fishers.

Water scavenger beetles carry a layer of air under their bodies, causing them to be shiny and reflective. Body length = 10mm.

Water scavenger beetle larvae (family Hydrophilidae) are less mobile than dytiscid larvae, preferring to wait among aquatic vegetation for prey to approach closely enough to grab with their sharp mandibles. Body length = 9mm.

True bugs are most likely to be confused with beetles, which also have hardened forewings and frequently a similar body shape. But in beetles the entire forewing is thick and tough, whereas only the front half of a hemipteran forewing matches that description. Most beetles lack piercing-sucking mouthparts, and in the ones that do (like predaceous diving beetle larvae), the mouthparts are differently shaped and don't originate in the middle of the head.

True bugs undergo incomplete metamorphosis, but of a different sort than we have seen in the insects discussed so far. The juveniles look almost exactly like the adults, except for the absence of wings. The change to adult form is gradual, throughout the five instars; there is no step involving an abrupt metamorphosis of a nymph into a radically different adult. Furthermore, the adults and nymphs live in the same habitats and feed in the same way. In contrast to most other aquatic insects, true bugs spend most of their lives as adults rather than as juveniles.

The most commonly encountered underwater true bug is the water boatman (family Corixidae). Some kinds live in the quieter margins of rivers, but the vast majority reside in the shallows of lakes and ponds. Like many of the other still-water macroinvertebrates, water boatmen are lovers of aquatic vegetation.

Water boatmen have a one-year life cycle. Eggs are laid in the spring, and after hatching the nymphs grow through late spring and summer. They become winged adults in late summer or early fall. Adults generally stay in the same habitat and continue with the same lifestyle as the nymphs. But they are capable fliers, and if the need arises—when a pond dries up, gets too warm, or is otherwise uncomfortable—the adults fly to other bodies of water. Water boatmen overwinter as adults, then in the spring they mate, lay eggs, and die.

Both nymphal and adult water boatmen have a cone-like beak that is more blunt than the piercing mouthparts of most other hemipterans, with a small hole in the end. The predominant feeding method is to stir up the bottom sediments with their front legs and then consume any organic matter dislodged, which may include algae, diatoms, small worms, or midge and mosquito larvae. They can also pierce plant stems and suck out the fluids.

In a manner reminiscent of aquatic beetles, water boatmen respire atmospheric oxygen through spiracles, or tubes, leading from outside to inside their bodies. Also like the beetles, their technique involves surfacing to capture an air bubble, which is held under the wings and the ventral part of the body by fine hairs. The air causes them to be very shiny. Because the layer of air is thin, it readily exchanges oxygen with the water, so under optimal conditions, a water boatman can avoid surfacing for long periods of time.

Water boatmen have an elongated, oval shape when seen from above. Three pairs of legs are each specialized

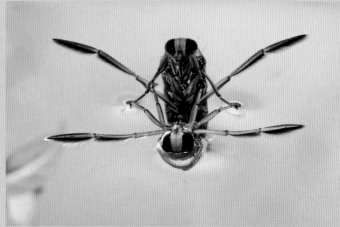

The best place to find water boatmen (Corixidae) is within dense aquatic vegetation. Body length = 7mm.

When viewed from below at an angle, a backswimmer hanging below the surface appears to be duplicated by its reflection. Body length = 13mm.

The side of a backswimmer that you seldom see from above, its back, is light colored.

for a different function. The front legs have fine hairs and are somewhat scoop-shaped for manipulating their food. The middle legs are used to hold onto vegetation. The rear legs are very long and move with simultaneous oarlike strokes to propel the bug forward in several-inch spurts. Some species have intricate patterns and colored eyes that are more attractive up close than they first appear from a distance.

Backswimmers (family Notonectidae) are the inverted cousins of the water boatmen. They have a perplexing habit of swimming upside down. Since they spend most of their time hanging out just below the surface, I guess they do it so they can get a better look at what's below.

If you are above the water you won't get a chance to see the dorsal surface of a backswimmer, because they usually maintain their inverted position at all times. If you pick one up and turn it over—be careful, they can inflict a painful bite—you'll see a much lighter color than on its ventral side. This arrangement is reversed from the usual aquatic insect color pattern, but then this bug is really into doing things backward. But it makes sense: backswimmers spend most of their time hanging at the surface, and a predator looking up from below will see a light bug against a light sky.

While backswimmers may look a lot like water boatmen, they have some significant differences. Most important, they are avid predators, like most true bugs—no bottom mucking for them. They'll eat anything they can catch: other insects, snails, tadpoles, and probably most often, water boatmen. Kinship seems to offer no protection in this case. In contrast with the modified mouthparts of water boatmen, backswimmers have the true piercing-sucking beaks common to most true bugs. They stab their prey—which is held with front legs ending in claws—inject their killing and digesting fluid, and then suck out the victim's juices.

The life cycle of backswimmers is very similar to the water boatmen. It has a one-year period, with egg laying in the spring, nymphal growth over the summer, and adults appearing in the fall and lasting into the next spring.

Like the water boatmen, backswimmers carry their own air supply when they dive. Some of it is stored in hair-fringed troughs on the ventral abdomen, and the rest is on the back and under the wings. They usually rest at the water surface with the tip of their abdomen breaking through and contacting the atmosphere. In a head-down position, they are constantly ready to sweep down with strokes of their long legs to seize any prey that might be spotted.

Both backswimmers and water boatmen are taken in large numbers by still-water trout. They are especially important food items in the fall, winter, and early spring, when they are mature and numerous during a period when other insects are small or in the egg stage. This is a good time to use a fly that imitates them.

FLIES

Still-water fly patterns could fill up a book by themselves, and of course they have. Shown here are some that stand out in my mind.

Bill Marshall's Callibaetis Emerger. Tied by my friend and fishing companion, and the illustrator of this book, this pattern mimics the most vulnerable stage of a *Callibaetis* hatch: when duns attempt to leave the nymphal exoskeleton just below the surface film. It came to my attention one day several years ago when Bill and I were fishing western Oregon's Gold Lake. Bill was catching trout. I wasn't. Putting pride aside, I rowed over to learn the secret of his success. This emerger was the ticket. After tying on one of the flies Bill gave me, my luck improved considerably.

Griffith's Gnat. This simple fly was developed by George Griffith, one of the founders of Trout Unlimited. It consists of just a peacock herl body wrapped by grizzly hackle. Often tied in tiny sizes—down to a hook size 26—that mere mortals cannot see on the water, it also can be fished successfully at up to a size 18. The smaller sizes represent individual adult or emerging midges, while the larger versions probably most often suggest clusters of mating adults.

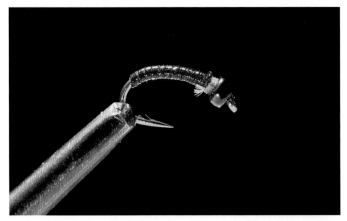

Red midge pupa. A tiny pupa pattern is often the most effective way to fish a chironomid hatch. This one, a size 18, was tied by Mike Caldwell of Boise, Idaho, to mimic the blood-red midges found in many lakes.

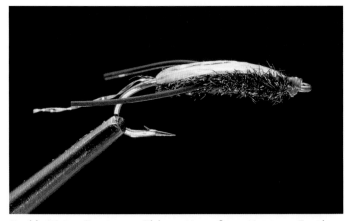

Burk's Water Boatman. This pattern from Umpqua Feather Merchants is best fished by coating the fly in powdered dry-fly floatant so it will be coated with bubbles, and then retrieved in short but quick strips.

Damselfly nymph. Effective damselfly nymph patterns should have prominent eyes and mimic the swimming motion of the natural.

Alexandra. The classic Alexandra was developed in Scotland in the 1860s. Originally called the Lady of the Lake, it was renamed in honor of Princess Alexandra of Wales, whose beauty was said to be legendary. The same can now be said of her fly. And it's not only a beautiful lake pattern, but also an effective one. Its impressionistic profile and flashing colors might suggest the movements of beetles, backswimmers, dragonfly nymphs, or even minnows.

Carey Special. This is a suggestive pattern originated by Tom Carey in the 1930s to imitate the dragonflies of British Columbia lakes. It should be fished slowly near the bottom, with twitches and pauses to mimic the motions of dragonfly nymphs.

12
Dog Day Doldrums

An investigation into the causes of the late summer trout-feeding slump

The local trout were in a feeding funk, and I was wondering why.

It happens every year about this time—late summer in my neck of the woods, western Oregon. The exact timing may vary somewhat from place to place, but most sections of the country experience a similar downturn in fish activity sometime during the summer. Was it the temperature? It sure felt hot to me, and without question some rivers and streams reach temperatures that cold-water fish find unpleasant. But many rivers stay well within the reported comfort zone of our finny friends. According to various sources, rainbow trout are most active in the somewhat ill-defined range of 55–65 degrees F. Studies on farm-raised rainbows show the fish grow fastest when the water is held at 59–62 degrees.

Oregon's McKenzie River is an example of a cold stream, and the section where I most often fish had been running in the range of 54–62 degrees over the prior month. No excuse there, it would seem, for fish to go on strike.

Next I considered the food supply and how trout may react to it. There was no doubt that visible hatches had tapered off dramatically from the spring and early summer. In comparison, it looked fairly dead out there now.

Oh, there was the occasional streamside caddis, and even a golden stonefly or two if one looked carefully. A good way to find these tardy goldens was to look for rocks at water's edge bearing a few nymphal shucks from recent hatches. They seem to favor certain rocks, ignoring similar nearby ones, and if you visited those places at dusk you just might have seen an adult fresh out of its shuck. You

The dog days of summer.

A golden stonefly is silhouetted in the fading light of dusk.

There may still be the occasional *Epeorus* mayfly spinner around in late summer. Body length = 11.5mm.

may also have seen the odd *Epeorus* mayfly spinner, that infrequent little yellow stonefly (slightly larger and less yellow than the numerous little yellow sallies of early summer) and whatever terrestrials may have fallen into the water.

But the only insects that I had seen in any abundance lately were some very small blue-winged olives. Between 9:30–10:30 A.M., the males had been gathering in the typical mayfly spinner cloud near the water, doing their up-down mating dance. They are so tiny that I usually can't see them unless they are backlit by the sun.

Interestingly, the females seem to congregate in their own resting area not far away, and watch the show a while before braving the boys. The disparity in form between males and females is a good example of sexual dimorphism; if I hadn't seen them together, I probably wouldn't have suspected at first that they belong to the same species.

But as far as I could tell the tiny BWO spinners were not contributing much biomass to feeding the fish. They

weren't all that numerous, and I had yet to see a fish rise to them. Strangely, I hadn't observed any of the duns, despite checking the water at various times of day. I suspected that they might be coming off right after dark. If the molt to spinners occurs within a few hours (as is the case for some species), the duns would never see the light of day!

To investigate that latter possibility, I set out one summer evening to see what bug activity might be taking place at night. As usual, nothing much was happening along the shores and water surface of the McKenzie while some rays of daylight remained. But about a half hour after dusk, my flashlight beam began to catch the stirrings of little creatures along the river's edge. To get a better view, I placed a fluorescent lantern right by the water. Soon, clouds of insects, mostly minuscule midges, were swarming around the light. But among them were, yes, a few newly hatched tiny *Baetis* duns, still showing the pale hues they wear when fresh from the confines of their nymphal encasements; confirming my hatch-schedule suspicions.

A few little yellow stoneflies may be found at the water's edge. *Isoperla*; body length = 9mm.

Tiny male blue-winged olive (*Baetis*) spinner. A friend once asked if I could put a small object in my bug photos to show scale. I decided it wasn't generally practical, but in a nod to Scott and those who think like him, in this photo I used a small match to help visualize how tiny these mayflies really are. Body length = 4mm.

Female blue-winged olive (*Baetis*) spinner. Body length = 4mm.

A gathering of female crane flies (family Tipulidae).
Body length = 8mm.

A female *Baetis* dun fresh from an evening emergence. Body length = 4mm.

The ventral side of a stonefly nymph amid rocks and bubbles.

Also congregated on a partly submerged rock in an area of shallow but fast current were a handful of gangly yellowish bugs. All lined up at the waterline, with their rear ends touching the water, these female crane flies were busy laying eggs and letting the current disperse them downstream.

I've since observed this phenomenon many times, and these bugs always seek objects projecting from brisk currents to gather for an egg-laying session. Such objects include the legs of a fly fisher wading the river or stream at dusk!

So maybe the paucity of daytime hatches explains why dry-fly fishing was slow. Perhaps most trout were just not looking up, at least during daylight hours, not expecting much food to be in that direction. The surface is a dangerous place for a fish, so better not to go there without good reason. But surely they have to eat, and there is always prey down under, right? Then why is nymphing also slow this time of year?

I decided to explore underwater to determine what food items might be currently available there. Let's see what I found.

From between the cracks of some rocks in a McKenzie River riffle, I saw a rather large nymph scoot by amid the bubbles above.

I followed it for a better look.

It was a large shortwing stonefly (*Claassenia sabulosa*) nymph, in the same family (Perlidae) as golden stoneflies and similar in size. The M-shaped (or W-shaped, depending on viewing angle) mark between the eyes of the nymph, in combination with gills between the tails, is the key to its identification. Shortwing stones are much less common in most places—including the McKenzie River—than the golden stoneflies, though if you look back at the top photo on page 134 you will see that the shuck on the rock was also derived from a shortwing. (The adult in the background, however, was a golden stonefly *Calineuria californica*.) I find shortwing stoneflies to be so interesting that I've devoted a whole section of the book to them, so I'll have much more to say about these intriguing bugs in chapter 13.

Getting back to my bug hunt among the cobblestones of the McKenzie's bottom, I came across a brightly colored caddis larva as it roamed the rocks in search of insect prey.

The free-living green rock worm (*Rhyacophila*) is common in riffle areas of cold streams, and I have found them often at other times of the year. But only a single one showed up during this hunting expedition. I did see a couple of very small, cream-colored net-spinning caddis larvae, but there weren't a lot of those, either.

Not many of the river's insects like being exposed to sunlight and predators, so I had to turn over a lot of rocks to find them (a maneuver that trout would find a tad difficult). I thought I might discover some crawler-type mayfly nymphs, especially *Ephemerella* (PMDs and others) that are usually common. But if they were around, they were making themselves scarce. The only examples of crawlers I found were two or three *Attenella* mayfly nymphs, the tattoo lovers of the insect world. At least that's what their multicolored designs look like to me.

In another case of common name confusion, *Attenella* adults are sometimes called blue-winged olives, just like the more common *Baetis* species and others. The nymphs have a habit of wielding their tails above their heads like scorpions, even stabbing them forward toward an antagonist. I doubt that very many predators are intimidated by that bit of bravado.

Now I flushed another strange-looking bug from its hiding place. What was it?

It was the first example I had found of the relatively uncommon stream-dwelling dragonfly family Gomphidae. Most dragonfly nymphs are residents of still or slow waters, so I was quite surprised to come across this one. And it was not at all happy to see me, continually trying to burrow down into the gravel or use its unique propulsion system to jet away, making photography a challenge. The nymphs crawl quickly, and in an emergency (like when a fish or photographer approaches) can squirt water out their rear ends to dart several inches at a time. Their bodies are covered with small hairs that collect stream flotsam as camouflage. Then hiding on the bottom, half covered with silt, they lie ready to spring out and seize passing prey—including even small fish—with long mandibles that fold up under their "chin."

Finding the bug picking to be slim in the rocks, I moved over to explore a clump of plants growing in moderate current. Here there was more to be found, including

Shortwing stonefly (*Claassenia sabulosa*) nymph.
Body length = 24mm.

Rhyacophila (green rock worm) caddisfly larva.
Body length = 16mm.

Attenela (yet another blue-winged olive) mayfly nymph.
Body length = 7mm.

Grappletail dragonfly (*Octogomphus specularis*) nymphs
prefer flowing water and gravel bottoms. Body length =
14mm (probably in the second year of the three-year
nymphal stage).

Abstract artwork appears on a large salmonfly
(*Pteronarcys californica*) nymph's dorsal thorax.
Body length = 36mm.

several small salmonfly nymphs that would be part of next year's hatch, and one large individual that looked like it just missed the emergence party of the previous spring.

In addition to a few small golden stonefly nymphs prowling the weeds for likely victims, the most abundant inhabitants were small humpless case maker caddisfly larvae (family Brachycentridae). They dragged around cases that look for all the world like skinny log cabins. These little guys moved constantly around the plants, reminding me of tiny grazing cows, and feeding nonstop. Whenever their paths crossed, they would pause for a half minute or so to battle over the immediate territory, and then go back to grazing.

Caddisflies of this type are often called grannoms, and this particularly common one (*Brachycentrus occidentalis*) is referred to as the Mother's Day caddis in some places. Besides crawling, grannom larvae have a fascinating habit

of attaching a silk thread to a rock and then repelling downstream until they can grab onto the next rock (chapter 3). These behaviors often cause them to slip into the current, drifting downstream right into the mouth of a lucky fish.

Observing all this led me to the conclusion that if I were a trout, I would try to position myself behind a rock just downstream of one of those weed clumps. And as an angler, I made a mental note to spend more time fishing exactly such spots.

Moving out of the weeds and back into the riffle rocks, by far the most common insects I found were some very small clinger mayfly nymphs of the family Heptageniidae.

The genus *Nixe* is one of several genera, including *Heptagenia, Leucrocuta,* and *Cinygma,* that aquatic biologist Rick Hafele groups together under the name "pale evening dun (PED) complex" (chapter 6). Particular

Battling grannom caddisfly (*B. occidentalis*)
larvae. Case length = 8mm.

A pale evening dun (*Nixe*) nymph.
Body length = 7mm.

species of *Nixe* go by common names like western ginger quill and little slate-winged duns, in case those may be more familiar terms to some. As Rick says, most of us won't know or need to know any more than the PED label.

These bugs lie flat as pancakes on the stones, letting the water slide over them so they can thrive in the swiftest of currents. They cling tightly and prefer the undersides of rocks, so not only are they hard for us to find and see, but the trout don't often encounter them either. Thus they are important to fish and fishermen only shortly before and during hatches.

We're near the end of my bug survey, but what about *Baetis* nymphs? I started off by saying that the only insects I had seen above water in any numbers lately had been tiny BWO spinners. So I thought I might find a lot of *Baetis* nymphs. I looked all around—in the riffles, in the weeds, under rocks, in fast and slow water. Only in the slower currents near the banks did I find a few small individuals, and they were so tiny that they strained the resolution of my macrophotography setup to the limit. Being less than 1mm wide, some of them were able to crawl through the holes of my seining net! So it's possible there were significantly more *Baetis* nymphs that I missed, but I think most of them had probably already hatched.

In fact, it's likely that most species had already hatched and died, and that is why we don't see as many bugs in or over the water at this time of year. Eggs and tiny early nymphs of the next generation are predominant during this period, and the total bug biomass is lower than in the previous few months.

If you're still with me after my diversion into the particulars of the fish-food menu, let's return now to my main point. Which is again, why are the trout off their feed? And especially in waters like the McKenzie, where the temperatures are close to the optimum range at this time of year?

After spending half a day gathering my evidence, I concluded that the trout food supply in late summer is significantly reduced when compared with spring and early summer; and not only above water, which everyone can see, but also below in the mysterious depths. True, my methodology lacked scientific rigor—I did not lay out grids and use statistically valid sampling techniques—but I think that the information obtained is probably qualitatively, if not quantitatively, in the right ballpark. So if the food supply is lower, shouldn't the (hungrier) fish be even more receptive to whatever morsel might drift by? Even more eager to take a chance on our imitative flies? Initially

A small blue-winged olive (*Baetis*) nymph that has broken off its middle tail. Body length = 3mm.

The behaviors of enigmatic trout can be difficult to figure out.

it would seem so, but then I thought further about energy balance and the choices a trout must make.

First, I noted that fish see lots of buggy flotsam streaming by, and their powers of discrimination are not so perfect. Witness the large amounts of debris found in stomach samples, not to mention how often they grab a clump of fur and feathers with a pointy wire sticking out of it. Let's be honest, they sample a lot of junk in the water. Second, moving into the current and back uses precious energy that must be compensated by the target of the move: a potential food item. Stringing those thoughts together: during periods when there is a lot of food in the water—along with the usual flotsam—moving to intercept an object that is the appropriate size and shape will pay off frequently enough to be energetically worthwhile; but at times when the ratio of real food to junk food is low, it will most often cost

more to move than to stay put. Late summer is probably one of those latter periods. The fish know to hunker down and wait for better times. It is only we anglers who don't know when to give up.

So there you have my tentative conclusion from an investigation sparked by musings on the usual late-summer fishing slump. I know that I'm not the first to go down this path, but it was fun doing my own analysis. Of course I could be wrong. Besides water temperature and food supply, there may be other important variables affecting feeding behavior, like light levels. (After all, it's usually much cloudier in spring, early summer, and fall than it is at summer's end.) Trout behavior is a complicated thing, and it is difficult to come up with definitive explanations for complex phenomena. But I, like you, can keep exploring, investigating, and researching. The fun is never over!

13
Of Wings and Water

The strange case of shortwing stoneflies and the origins of flight

To see the real West, we headed east. My wife Susie and I left western Oregon's lush McKenzie Valley on a fine September morning, traveling through the state's arid eastern portion and continuing our journey toward Idaho and the rising sun. After crossing the Cascades, we found ourselves traversing hundreds of miles of sparsely populated but dramatic high desert country that could have been taken straight from an Old West movie. Our ultimate goal was eastern Idaho, where we would fish the famous South Fork of the Snake River and its not-so-famous shortwing stonefly hatch. Ever since I had found some shortwing nymphs in the McKenzie River (see chapter 12), where their numbers are modest, I had been enthralled with this strange but comparatively unknown relative of the golden

stoneflies. Now I was headed to a place where the hatch was both heavy and a primary target of the local trout.

We met up with our friends Mike and Pat who flew in to fish the South Fork and nearby Wyoming waters with us. Both are enthusiastic fly fishers but, living in dry southern California as they do (and we used to), they don't get nearly as much practice as those of us residing in Oregon. We spent two days fishing with South Fork Outfitters guides Ed Emory and Sue Talbot. Both days we floated the upper part of the canyon section in Swan Valley.

Susie and I teamed up with Ed the first day, and we fished his recommended setup of an outlandishly big, almost grotesque, Chernobyl Ant on the surface, coupled with a size 20, sparsely tied bead-head nymph on a 24-inch

Bitterroot River. The larger rivers of western Montana, Idaho, and Wyoming provide some of the best habitat for shortwing stoneflies.

The colorful Westslope cutthroats of the South Fork eagerly take shortwing stonefly imitations.

Fishing can be great when shortwing stoneflies are around, but regardless of the catch rate, a good time is assured in an environment like the South Fork of the Snake River.

MARGIT SUSAN THOMASON

dropper. Though I didn't keep track, Ed estimated that I caught about thirty trout in the 14- to 17-inch range, more than half of them cutthroats and the rest rainbows except for a few smaller browns. And I missed or lost at least as many, with lots of fish knocking the big Chernobyl Ant aside in their rush to hit it. (Ed thinks that many fish purposely thump these big flies, which they mistake for spry shortwing stoneflies, in an attempt to drown them so they'll be easier to catch.) Susie hooked a few fish, too, though she preferred to spend most of her time watching the abundant wildlife, or playing with Ed's dog. In the other boat—guided by Sue—Mike and Pat were catching their share of trout too; especially considering that they don't get to fish very often. Our second day on the river, we would split up into a girls' boat and a guys' boat, and Mike would have the hot hand that day.

These Snake River cutthroats are a beautiful golden pink fish, much more colorful than the coastal cutts we have around the Cascades. And they take those huge—up to size 6, 4X long—Chernobyl Ants with gusto.

No ant is anywhere near that big of course, so what are the fish really mistaking the imitation for? In some places it might be taken for a grasshopper, but it is by far most successfully employed in those areas with large populations of shortwing stoneflies.

I was keen to observe and photograph some shortwing adults—up to that point I had only seen the nymphs—and if you looked in the right places along the banks of the South Fork, they were thick. The right places were shores lined with loose rocks three to six inches in diameter. (Those were also the spots where Chernobyl Ants were most effective on the fish.) Turning over the rocks would reveal the bugs, mostly males, scampering everywhere. It's easy to differentiate shortwing stonefly males from females, because there are remarkable differences in their appearance and behavior. The males have much smaller wings that are very short and nonfunctional; they are flightless. And Ed confirmed what I had heard about the females: while they can fly, they rarely do.

THE SHORT STORY OF THE SHORTWING

Other than the remarkable dimorphism of wing structure, in many respects the shortwing stonefly (*Claassenia sabulosa*), which is occasionally referred to as the giant golden stone, is typical of its clan. It undergoes incomplete metamorphosis (chapter 3), follows the general stonefly body plan, and prefers the well-oxygenated aquatic habitats imposed by the characteristically inefficient stonefly respiratory system (chapter 7). Shortwings belong to the family Perlidae that includes some of the most well known of the

Female shortwing stoneflies have fully developed wings, and look much like a golden stonefly without its colors.

Male shortwing stoneflies have stunted wings and are unable to fly.

Side-by-side comparison of male and female shortwing stoneflies reveals the discrepancy in overall size and wing development. Male body length = 21mm (upper); female body length = 31mm (lower). The females' wings extend well past the rear of the abdomen, while the wings of males terminate far short of their posteriors.

Shortwing stonefly nymphs can be identified by the combination of gill tufts around the legs and between the tails, and an M-shaped mark on top of the head. Body length = 24mm.

stoneflies, the golden stones (chapter 9). And the adult females are about the same size as, or even a tad larger than, the goldens. In fact, shortwings look so much like golden stoneflies that it would be easy for the first-time observer to confuse them—at least the females. Female shortwings are darker on their dorsal sides, and lack the yellow-orange undersides of the goldens.

C. sabulosa is a western species, but it is widely distributed within that region. The species has been recorded from British Columbia and Alberta down through the Rocky Mountains and Cascades to Arizona and New Mexico, and east to northern Manitoba and northern Ontario. The largest concentrations are probably in sections of Montana, Wyoming, and Idaho. Most of the larger, cooler rivers in the Northwest support at least small populations.

Shortwings prefer a habitat similar to their sister golden stoneflies, and they may often be found in the same areas. *Claassenia* nymphs strongly resemble the goldens, but can be differentiated from *Hesperoperla* and *Calineuria* nymphs with which they are often collected, on the basis of gill structure and head markings. *Calineuria* nymphs are a little smaller, about 25–30mm long at maturity, have feathery gills at the base of each leg, and no gills on the abdomen or between the tails. *Hesperoperla* nymphs are a little larger, about 28–35mm long, and have two gill tufts between their tails in addition to the ones near the legs. Moreover, *Hesperoperla* nymphs have a light-colored, hourglass-shaped mark on the top front of their heads. This mark is helpful in distinguishing *Hesperoperla* from *Claassenia*. *Claassenia* nymphs have gills similar to those of *Hesperoperla*, including between the tails; but the mark on their heads is in the shape of the letter M, rather than like an hourglass.

The predatory nymphs are extremely active in the riffle areas of the rivers they inhabit, constantly searching for prey. Usual victims include helpless midge larvae, as well as more mobile mayfly and caddisfly larvae. Shortwing stonefly and perlid nymphs in general take a big toll on the populations of other insects, and have been doing so for millions of years. Some interesting research has shown that many of the targeted victims have devised escape responses specifically aimed at perlid predators. If the scent of a perlid nymph is detected in the water, targeted species will usually flee or hide. The scent of other non-perlid stonefly nymphs does not elicit the same response.

Emergence of shortwing stonefly adults begins as early as June in some locales, and can extend into October. In a given river the hatch usually goes on for several months, a

A pale teneral adult (male) shortwing stonefly that has just emerged from the nymph.

distinct boon to anglers who are accustomed to timing the short-duration hatches of many other species. This also means that trout are conditioned to look for shortwing adults over a large part of the season. The hatch begins after dark when nymphs crawl from the water, and the males always emerge first. Shortwing stonefly nymphs rarely venture far from the water's edge, and prefer the exposed portions of partially submerged rocks as their hatching platforms. They don't march off in search of vertical structures like trees or bushes, as golden stoneflies and salmonflies often do. Compared with other stoneflies, shortwing emergence is a very quick affair, particularly for the males. Once the nymph has planted its feet on terra firma, the actual splitting and exiting from the exoskeleton by the teneral (freshly hatched and still soft) adults takes only a few minutes. The newly emerged male is still soft and pale, but he doesn't waste much time just waiting around.

Male shortwings are not only quick emergers, but unlike most other stoneflies they are extremely energetic and immediately active. They begin scurrying like cockroaches over the rocks at the edge of the water, looking for any females that may be crawling ashore. When they find one, the males are so eager to mate that they can't even

wait for the female to exit her nymphal shuck. There are reports in the scientific literature that males of several species of stoneflies with short wings are, for some reason, abnormally libidinous. In the photo on the next page, a female shortwing stonefly is in the process of emerging from the nymphal exuvium (skin). Note the darker male on her back even before she gets herself free!

The male shortwing usually guards the female, to fend off other males, while she gets out of her old clothes. As soon as her abdomen is exposed, he will begin mating. Often, the male will hang around to guard the female to make sure no other males mate with her. But like randy males everywhere, he will sometimes go off looking for other emerging females. Studies have shown that an unguarded female may mate as many as nine times with several different suitors before the evening is over.

You may recall from earlier chapters on stoneflies that males of many species tap a little drum rhythm to call for females, and females respond with some rhythms of their own. That's how they find each other after they've moved into the bushes, trees, and surrounding countryside. Like other stoneflies, male shortwings have a drumming appendage, called a hammer, on their abdomen. But they don't use it. These guys are too impatient to tap and wait

A very pale, yellowish female shortwing stonefly adult begins to emerge with the nymph half in and half out of the water. An eager male has climbed onto her back to claim her even before she is free.

A few minutes later the female, having finally shaken off the male, has then found a spot to rest, harden her wings and exoskeleton, and begun to darken in color.

By the next day the female shortwing has taken on the typically dark shades of a mature adult.

for a gal to respond; their waterline-searching habits have rendered drumming superfluous.

If the emergent female shortwing manages to get free of the males, she'll usually head for a crack in the rocks to rest while her exoskeleton hardens. The newly hatched teneral adults are not only still soft, they're also much lighter in color than mature stoneflies. It takes a while before they darken to the shade we see in adult stoneflies during the daytime. (Note that the male on the emerging female's back in the accompanying pictures had already darkened considerably by the time she arrived.)

Adult shortwings don't venture far from the water, usually not more than about three feet away. They are almost always in areas with lots of jumbled rocks in their preferred size range. Where the shoreline of a river varies from a few rocks, to a lot of big rocks, to gravel, and then to three- to six-inch rocks, the adults will be found primarily in the last mentioned locale. (And the nymphs will be most abundant in water adjacent to those areas.) These bugs won't often be out running around in the open for you to see them during the day. You'll have to search among shoreline cobble, turning over stones. A good way to find out if you are in the right area is by looking for exuviae along the banks. If you see lots of discarded shucks just a few inches from the waterline, with that telltale M mark on the head, you've found shortwing territory.

The two hours just before dark are party time for shortwing stonefly adults. That's when males come out from their hidey-holes to watch for female beach parties, and it's when mated females engage in their egg-laying mission. Both sexes often end up on the water. Males scamper with amazing speed across the surface, from one exposed rock to another onto which an enticing young female nymph may emerge from the depths. Gravid adult females also scurry between those rocks, dragging their abdomens and dropping eggs as they go. Females can fly, but they don't take to the air very often. They were born to run.

So what is it with these roachlike running stoneflies? Females that can fly, but don't? Males that have somehow lost half their wing surface and are permanently grounded? It gets you thinking about how and why bugs fly, under what circumstances insect flight first arose, and what role these strange stoneflies with their midget wings may play in the big picture. At least, that's what it gets me thinking about. So let's head off again onto a buggy tangent that will have no bearing on your fishing, but will hopefully lend some insight into one of nature's interesting little mysteries.

SMALL WINGS AND THE ORIGINS OF FLIGHT

True powered flight (as opposed to gliding) is known in just three groups of living animals: bats, birds, and insects. Of the three, insects preceded the other two groups into the air by millions of years. They also solved the problems of flight in a very different way. Birds and bats gave up limbs that were pressed into service as flying gear. Only insects mastered aerial locomotion without losing the use of their legs.

Though the process by which animals developed the capacity for flight is not completely understood for any of the groups, the vertebrates can be seen to have had a "leg up" on many of the problems that would have presented themselves. That's because they cannibalized existing structures (legs) that came pre-equipped with versions of some of the required parts. A moving, flapping wing must be articulated; that is, possessing joints that allow movement in the needed directions and prevent it in others. It must have been a relatively uncomplicated process (compared with the situation in insects) to modify vertebrate joints in a way that would allow them to operate as wings. Gliding flight, with its lower energetic and muscular demands, may have been the first step toward vertebrate-powered flight. Selection for animals that could fly farther, faster, and higher would presumably have led to improvements over time in wing articulation, aerodynamics, strength, weight ratios, etc.

While it may have been a big advantage for flying insects to retain the use of all their legs, it presents us with a bigger conceptual problem. Wings don't just pop into existence in a single de novo mutation, fully formed and functional. Their structures are far too complicated to have evolved in a single, rapid step. So how does a swimming or crawling proto-insect develop proto-wings? That is, rudimentary structures that don't allow flight, but do provide some advantage to the owner, and the improvement of which, by natural selection, will gradually lead in the direction of true flight? That can become equipped over time with aerofoil surfaces, articulation, and flapping power, while each incremental step provides some advantage that can be maintained by selective pressure? All without the use of a leg—possessing the rudiments of some of those properties—as a starting point?

Unfortunately for us, the known fossil record sheds little light on those questions, because there is a gap in the crucial period between the times arthropods ventured onto land and the development of winged flight. What we can learn from the record is that primitive arthropods—precursors to the insects—began invading land sometime prior (probably much prior) to about 420 million years ago, when the earliest recognizable fossils already resembled modern relatives. Hexapods (including insects and their close relatives) are scarce among the fossils until about 290–325 million years ago, when insects suddenly appear in great richness and variety but already in their relatively modern forms. The suddenness is due to the onset of conditions favoring fossil preservation; conditions that didn't exist in the preceding period. The insects were undoubtedly around prior to that time, but their existence was not being recorded in fossils. What happened during the gap of some 95–130 million years that led from early arthropods to winged insects? Just what steps were involved in the evolution of those remarkable wings? Fossils discovered thus far have been unable to tell us much about it.

Based on largely circumstantial evidence, scientists have come up with several theories over the years to explain the steps that may have been involved in the evolution of insect flight. Most of them postulated the advent of thoracic appendages, in the positions now occupied by wings, with functions that did not initially have anything to do with flying. With time, the new appendages are proposed to have evolved into structures that gradually gained more of the properties of wings. The most important difficulty with most of the theories has been their assumption that a fixed (unhinged) proto-wing and gliding flight were steps that preceded evolution of an articulated wing and flapping flight. Yet many scientists see little to support the notion that fixed wings in insects or their ancestors ever existed, based on findings in numerous biological fields and in paleontology.

Then some years ago along came the currently prevailing theory, which neatly solves the problem of fixed wings evolving into articulated flapping structures. It does so by postulating that, as in bats and birds, insect wings developed from a preexisting articulated appendage; so there was never a time when a gliding insect needed to evolve into a flapping one. The proto-insect appendage was not a leg *per se*, but rather a gill plate. Many living juvenile aquatic insects have gills and gill plates on their abdomen

and/or on their ventral thorax, and fossils show that early insects also had gills on their dorsal thorax in the very positions now occupied by wings.

But like most good theories, this one raised new questions even as it solved old ones. The overall principle that articulated gills served as precursors to wings may be well supported, but what drove the transition? Intermediate steps must have been involved, in which the gills morphed into winglets, not yet capable of full-powered flight yet providing enough of an advantage for natural selection to increase their incidence within the population. What benefit might flight-incapable small flapping wings confer to their bearer?

This is the point where the subjects of this chapter, shortwing stoneflies, finally get to play a role in the story. While flightless, abnormally small-winged (brachypterous) insects are not common, they are also not really rare, especially among stoneflies. It turns out that in at least some of the brachypterous stoneflies, while the small wings don't support actual flight, they do allow skimming. These insects move from one point to another over the water surface by rapidly beating their wings for thrust—forward motion—rather than height. The inefficient wings provide just enough lift to get most of the bug's body out of the water, so that it can move across the surface with only its legs and rear end dragging. In that way it minimizes its exposure to, and time spent in, the water, where drowning and predation from below are serious risks. It is pretty easy to see how skimming would be an advantage over no aerial capability at all. The behaviors of living brachypterous stoneflies offer examples of what could have been intermediate, increasingly functional stages along the evolutionary path to full-powered flight.

The scenario envisioned for evolution of winged insects goes then something like this. Early proto-insects were aquatic, as were all of the original arthropods. Some types had different numbers of legs and leglike appendages, including gill plates, on various parts of the body—particularly on the dorsal thorax. (Modern biological studies have shown that gills and most other arthropod appendages are really modified legs, growing from similar embryonic tissues, and capable of sprouting in inappropriate spots on the body via a simple mutation in a regulatory gene.) A number of these proto-insects used their rapidly movable gill plates, including those on the dorsal part of the thorax (where wings are now attached), for propulsion through the water. As land around the lakes, swamps, and rivers became habitable, some of these proto-insects began to venture above water. In those early days there would have been few predators on land, providing plenty of incentive to move ashore.

Westslope cutthroat trout are suckers for big dry flies when shortwing stoneflies are around.

Adult shortwing stoneflies, like this female, are light brown or tan underneath.

Some of the adventurers continued to use their flapping gill plates to move on the water surface. Those individuals with bigger and better functioning flaps had a survival advantage over their siblings, and as a result left more descendants. In a similar manner, flapping gills gradually turned into more efficient winglets, with improved structures, strengthened muscles, and improved physiology to move them. Eventually, the process led to the development of true wings and powered flight. Movement through air was such a huge advantage that winged insects rapidly outcompeted their flightless brethren, pushing them into extinction as the true insects diversified and radiated into almost every niche on the planet.

Just think about it. The ancestors of fly fishing's own aquatic insects are now thought to have played a central role in the development of flight, one of the most notable achievements in the history of life on earth. One more interesting aspect of our sport, and a good conversation point for cocktail parties. But now let's get back to some information about shortwing stoneflies that may be useful where it counts the most—on the river.

FISHING THE SHORTWING STONEFLY HATCH

Most large rivers in the Northwest and Rocky Mountain regions produce at least moderate numbers of shortwing stoneflies, and wherever they occur, they are big morsels sure to interest trout. A few places have exceptional hatches, and in those areas the fish really key on them. Two such places that stand out are the Yakima River in Washington, and the South Fork of the Snake in Wyoming and Idaho. Those are places with ideal habitats for these bugs: loosely piled stones in the preferred size range.

Since the nymphs spend two to three years in the water before hatching, there are always some sizable individuals at any season, even right after a hatch. It also means multiple size classes, so both large- and medium-size imitations should be carried along when visiting shortwing territory. Like their cousins, the golden stones, shortwing nymphs are active hunters, and their roaming lifestyle in search of prey gets them swept into the drift. Any drifting insect is in turn preyed upon by trout, and a snack this big is bound to be an irresistible delicacy. Since shortwing nymphs live in

A big, improbable Chernobyl Ant is one of the best patterns to use when shortwing stoneflies are hatching.

comparable places and look very similar to the golden stones, the same patterns and tactics used for those species can be employed in shortwing waters.

When it comes to adult shortwing stoneflies, appearances and behaviors move away from their golden relatives. Adult shortwings are dark brown, almost black on their dorsal surfaces, but their undersides are a light brown or tan. When fishing dry-fly imitations, you want to represent the size, silhouette, legs, and ventral color of the naturals. As you can see in the photograph of a shortwing stonefly on the preceding page, the ventral color is quite different from golden stoneflies.

When golden stoneflies are hatching, trout see far more of the females than males. That is because while both sexes inhabit the bank vegetation, only the females fly back over the water—and frequently fall into it—during egg-laying flights. So just the occasional male will find itself in the drink. Shortwing stonefly adults, on the other hand, rarely or never fly, don't climb the vegetation, and stay within two to three feet of the waterline; but *both* sexes scramble across the water surface near shore. Since the males are considerably smaller than females, as well as more active, it's a good plan to carry patterns in sizes that match both sexes.

The best time to fish dries is the two hours preceding dark. That's when females run across the surface from one exposed rock to another, dropping eggs into the water as they go. Males engage in similar activity, but for a different purpose: looking for freshly emerging females with which to mate. All this scampering on the water can drive trout wild. Even at other times of the day, the fish remember these bugs and will often hit big dry flies that imitate them.

While dry-fly patterns that succeed during golden stonefly hatches will also work for the shortwings with appropriate modifications in color, the odd foam patterns dubbed Chernobyl Ants are often the go-to fly on those rivers with big hatches of these bugs. The body shape presents a realistic silhouette, the rubber legs have lots of movement, and most importantly, they work.

14
Swim Before You Crawl

The large swimmer mayflies crawl out of the water to hatch

In this chapter we'll take a look at some large mayflies whose nymphs are exceptionally good swimmers—but rather than following the typical mayfly pattern of emergence at the water surface, these nymphs usually crawl out on rocks or partially submerged vegetation to hatch. Like the smaller swimmer nymphs (such as *Baetis* and *Callibaetis*), large swimmer nymphs are very streamlined and possess tails with interlocking hairs that increase their propulsive capabilities. With larger size comes greater strength, allowing some of these mayflies to swim upstream against even relatively stiff currents.

I would have liked to open this chapter with an exciting fishing story in which the large swimmer mayflies played a major role, but the truth is that I have yet to cross paths with trout selectively feeding on these bugs. We all need something to look forward to, right? To be fair though, two of the three types of large swimmer nymphs offer few fishing opportunities in western North America, where the bulk of my rod-in-hand wanderings have been concentrated.

The large swimmer mayflies—with body lengths in the 10–20mm range—all have nymphs with three tails and adults with two. They fall into three families: Isonychiidae,

Fly fisher Barry Olson tries his luck on Oregon's North Umpqua River, home to magnificent native steelhead and large swimmer mayflies.

A slate drake (*Isonychia*) female spinner is both large and fast. Body length = 20mm.

Siphlonuridae, and Ameletidae. Each family includes a single genus of some consequence to anglers: *Isonychia* (slate drakes or leadwings), *Siphlonurus* (gray drakes or black drakes), and *Ameletus* (brown duns), respectively. Of the three, *Siphlonurus* occurs very commonly in the West—though the waters with large superhatch populations are limited—and is the only one offering noteworthy fly-fishing opportunities in the region. Several *Siphlonurus* species are also found in the Midwest and the East, where the hatches are usually considered minor. *Ameletus* is widely distributed throughout the West, and to a lesser extent the Midwest and East; but it is not considered very important to fly fishers in any part of its range. *Isonychia* is found across North America, and several species have great fly-fishing significance in the East and Midwest. In the West, the genus has only limited importance, primarily because of the narrow distribution of two species: *I. velma* near the coast, and *I. sicca* in the northern Rocky Mountains.

You may have concluded from the preceding paragraph that most of these large swimmer mayflies are too restricted in range or overall importance to bother learning about them. But there are times and places where each of these bugs is the top priority of the trout at hand, and it is always

best to be prepared for those situations. After all, some of these insects are very large indeed, and when the opportunity presents itself, we can be confident that trout will be taking advantage of it. Not only that, but the large swimmer mayflies are fascinating creatures in their own right.

ISONYCHIA (SLATE DRAKES, LEADWINGS)
In my part of the country, the West, significant populations of the slate drakes (*I. velma*) occur chiefly in the coastal streams of northern California and southern Oregon. Primary hatches are in the fall; that's why this chapter is situated near the end of my seasonal arrangement, even though the other two genera discussed here hatch at different times of the year. (I considered the similarities between the families more important than the different times of year in which they hatch.) Hatches of a different species, *I. sicca*, are found in some areas of the Rocky Mountains, most notably the Lower Yellowstone River. Those hatches arrive earlier in the year, around June. The Midwest and East experience much more widespread and significant hatches of the *Isonychia*, from June to September; with *I. bicolor* being the major species.

Slate drake duns emerge on rocks in shallow water, sometimes in massive numbers.

Isonychia nymphs are very strong swimmers, capable of moving against heavy currents, and the largest populations occur in faster rivers. The nymphs have long hairs on the inside edges of their front legs, and this sets them apart not only from the other large swimmer nymphs, but from all other mayflies. They have a habit of anchoring the middle and back legs to the bottom substrate, then filtering the water with the hairs on their front legs as if with a net. Besides being consumers of plankton and other plant matter, *Isonychia* nymphs are unusual among mayflies in that they are partially carnivorous, feeding on small insect larvae as well.

My first encounter with slate drakes was on the Chetco River in southern Oregon, just north of the California border. The Chetco is noted for its big salmon and steelhead runs. We had driven upriver from Brookings on a fine warm October morning, and were exploring the river around Loeb State Park, when I was suddenly buzzed by some enormous speedster spinners. These were the fastest flying mayflies that I had ever seen, and among the largest. The only bigger mayflies in the West are the burrowers (*Hexagenia limbata* or hex) and *Ephemera simulans*. I would later learn that my impressions were accurate; not

only are *Isonychia* nymphs the speed champions of the watery realm, but the spinners can give dragonflies a run for their money in the air.

Many of the coastal rivers where the slate drakes have a big presence don't support large populations of resident trout. So the opportunities for fishing *Isonychia* imitations to garden-variety trout in that region are limited. But bigger quarry are a possibility—think steelhead.

Whereas most anglers who fish for steelhead employ wet flies, either swinging specialized streamers or drifting big nymphs, these anadromous (migrating to and from the sea) members of the trout family can be induced to rise to a dry fly. Many steelhead aficionados feel that the ultimate experience in fly fishing is witnessing the explosion of a huge steelie on a waking dry fly. Now, it just so happens that fall is the time when steelhead dry-fly fishing is at its best. That's also when two very large insects, the October caddis (chapter 15) and the slate drake mayflies, are on the water. Coincidence? Maybe, but given that steelhead are really just big rainbow trout that went to sea for a while, it seems quite possible that there's a connection.

It was on one of the most famous steelhead rivers in the world, Oregon's North Umpqua, where I encountered the

1

When ready to emerge, an *Isonychia* nymph crawls from the water and takes a firm grip on the rock it has selected. Body length = 15mm.

2

The first step is splitting the nymphal thorax, and the dun begins to push through the opening.

5

Free at last, the dun turns for a look at the shed exoskeleton.

most amazing *Isonychia* hatch I've ever seen. About two o'clock in the afternoon I came upon a section of the river where hundreds of big nymphs were swimming into the shallows and climbing out on the chalky white rocks along the bank, where the duns were emerging and proceeding to sun-dry themselves before flying away.

I came back the next day at the same time with my camera, and luckily the whole scene was repeated. Pre-sented here for your enjoyment is a series of photos depicting the emergence of a dun from one of the many nymphs that entertained me that day.

I know you are wondering whether I caught any fish from that most revered of steelhead rivers. The answer is yes; a 32-inch twelve-pound beauty, which broke off the tip of my rod just as I landed it. (OK, fish don't break rods; people do.) Just a quick lift for a photo, and then it was

3

Slowly the wings and legs are extracted, but in the midstages neither is completely free.

4

Once the dun's legs are released, they can latch onto the rock and help pull out the wing tips and tails.

6

With the river in the background, a dun dries itself in the sun before flying off.

released and back on its way upstream toward the spawning grounds. That fish was caught swinging a traditional steelhead wet fly, not on a dry—but that is my next goal.

SIPHLONURUS (GRAY DRAKES)

Siphlonurus mayflies (usually called gray drakes, but sometimes black drakes, especially when spinners are the subject of discussion) have rather mysterious habits. The nymphs are often not where you expect to find them, and when you do come upon substantial concentrations, it is frequently in an area away from the locations where large numbers of the big dark spinners are observed. Duns can be even more elusive. Many experienced fly fishers have rarely observed a *Siphlonurus* dun. I count myself among them!

Here's an example. I regularly see fair numbers of the big, size 12 or larger gray drake spinners on the lower

Male gray drake spinners (and duns) have huge eyes characterized by the presence of a dark horizontal band in the middle, flanked above and below by lighter bands. The presence of these banded eyes is a quick way to identify them.

Gray drake (*Siphlonurus*) male spinners are known for going large: including forelegs, hindwings, and tails. Body length = 17mm.

Gray drake nymphs migrate into shallow areas with vegetation and bottom debris when almost ready to hatch. Body length = 16mm.

McKenzie River during early summer to mid-summer. Yet for years I never saw a dun, nor ever observed a *Siphlonurus* nymph, during any of my bug-collecting forays. I looked for the nymphs in fast riffles, in slow pools, along banks, and in aquatic vegetation. In areas of big boulders, small cobble, gravel, or sand. Nothing. Yet I knew those spinners had to be coming from somewhere, and probably from not very far away.

Then one late spring day I happened to be checking a pool in a small, intermittent, troutless stream that runs through my property. About a quarter mile down from my place, it joins the McKenzie River. The stream runs during winter and spring, then shrivels until the surface flow stops altogether before the end of summer. Isolated pools remain until the fall rains get the flows started again. The shallow water warms quickly and can be into the 70-degree range by early June in some years. The pondlike areas hold good numbers of dragonfly and damselfly nymphs, as well as some *Callibaetis* mayflies, backswimmers, and midges; not to mention mosquitoes and tadpoles. It is shallow and heavily vegetated, becoming almost choked with weeds and water plants by mid-summer.

On this day I swept a collecting net through some weeds just off the bank, and to my surprise it came up teeming with wriggling swimmer nymphs. A close examination revealed they were the long-sought juveniles of the gray drakes!

Judging from their size and the stage of the developing wing pads, I estimated that these nymphs would be hatching within a week or two. So I kept an eye on the spot, checking it every few days for signs of the duns; but none were to be seen. After some of life's other demands distracted me for a bit, I returned two weeks later and seined the water again. There wasn't a *Siphlonurus* nymph to be found anywhere! The sneaky little rascals must have slipped out of the water and molted to duns while my back was turned, and then disappeared into parts unknown. The duns have so far failed to reveal themselves. I've encountered only a single individual, and that one was missing some legs, so I decided to wait for a more photogenic example on which to train my camera. I'm still waiting.

By the most authoritative accounts, gray drake nymphs are to be found in fishable numbers mostly in fairly slow rivers with sandy, vegetated bottoms, or in such sections of faster freestone rivers; as well as in some lakes. During most of their nymphal existence, they are thus in areas where fish have access to them, and no doubt often find themselves on the inside of a trout's belly. When the siren song of impending emergence comes calling, the nymphs migrate with their characteristic darting motion toward shallow water. Very shallow, very weedy water, as it turns out. They may often get stranded there, as in my stream when flows drop to leave only isolated pools. When the

time is right, the nymphs usually leave the water by crawling onto emergent vegetation or rocks, and molt into duns. From all reports, this seems to happen mostly at night. The duns prefer emerging in areas with nearby tall trees, where they are reported to fly and molt again into spinners within a few days. Duns are thus rarely available to trout, and also rarely seen by anglers.

The periods when *Siphlonurus* nymphs are engaging in their mass migrations to the safety of the shallows is the best time to imitate that stage. Since they swim in rapid, six- to twelve-inch darts, a similar motion should be imparted to the artificial by quick stripping and brief pauses.

Gray drake spinners are clearly the most important stage to fly fishers, particularly on those waters where they occur in great enough numbers to elicit selective feeding. Even though they may have recently emerged from nymphs that were living up the side channels and in stagnant pools away from the primary flows, the spinners return to the main currents and riffles to lay eggs. So spinner falls occur in trouty water. That's the time to employ the big spinner patterns, but be prepared for a lot of competition from the numerous naturals.

AMELETUS (BROWN DUNS)

If the habits of *Siphlonurus* mayflies are mysterious, then their *Ameletus* cousins are downright inscrutable. Many fly-fishing books don't cover them. You never see a magazine article about them. Most anglers have never heard of them. Even the scientists are fuzzier on the details of the *Ameletus* life history than they are for most other mayflies. Yet in many clean, cool rivers in the West, and some in the East, it isn't difficult to find decent numbers of the nymphs. Why can't these bugs get any respect?

At least for fly fishers, the answer lies mostly in their relationship to trout, or more accurately, the lack thereof. While the nymphs can be locally abundant, most often they hang out in places where there are no trout, or trout would have a hard time getting at them. That's because although they are almost always found in cold, flowing water, *Ameletus* nymphs prefer the shallow, gravel areas or the sandy margins right up against the shore. It's not unusual to collect them in four inches of water. That's pretty skinny water for a trout that anyone would be interested in catching.

Despite their tendency to stay away from trout-inhabited areas, *Ameletus* nymphs are among my favorite aquatic macroinvertebrates. I find them in greatest abundance and largest sizes on my local rivers in January and February. (In fact, I considered placing the discussion of *Ameletus* mayflies in the chapter on bugs of winter. But their relationship to the other large swimmer nymphs won them a place here.) This is a period when winter rainstorms regularly soak the Pacific Northwest, often inducing spikes in river flows. Marginal shallow areas that were previously off-limits to bigger trout now suddenly become their places of refuge. And what are they going to find to eat there? Among other things, *Ameletus* nymphs that had become a little too smug about their choice of a safe place to live.

Another place where trout and *Ameletus* nymphs occasionally come into contact are undercut banks along meadow streams. Both creatures favor such habitats. Although the evidence is slim, you just know that is a situation where the smaller species will get eaten. So there is more reason to consider fishing with *Ameletus* nymph imitations than most anglers suspect.

But that's not the main reason I like them so much. I just think they are really cool looking. Not only do they sport striking colors arranged into exquisite patterns, but up close, they resemble nothing so much as an alien who just stepped off his spaceship.

While the relationship between *Ameletus* and *Siphlonurus* nymphs is readily apparent, there are some differences that make it easy to distinguish them once you know what to look for. Probably the easiest differentiating characteristic to see is gill structure. *Ameletus* nymphs have simple, modest, oval-shaped gills. The gills on *Siphlonurus* nymphs, on the other hand, are much larger, and are doubled on at least abdominal segments one and two (nearest the thorax and legs).

If *Ameletus* nymphs are only occasionally available to trout, what about the duns? Unfortunately they follow the pattern of the other large swimmer mayflies, with nymphs crawling out of the water to emerge. If a nymph that is ready to hatch isn't already in shallow water, it migrates there, then finds a plant, stone, or stick to crawl up to the water surface.

It may stop when it is halfway out of the water, or it may continue crawling for a few inches. Then it molts to the dun. So there is no open water hatch, and trout never get a look at the duns, unless it's a very windy day and some of them get blown into the water. (I have seen a couple of duns floating down the river, but that's the rare exception rather than the rule.)

After a few days of resting on shore, the duns molt to spinners. Amazingly, that's about all we know about them. While isolated spinners are occasionally observed, like the ones pictured on the following pages, there are no reports of spinner mating swarms, either in the angling literature or scientific publications. There is conjecture that mating occurs very high in the air, out of sight, or even while perched in trees and bushes. We just don't know. And the method of egg deposition is also in question. Spinners are virtually never seen on the water surface, leading to speculation that females dive underwater to lay eggs, and then drown there so we don't see them. Another subject for investigation.

Ameletus nymphs resemble their *Siphlonurus* cousins, with a similar swimmer body and head shape, but have cleaner lines. Note the dark band in the middle of the tails. Body length = 14mm.

I call this shot of an *Ameletus* nymph "The Space Alien," for obvious reasons.

To help determine identity, compare the larger, more elaborate gill plates of this *Siphlonurus* nymph with the smaller, simpler ones of the *Ameletus* nymph in the photo on page 158.

When viewed very closely a female *Ameletus* dun is a striking creature.

Ameletus duns can sometimes be observed on streamside vegetation, but rarely on the water surface. Body length = 12mm.

Ameletus spinners lose the dark crossbars in the wings of the duns, but sometimes have smoky, clouded areas near the front edges. Males have very large eyes that touch on top, and partially clear abdomens.

Bottom line: *Ameletus* nymphs are very interesting to observe and may occasionally be worth imitating in specific situations. Trout rarely see duns, except maybe a few on windy days, so selective feeding is very unlikely. We don't have a clue what the spinners are up to, but we do know that you (or trout) probably will not see them on the water. So marvel at the mystery, but don't worry too much about finding yourself in a situation where trout are feeding on *Ameletus* mayflies and you have nothing in your box to match them.

The habits of *Ameletus* spinners, like this female, are a mystery. Body length = 14mm.

Pheasant Tail nymph. The PT is one of the best-known and oldest of modern nymph patterns, and you won't find many fly fishers without a good selection of sizes and variations in their go-to box. Originally designed by Frank Sawyer and described in his 1958 book *Nymphs and the Trout*, it was intended to mimic the small *Baetis* swimmer nymphs of his native English streams. It is no less effective on this side of the pond.

Parachute spinner. This is a useful pattern for those situations where a good spinner fall of gray drakes is encountered. The one pictured employs a loop-wing in the style of Bob Quigley, but when visibility is more important than realism, a white calftail or poly-yarn wing tied as a post can be substituted.

FLIES

Since the fishing opportunities provided by all three families of the large swimmer mayflies—with the exception of gray drakes—lie mostly with the nymph stage, there is not much need to worry about flies that specifically mimic the other stages. Most of the usual suspects among mayfly nymph patterns will prove effective at times. But the standard Pheasant Tail nymph is a good choice because of its slim profile and prominent tails, both features of swimmer naturals.

Gray drake spinners (called black drakes in some places) are an important exception where the adult stage can present a chance for excellent fishing. The Williamson River in southern Oregon comes most strongly to mind. Blizzard spinner falls and many rising fish are common there during early summer. The fly pattern most recommended for that situation is a dark parachute spinner in a size 12–14.

Up to a hundred or more native steelhead in the 6–20 pound range stack up each fall in a favored pool of a North Umpqua River tributary. When winter rains increase the flows, their upstream migration to the spawning grounds continues. Fishing with large, waking dry flies is popular on the North Umpqua, a river that has a good population of large *Isonychia* mayflies.

15
The Halloween Hatch

The big October caddis tempts even the largest trout

October is the month of goblins and ghosts, pumpkins and pie, candy corn and Trick 'r Treat. It sports its own team colors—orange and gold. And in keeping with the team spirit, the month's mascot—at least in the eyes of many fly fishers—blends right in with its own seasonal hues, visible in the photos on the next page.

I don't think we can know exactly how a bug will look to any particular fish. In a stream with a dark bottom, little light will be reflected back up to illuminate the insect's underside. Conversely, a light bottom in shallow water will serve as a better reflector. Riffled water will provide its own distortions. And importantly, we don't know how well a trout's eyes and brain can compensate for disparities in light levels. It may perceive a dimly lit bug's belly against a light background quite differently than we do.

Whatever the viewing angle, this has to be considered one of the most attractive of the caddisflies—if *attractive* is a term that can properly describe any member of this clan. Even more striking than its appearance is its size. October caddis—or fall caddis or orange caddis or great orange sedge or, most unambiguously, *Dicosmoecus*—is one of the biggest bugs in the West. They reach lengths of 35mm (1^1/$_2$ inches) or more, and their fat juicy bodies are enough of a mouthful to tempt even the largest fish into passionate pursuit. Among those dedicated dry-fly fishers who selectively target the largest of the trout family, the October

Washington's Twisp River appears dressed for Halloween.

October caddis (*Dicosmoecus* sp.). Body + wings = 32mm.

Turn an October caddis upside down and its brightest colors show up.

Of course, the October caddis's hues will appear a lot less vivid when seen from a fish's perspective: viewed ventrally and backlit against a bright sky.

caddis emergence is often the most anticipated hatch of the year. Even steelhead seem to be more surface-oriented than usual when the big adult caddisflies are around.

Since I'm throwing a smidge of Latin at you, let's get that over with and place these insects into their organizational cubbyhole within the caddisfly classification system. The bugs we call October or fall caddis in the western United States are in the genus *Dicosmoecus*, and include two important and very similar species, *D. gilvipes* (most common in the Pacific Northwest), and *D. atripes* (more common in the Rocky Mountain region). They are among the largest members of their family, Limnephilidae, also known as northern case maker caddisflies.

These bugs have lots of relatives at family reunions; the Limnephilidae family is very large, with about one-quarter of North American caddisfly genera claiming membership. What they have most notably in common is a larval case that is roughly tubular in shape. But as you might expect from such a diverse family, those cases are built from a wide variety of materials—sticks, leaves, pebbles—and assume many different forms. The kinfolks that build them have moved into a lot of different neighborhoods, from riffle to pool, from pond to roaring river.

THE AQUATIC STAGES

Now to fully appreciate the October caddis story, let's back up a bit, to a time when the *Dicosmoecus* youngsters are still crawling around the river bottom. That would be from winter until about mid-summer to late summer. If you're stomping around the margins of a riffle in a western freestone river in July or early August, turning over rocks or kick seining to see what fascinating fauna may dwell there, you just might come across a few—or more—critters with black heads sticking out of pebble tubes.

In the later larval stages, like the one shown here, October caddis cases are constructed of pebbles and rock fragments held together by a sticky silk that the caddis secrete from glands in their mouths. If you put on a diving mask and take a dip or, more comfortably, use a handheld viewing device with a window that lets you see underwater while remaining dry yourself, you may see these bugs crawling about in the spaces between the cobble.

At the risk of breaking our train of thought here—which if you haven't recognized it, is an overview of the October caddis life cycle—I'm going off on a fascinating tangent for a moment. When you think of caddis, what word or characteristic jumps first into your mind? I bet it's not silk. Were you surprised when you read above that this

October caddis cased larva. Case length = 31mm.

October caddis larva outside its case.
Body length = 29mm.

October caddis peeking pupa.

bug uses it for constructing its case? Well, I was, the first time I learned about it.

The one striking thing that all caddis have in common is that juveniles make and use silk; they are the silkworms of the underwater world. Case makers like *Dicosmoecus* use it as glue to bind the bricks of their mobile homes, and to line the interior. Net-spinning caddis larvae use silk to build elaborate webs, as spiders do, to catch particles or prey swept in by the current, and to construct their attached shelters. And the last group of caddisfly larvae, the free-living ones like green rock worms (*Rhyacophila*), trail a thread of silk as they roam the bottom; it serves as a lifeline in case they get swept into the current, or decide to repel into it. All of them build silk cocoons, not unlike a butterfly, when it comes time to pupate and transition to the adult.

Many entomologists believe that silk is the key to the great success of caddisflies in colonizing so many freshwater environments. There are more varieties of caddisflies than any other type of aquatic insect. The imaginative uses of silk have helped them exploit almost every available niche.

Getting back now to our October caddis larva crawling around the stream bottom—just what is it doing down there? Making a living, of course, by looking for detritus or decaying leaves to shred. But what they like the most is

the delicious fungi—think caddis mushrooms—that grow on and break down dead organic matter. In an ironic aquatic version of "man bites dog," the fungus can turn the tables. If you chance upon a caddis case all covered with a feltlike fuzz, that fuzz is actually a fungus that is feeding off a dead larva or pupa inside.

As suggested by the photo on page 165, while the *Dicosmoecus* larvae are dragging around their heavy cases, they generally expose only their dark heads and legs. The bulk of the body remains protected inside the case, and at the first sign of trouble, like a turtle, they quickly pull everything inside.

So do trout eat these big cased larvae, stones and all? If you do a little reading in magazines and fishing books you will find differing opinions. From my review of the scientific literature, the evidence suggests that in most fairly clear streams, cased *Dicosmoecus* larvae are rarely on the trout menu. Under these conditions trout feed primarily on the drift, which is food brought to them by the current as they remain stationary in their holding positions. Heavy pebble cases don't drift in anything short of a roaring flood. However, in cloudy water, trout may be forced to go hunting for food. Since trout are primarily sight feeders, in cloudy water they can't see far enough to determine what's coming down the chow line in time to intercept it. In a

October caddis late-stage pupa within cutaway case.

study in California's usually turbid (due to glacial runoff) McCloud River, researchers found that trout in that stream resorted to rooting around on the bottom for food, and cased October caddis larvae became a major prey item found in stomach samples.

If you decide that it's worth a try imitating a cased caddis, take a look at Jeff Morgan's interesting article "Caddis Larvae—Part I" in the Westfly.com website archives for suggestions on fly patterns.

Does an October caddis larva ever leave its case? Not often, but it does happen in some circumstances. For instance, it will reluctantly abandon a case if it becomes stubbornly stuck and it can't work it free. If you were there when that happened, something like this is what you would see: a black head and brownish thorax attached to a gill-covered, pale cream abdomen that looks very naked indeed. (And they seem to act naked, too, as if they are embarrassed to be seen.)

Every caddis larva goes through a series of stages (instars) as it grows, and at several points along the way a *Dicosmoecus* youngster must move out of its now-too-small home and build a larger one. Many caddis species undergo "behavioral drift" at this time, which usually occurs during twilight (dusk or dawn) or at night. Doing it in the dark makes sense, as they are unusually vulnerable to predators while drifting; no need to make a sight-feeding trout's job any easier. Behavioral drift is also believed to be a mechanism for dispersing the bugs throughout a river system, so that they may exploit all the habitat opportunities and avoid calamity if a disaster strikes any particular locale.

Of course fly fishers may also be eager to take advantage of caddisflies' tendency to abandon cases and drift freely. That's another good reason to be on the stream during twilight hours. But for the October caddis larvae in particular, there may—or may not—be a bonus period. The renowned Gary LaFontaine, king of the caddisfly, and author of the highly respected and comprehensive volume *Caddisflies*, wrote in that book that *Dicosmoecus* larvae exhibit the unusual habit of drifting during the daytime (around 4 P.M.) in early summer. He believed that was a golden opportunity to fish uncased larval imitations with great chances for success.

The occurrence of the *Dicosmoecus* larvae midafternoon drift is often restated in the fly-fishing literature. It would be great if that daytime drift really occurs—and I'm not saying that it definitely doesn't. However, I can't find much evidence for it. LaFontaine cited a single 1972 scientific reference for the phenomenon, which actually doesn't mention daytime *Dicosmoecus* larval drift; and I haven't yet uncovered any other references to support it. Trout

October caddis pupal shucks accumulate on favored rocks.

stomach sample data that I've seen don't point in that direction, and it would certainly be out of the ordinary for a caddisfly. Still, I'm hoping he was right, and that someday I'll encounter a midday October caddis larval drift and the great fishing that should accompany it.

Let's move now from the larva to the pupa stage. Unlike mayflies or stoneflies, caddisflies go through complete—rather than incomplete—metamorphosis (chapter 3) and don't enjoy the luxury of proceeding directly from nymph to adult. They have to put in their time in an inactive pupa phase, sealed into their cases or shelters, and not feeding or moving about; just slowly undergoing an extraordinary transformation.

Usually by about mid-August, most of the October caddis larvae will have attached their cases to the undersides of rocks near riffles, sealed off the entrance with a layer of silk, and settled into a period of variable duration called "diapause." During this interval of up to a few weeks, nothing much happens; progression from larva to pupa is delayed to allow all the larvae to synchronize. At some point, temperature and light conditions are right to give the green light for pupal development to commence.

If you pull a *Dicosmoecus* case off the underside of a rock late in its pupa phase, then remove the tough silken seal at the larger end and take a peek inside, you'll see an orange face and a pair of big pupal eyes staring back at you. I carefully cut away the side of a case so we could get

a good look at the late-stage pupa inside. It was quite amazing to see all the structures of the pupa tucked up compactly inside the case.

Even with the case cut open, when reimmersed in water the pupa stayed calm and continued the rhythmic body motions it uses to pump water through the pores in the case and over the gills on its abdomen. Notice the long brush-like hairs on its middle leg. We'll see them put to good use shortly. (The rear legs—recall that as in all insects, there are three pairs—in caddisfly pupae are not entirely free, and are bound close to the body. They are therefore difficult to see without close examination, and are not of much use to the pupa for locomotion.)

HUNTING FOR THE ELUSIVE HATCH

For years I had observed adult October caddis on the river, collected larvae and pupae, and had seen numerous discarded pupal shucks on the partially submerged rocks at water's edge. But I had never observed a hatch in progress. I knew that it happened sometime between dusk and dawn, at least on local streams in western Oregon, because that's when the pupal shucks appeared on the rocks. I wanted to know more about this fascinating bug. So 2007, I decided, would be the "year of the October caddis." If Gary LaFontaine could devote the four years preceding the publication of his *Caddisflies* book to the bug, then I could at least dedicate a couple of months to the project.

Starting in August, I set out to monitor the *Dicosmoecus* population of my home waters, the middle McKenzie River, and to keep a detailed journal of events. I noted a single adult that appeared on the bankside foliage on August 16, the earliest I had ever seen one show up. It turned out not to be a harbinger of an early hatch, but rather just one very confused bug whose internal clock had gone awry. I wouldn't see evidence of another hatching adult for almost a month.

If you want to find a place where lots of October caddis will be hatching during the night, how do you find it? Answer: you find a spot where lots of them have already been hatching. When these insects hatch, it is clear that at least much of the time, they crawl out on half-submerged rocks or sticks; then leave their pupal exoskeletons behind for bug sleuths like me to find. And they have their favorite rocks, too, like the one pictured on page 168. Many times when two apparently similar rocks are right next to each other, the vast majority of pupa will pick just one of them. The preferred rock usually remains a favorite, night after night. It makes no sense to me, but it's useful if you want to be at the right place to see it all happen.

I soon found out that being at the right place is one thing; being there at the right time is quite another. Night after night I sat watching, flashlight or lantern in hand. One hour, then two hours passed; but nothing happened. I tried varying the time I was there: beginning at dusk, one hour after dusk, or two or three hours later; yet no success. Some nights I was out until midnight with no action. But when I would come back the next morning, sure enough, there would be fresh shucks. It began to seem as if they were obeying the Observer Principle: aka "a watched pot never boils." Did they know I was there? Did they wait for me to leave?

I tried sitting in the dark, just turning on a light occasionally to check if anything was happening. Some nights I sat there in the rain. Once my wife brought dinner out for me to eat at my post, so I wouldn't have to leave and possibly miss something. She said I was nuts, and that if people knew what I was going through to see and photograph this event, they wouldn't believe it. But in truth, it wasn't so bad. I was well dressed for rain, and managed to keep warm. In some sort of perverse way, it was actually enjoyable to be out there while nature tested my mettle.

In the end, persistence paid off and I got what I was after. I saw the hatch happen enough times to learn a lot about how it works. If you're not willing to go out there and devote the time I did, then here's the CliffsNotes version.

When they're getting ready to pupate, the *Dicosmoecus* larvae migrate to certain areas. They tend to congregate out of the main current of the riffle, in still moving but somewhat slower water, about eight to twelve inches deep. (Actually, I can't say whether they are found at depths greater than about two feet; it was too difficult for me to survey deeper than that.) I found them to be most abundant in areas two to four feet from shore or gravel bars. They favor rocks averaging the size of a grapefruit, and they seem to like company—many times several or lots of them will attach their cases to the same rock.

The cases are attached at their larger ends to the rock, next to the pupa's head, and the act of attachment also seals that end. When they hatch, they cut through the attachment point, and more often than not the case falls off the rock. But sometimes it stays connected; in the photo below of the two cases, the pupa in the one on the right has already hatched and left an exit hole near the end, but the case is still loosely hanging on.

Immediately after pulling itself from the case, the pupa will often rest for a few moments on the case or on the bottom, seeming to gather its strength. Then it usually starts swimming—slowly, rather clumsily, but with strength. This is where the brushlike hairs on its middle legs come into play. They look like oars, and that's just the way they function. If you imagine the surge-pause, surge-pause motion you would experience if rowing a boat—or if you have ever seen a water boatman bug swim—then you will have a good idea of the motion of a swimming *Dicosmoecus* pupa. It moves toward shallower water and the surface. Most of the time it finds a partially submerged rock or stick, and quickly climbs out of the water. Now and then, a pupa may not find something to climb out on before it gets too tired to keep swimming. Then it either emerges on the surface of the water—or it sinks back to the bottom to rest a bit, before it starts swimming and tries again. Occasionally this lasts quite some time, but most often it takes only a minute or two. Eventually, the pupa finds a suitable spot to climb out of the water, and then the remarkable metamorphosis to an adult takes place.

October caddis pupal cases in situ.

A resting October caddis pupa, shortly after exiting its pebble case. Body length = 24mm.

Swimming October caddis pupa, seeking a suitable emergence location.

A few moments of pushing, and the pupal skin pops open at the dorsal thorax. The adult inside begins to push through the opening.

In my observations, the hatches always occurred after it was completely dark, and before it got light in the morning. It was usually within one to three hours after sunset, but sometimes it was after midnight. Occasionally some would hatch just before dawn. The bugs seemed to come in bursts; one batch might hatch at 8 P.M., and another at 10:30 P.M. on the same night. But there was no discernible pattern. There could be an emergence at 10:00 P.M. one night, and at 8:30 P.M. the next, and after midnight the night after that. It's a

far cry from the punctuality of March brown (*Rhithrogena*) mayflies in the spring, when you can virtually set your watch according to the time the hatch begins.

Of the anglers that I've communicated with in Oregon and Washington, none have seen October Caddis adults emerge during daylight hours, when it's still light enough to fish the hatch. This is in contrast to LaFontaine's observations as related in *Caddisflies*, where he wrote that the hatches usually occurred in the late afternoons and

3

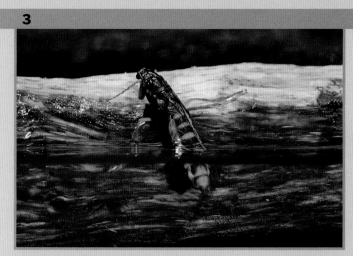

October caddis pupa exits the water.

4

Once out of the water, the pupa wastes no time before setting its feet and getting the emergence started.

6

As soon as the legs of the adult are out, they can grasp the stick or rock, and pulling joins pushing to help extract the wings.

7

When the wings get free, they immediately pop into their fully inflated position. No waiting around like you see for the rather slow inflation of a newly hatched stonefly's wings. The adult caddis does usually take a breather, posing by its old skin for a while, before crawling or flying away.

evenings, and the pupae offered a fishing opportunity. It's possible that these bugs hatch at different times on different waters, explaining the discrepancy.

But in the rivers and streams where I've fished and observed the *Dicosmoecus* hatch, I'm forced to question the rationale for using flies that imitate the pupa stage. I'll admit to having occasionally used them myself, with some limited success. But I'm not convinced the trout that took them actually believed they were October caddis pupae.

The hatch occurs almost exclusively at night on these streams, at times when sight-feeding trout would not likely see them. Pupae escape from their cases in the shallows, where there are few trout, and most of them crawl quickly out of the water to complete emergence. A few late-night emergers may still be in the water at dawn, but for the most part, I think trout seldom see a pupa or a newly hatched adult.

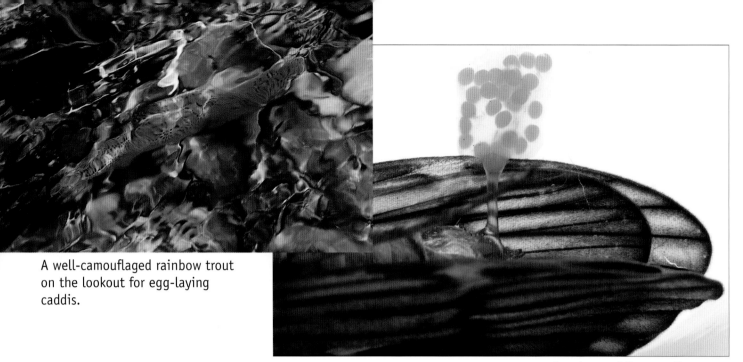

A well-camouflaged rainbow trout on the lookout for egg-laying caddis.

October caddis extruding eggs.

THE END GAME

There is no question, however, that trout see the adults later on. An adult October caddis may live for two or three weeks before returning to lay eggs, and then falling into or skittering on the water. That's when they drive the fish wild. On some rivers there are a lot of these big bugs, but even where their numbers are more modest, like on the McKenzie River, fish are keenly aware of them. The peak of the hatch occurs here during about the last week of September and the first week or two of October. Good numbers of adults will be around until the end of the latter month, and a few on into November.

While some adults may be active around the water at almost any time of day, especially if it's warm and sunny, late afternoon from about 4 to 6 P.M. is when most of the egg-laying activity takes place. These bugs seem to be attracted to the sound of rushing water and the sight of a broken surface, so look for runs with those characteristics and with good trout lies within them or at the margins. Egg-laying females tend to congregate in bushes and trees adjacent to such locations, and frequently fly out over the water with their distinctive bobbing, predator-avoiding flight pattern. Then like a kamikaze dive-bomber, from a height of six to eight feet, they suddenly plummet straight down for the water. Usually for only a second or two, but sometimes longer, they remain on the surface as a batch of eggs is released—and then pop back up into the air. This process is frequently repeated several times.

A large orange Stimulator may be just the ticket during the October caddis hatch.

If there are trout nearby, the result will often be a sudden explosion of spray. A miss, followed by second and third attempts, is not uncommon. Apparently a bug this big is worth a lot of effort to a hungry fish. I've even seen them try to snatch an escaping bug out of the air!

So this fall, don't hesitate to tie on a big October caddis adult imitation—maybe a size 8 orange-bodied Elk Hair Caddis or Stimulator—and dance it across the water. A dead-drifted fly will draw strikes, but twitching one to copy the antics of the natural often excites even reluctant fish into action. You just might be rewarded with the biggest fish of the year—maybe even a steelhead.

16
Bugs of Winter

For those willing to brave the cold, blue-winged olives and other insects are still hatching

When the days are short and the snow flies, many of us retire to the hearth, catch up on our fly tying, and read books like this one in preparation for the next season. Trout may like cold water but they have their limits. Below a certain point, even the hardiest salmonid holes up and becomes lethargic. Terrestrial insects all but disappear. Hatches are few and far between, even though beneath the water, juvenile bugs flourish. Along the Pacific Northwest coast, where winter brings more cold rain than snow, a hardy breed of die-hard steelheaders dredges the depths for winter-run fish. But most (more sensible?) trout anglers look ahead to spring.

Yet for those willing to brave numb fingers and iced-up rod guides, the winter season does offer a few opportunities to fish a dry fly. Blue-winged olive (BWO) mayflies are frequently the season's saviors, sparing the dry-fly purist the ignominy of dragging a nymph. Tiny midges seem oblivious to weather or time of year; some of them always seem to be hatching. A plucky group of winter stoneflies, representing several families known collectively as the small brown stoneflies, specializes in cold weather emergence. And as winter winds down, on many western rivers the emergence of medium-size *Skwala* stoneflies gets anglers' blood flowing again.

Snow and cold are no deterrents for some hardy insects.

BLUE-WINGED OLIVES (*BAETIS*)

Those most contrary of mayflies, the blue-winged olives, are in their element when the skies open to dump rain or snow. The BWO clan seems to take perverse pleasure in choosing the most inclement weather to leave the water, eschewing sunny days in favor of wind and precipitation. That's usually true even when the hatch is in a season other than winter—which it frequently is. In fact, many species in this group are multibrooded, with two or even three generations per year. Given the large number of species, with differences in timing of emergence, on many streams it seems that at least one of them is always hatching. Thus it would have been appropriate to cover them in any chapter, at any point in the year. But the fact that so few other insects hatch in winter gives the blue-winged olives special significance during this season.

We first encountered blue-winged olives in chapter 1, where they were featured in a photographic depiction of the unique mayfly dun-to-spinner molt. BWOs belong to the swimmer group of mayflies—the other groups being clinger, crawler, and burrower. They are further assigned to the subgroup "small swimmers," along with the *Callibaetis* mayflies covered in chapter 11. In the typical mayfly manner, small swimmer mayflies hatch at the water surface, rather than by first crawling out of the water like the large swimmer mayflies do (chapter 14).

All of the blue-winged olives that we are considering here are members of the family Baetidae; though members of other unrelated families sometimes go by that designation. The Baetidae family is extremely diverse in species, habitats, and habits. By the latest count—as reported in the Mayflies of North America Database on Mayfly Central, a website maintained by the Department of Entomology at Purdue University—Baetidae is represented by 155 species in twenty-three genera on the North American continent. By the time you read this, however, the numbers will probably have changed. That's because the taxonomy of the Baetidae is very complex, and seems to be in a constant state of flux as entomologists discover new information and revise family relationships. It's impossible, as well as unnecessary, for a fly fisher to keep up with the latest scientific nomenclature of this group. The most important genera are usually taken to be *Baetis, Acentrella, Diphetor*, and *Plauditus*. Most anglers just call all of them *Baetis*. Rick Hafele refers to them as "the *Baetis* complex" or "the BWO complex," a good compromise.

Whatever you call them, mayflies of this group are found only in moving waters, or those portions of lakes where creeks enter or exit. There are species that reside in almost any type of flowing water, but the greatest variety and largest numbers are found in shallow riffle areas of freestone streams, or in highly vegetated spring creeks and dam tailwaters. Hatches can occur at almost any time of year. In colder latitudes and altitudes there may be two generations, one in the winter/early spring, and another in the fall. Where the water is warmer, with accompanying faster growth rates, a third generation may hatch in the summer. Blue-winged olives also tend to hatch in large numbers. As a result, these mayflies are extremely important to trout and fly fishers—arguably the most important of all hatches.

BWO nymphs vary somewhat in their exact shape, but all of them retain the overall streamlined swimmer-mayfly contours. Most of them have three tails, with the middle one usually being shorter than the outer two; but a few species have just two tails. There are two rather long antennae, at least twice as long as the head is wide. Body lengths of mature nymphs are in the 3–10mm range. During development the nymphs may go through as many as twenty-seven instars. After each molt, it takes a while for the new exoskeleton to harden and assume its normal dark color; during that period the pale nymphs are highly visible and vulnerable to predation.

BWO nymphs feed primarily on algae and diatoms that grow on the surface of shallow rocks and vegetation. They flit from one spot to another in short one- to two-inch spurts, clutching the substrate at each stopping point to hold their positions in the current. Such behavior puts them into the drift at a high frequency. Drifting puts them in harm's way—at the mouths of waiting trout.

During the winter and early spring, BWO hatches tend to come off in the early afternoon, usually in the 12 P.M. to 2 P.M. range. If it's raining or snowing hard, all the better. During the prehatch and hatch periods, nymphs, emergers, cripples and duns may all be important, one after the other; or trout may concentrate almost entirely on just one stage. During the early part of a hatch, the nymphs become agitated and climb to the top of rocks and plants, then start making some trips to the surface.

These small nymphs with their low mass have a hard time breaking the surface tension, especially on smooth water. Maybe as a consequence, BWO emergers seem to have a higher than normal failure rate, with consequent high proportions of crippled duns unable to completely free themselves from the nymphal shucks, or to unfurl folded wings.

Some of my experiences with winter blue-winged olives have made me wonder about the wisdom of their choice in emergence weather. I've seen huge hatches with duns almost carpeting the river surface during a driving rainstorm, when half of the duns were beaten flat and drowned by the deluge, and the other half floated hundreds of feet without being able to get into the air. There must be some powerful reasons for avoiding sunny days to compensate for casualties like that.

Baetis nymphs are good swimmers. Body length = 8mm.

Many blue-winged olives experience difficult emergences, becoming crippled and unable to leave the water.

Female *Baetis* duns have smaller, less colorful eyes than the males. Body length = 8mm.

The tails of male *Baetis* spinners can be more than twice the length of the body. Body length = 8mm.

The stalked, divided (turbinate) eyes of male baetids, specialized for upward vision using UV light, are the most exaggerated of any mayfly family.

Female BWO spinners, even without big divided eyes, are remarkable in their own right. Body length = 8mm.

BWO duns that survive the water-to-air transition make their way to shore where safe resting spots await them. Depending on the species, the duns may be various colors—not always blue-winged or with olive bodies. (In fact, I would call the wing color gray in the majority of the species I've observed.) They always have two tails. Hindwings are either very small and slender, or missing altogether. As for the nymphs, dun body lengths are about 3–10mm.

Spinners have clear, unmarked hyaline wings. As usual for mayflies, the males' forelegs and tails are very long compared with the females. The middle portion of the male abdomen is often white or translucent, so you can see right through it. As discussed in chapter 4, male *Baetis* eyes are large and divided, exhibiting a marked turbinate structure—the most striking example of this phenomenon of all the mayfly families.

For the dry-fly fisher, duns are usually the primary stage for imitation. That is true for mayflies in this group too, but emergers and cripples play a more significant role than usual. Even nymphs get into the surface action, due to the extended time they spend just under the film. A Pheasant Tail nymph tied as a short dropper off a dry is a good combo for this situation. The dry fly employed can be one of a number of patterns, with size and color being the most important variables. The flatter and slower the water, the more realistic the imitation should be, as picky fish get a longer look. Emergers are my number one all around choice. Two productive patterns are a parachute dun tied by Pete Olson of Bend, Oregon, and Bill Marshall's Altoid Emerger, illustrated at the end of this chapter. Spinners are only occasionally important to imitate, and in my experience those times seldom occur during the winter.

MIDGES

Wherever there is water, and whatever the season, there will be midges. A description of these small members of the true-fly family (Chironomidae) was covered in some detail with the still-water bugs in chapter 11. For moving-water aficionados, winter is the time when most of us start to pay more attention to this class of insects—for the simple reason that beyond BWO mayflies, surface-hatching bugs are hard to come by. As for still-water fishing, the pupae are the most important stage to imitate. But mating adults buzzing over the water and crashing in clusters to the surface can provide the occasional opportunity to tie on a true dry fly. A Griffith's Gnat is a good choice. Tactics are similar to those described for still-water fishing.

Midges come in various sizes and colors, including bright green. Males have plumose, or feathery, antennae, whereas female antennae are unadorned. Body length = 5mm.

A Banded Stonefly (*Prostoia besametsa*), of the Nemouridae family, in profile.

STONEFLIES

A remarkable group of small stoneflies defies convention and chooses the cold days of winter to set foot on land. The group includes representatives from the families Nemouridae, Leuctriidae, Capniidae, and Taeniopterygidae. You may hear them referred to as the small brown stonefly complex or the winter stoneflies or several other local monikers. Not all members of these families emerge during winter; some species continue exiting the water into the spring. But in many places, it is not unusual for the intrepid fly fisher to spot small dark stoneflies against the white background of a snow-covered stream bank in January or February.

The tiny newborn nymphs of many of the winter-emerging species go into diapause (something akin to hibernation) right after hatching from their eggs. The nymphs wake up in the fall, just when the nearby trees are shedding their leaves into the water. The timing is no accident. Leaf packs on the bottom of streams are often the prime food source for these bugs. In some areas it is estimated that winter stonefly nymphs are responsible for a major portion of the breakdown of leaves to small particles. The now-active nymphs go on feeding and growth sprees that will lead them to maturity during winter or early spring.

Winter-emerging stoneflies typically leave the water on sunny days, during the afternoons when the most heat is available. Their dark brown or black colors are designed to absorb as much of the sun's energy as possible. Some of them further ameliorate the effects of the cold by building small burrows in the snow and ice.

Flying is a problem for insects that emerge from the water in winter. It takes a lot of energy to operate flight muscles, and cold muscles have difficulty generating much power. Since insects are cold-blooded, with body temperatures near those of their surroundings, they can't generate enough heat on their own to fly very far or fast. So most winter stoneflies are poor fliers, and would rather run than fly. In fact, as we learned in chapter 13, some of them have severely truncated wings that prevent them from flying at all. As a consequence, they rather easily fall or are blown into the water. But their quick feet allow them to skitter across the water back to the safety of shore, unless a trout gets them first.

Winter stoneflies are small, generally in the range of 3–10mm excluding tails, wings, and antennae. Flies to imitate them should be in the corresponding range. Good places to cast them are near overhanging vegetation where the naturals are present.

All right, time for a show of hands. How many of you have heard of *Skwala* stoneflies? If you raised your hand, count yourself among the more well-informed of the fly-fishing community. Either that, or you live in one of the

Skwala stoneflies will attempt to hide in vegetation if there is any around the stream when they are hatching.

areas where local publicity has made them hard to miss. This is a fairly unknown hatch, with little coverage in angling books or magazine articles. Perhaps that's why the bug hasn't acquired an appellation that's stuck beyond the name of the genus, *Skwala*. But it's gaining in popularity in a few places with good populations, most notably on eastern Washington's Yakima River and western Montana's Bitterroot, Clark Fork, and Rock Creek. The Bitterroot in particular is developing a reputation for fine angling in the late winter and early spring, using flies that are large enough to actually be seen on the water surface by the majority of anglers.

While not in the semiofficial winter stonefly families listed above, stoneflies in the genus *Skwala* start appearing on many western rivers by February, and even earlier in some places. These perlodid stoneflies—related to the small yellow stoneflies of late spring and summer—are considerably larger than the other stoneflies that hatch in winter. They would be considered only medium-size when compared with the entire Plecoptera spectrum, but at body lengths of about 18mm, they are a still a big mouthful for fish accustomed to blue-winged olive mayflies, midges, and the winter stoneflies of the preceding months.

There are two North American species of *Skwala*— *S. americana* (formerly *S. parallela*) and *S. curvata*. Both are found in the West, with the highest concentrations reported in western Montana and eastern Idaho, but with a substantial presence in northern California, Oregon, Washington, and several of the Rocky Mountain states. Hatches may begin anywhere from January to late March, depending on the climate and weather patterns. In western Oregon, where some green streamside vegetation persists year-round, a careful examination during February will often reveal some little black-and-yellow heads peering out from under the weeds.

Skwalas belong to the family Perlodidae, and like many members of that family, the nymphs are hunters. Any smaller insect in *Skwala* territory had best watch its back. Mature nymphs are about $3/4$ inch long, not counting antennae or tails. Similar to others of their ilk, they prefer fast, cold water and in many places are the most common stonefly nymphs to show up in sampling nets. Before the trees have grown their leaves, a casual look into *Skwala* water is likely to reveal a peaceful scene of rocks and crannies with little obvious activity. Don't be fooled. Crouching carnivores lurk here, ready to pounce on the unsuspecting.

Skwala nymphs are amber and black, with distinctive patterns on their dorsal surfaces. There are no gills on the thorax, but there is a pair of fingerlike gills in the ventral "neck" area. Groups of thin hairs are present on the back of the head and the top of the thorax. The tails are covered with a single row of fine hairs.

Like other perlodids, *Skwala* nymphs have intricate patterns on their dorsal surfaces.

Skwala adults are brown on top with some orange around the head, and have diagnostic long tails extending well past the rear of the wings. Body length = 18mm; tails = 16mm.

When the time to emerge approaches, *Skwala* nymphs step up their active lifestyles in a mass migration to the shore. You can bet the nearby trout, even in their semi-lethargic winter state, don't fail to notice when these big morsels begin to move. After all, they will have detected the slight increase in water temperature and realized that the time for more substantial meals is arriving. Even before the hatch, *Skwala* nymph imitations are in order.

The nymphs start crawling out in late afternoon or evening. You'll know they're hatching by the shucks they leave behind on rocks and bridge abutments. There are rarely huge visible numbers of the adults, like during a salmonfly hatch. You often have to poke among the rocks and weeds to find them.

Adult *Skwalas* are about $3/4$ inch long, or 1 to $1^1/4$ inches if you include the wings. Tails are extremely long, about $1/2$ inch, and extend well beyond the wings; this is a quick way to identify a *Skwala* stonefly at a glance. They have an overall brown color with orange markings on the dorsal head and thorax. If you flip them over, you'll see the colors of black and yellow.

As for most stoneflies, the best opportunity for trout to munch on the adults is when they return to the water to lay eggs. It generally happens in the late afternoon and evenings for *Skwalas*. On some rivers trout seldom rise to surface bugs in the winter. But on others the *Skwala* hatch can provide some welcome dry-fly action for six to eight days during a season when it can otherwise be hard to find.

Trout fishing in winter is not for everyone. On the coldest days in areas with the most extreme climates, only the truly dedicated venture out. But in milder climes and on warmer days, a trip to the local stream or river may be just the thing to break the hold of cabin fever.

FLIES

Much of the action during cold weather is likely to be subsurface. Nymph imitations of various sorts that have been covered in other chapters will also be good choices during this season. For *Baetis* nymphs, it's hard to beat the Pheasant Tail nymph discussed in chapter 14, using sizes appropriate for these small bugs: hook sizes of 16–20. The rubber-legged golden stonefly nymph shown in chapter 9, and the Possie Bugger of chapter 8, in sizes 12–16, are good choices during *Skwala* season and as general search patterns.

But for those really craving some winter dry-fly action, here are a few proven patterns when winter stoneflies and blue-winged olive mayflies are on the surface. Imitation of adult midges can be accomplished with the same flies described in chapter 11.

The bottom side of an adult *Skwala* is yellow and black.

Black Elk Hair Caddis. The EHC that is a workhorse during caddisfly hatches is also a good choice when the dark winter stoneflies are emerging and returning to the water. When tied in dark colors, and with the bottom hackle trimmed, it does a credible job mimicking the brown or black adults.

Yellow rubber-legged Stimulator. There are a number of patterns that fish well during *Skwala* season, but a Stimulator in sizes 10–14, with or without rubber legs, and tied in yellow to match the color of an adult *Skwala*'s underside, has worked well for me.

BWO parachute. Blue-winged olives tend to be the insect that draws trout to the surface during the winter more often than any other bug. In fact, that assertion can probably be extended to the other seasons as well. A small BWO parachute pattern, like this one tied by Pete Olson of Bend, Oregon, is an excellent choice at any time of year.

Hook: TMC 206BL #16–18
Thread: UNI 8/0 olive dun
Tail: Dark dun Microfibetts, split, two per side
Dubbing: Hareline mink SLF-Callibaetis
Wing post: White poly yarn
Hackle: Dark dun

BWO emerger. When the going gets tough, it's usually a good idea to turn to an emerger pattern during a Baetis hatch. Bill Marshall's pattern has developed a cult following in parts of Oregon, where it is usually referred to as the Altoid Emerger, after the mint tins that Bill uses as containers when he gives them to friends.

Hook: Curved emerger #18–22
Thread: Olive 8/0
Tail: tan mallard (sparse)
Wing post: Deer hair
Rib: Copper wire, very fine
Body: Thread
Hackle: Grizzly or badger
Thorax: Olive dubbing
Head: Thread

17

A Fish-Eye View of Insects and Flies

Fish vision and slant tanks

Throughout this book there has been a pronounced focus on the visual. You've seen lots of photographs of insects from various angles. One of the most common requests I get from fellow fly fishers is to display the underside of an insect—the view that a trout below it is presumed to care most about. I have, in some cases, included that ventral view throughout the chapters, and I've gone farther at times to picture the insect from underwater as it sits on the surface, using a specially constructed slant tank, which was briefly discussed in chapter 5. In this

final chapter, I'll consider fish vision in more detail, and provide insight into the uses, strengths, and weaknesses of slant tanks as tools for determining what an insect or artificial fly looks like to a trout.

During the first half of the twentieth century, how an insect or fly looks to fish received minimal perceptive attention from fly-fishing authors. The situation began to change in the 1970s. Mark Sosin and John Clark devoted an entire chapter titled "Seeing" in their book *Through the Fish's Eye*. Then in 1976 Pennsylvania angler Vincent Marinaro

How fish see underwater in varying light levels and colors is of great importance to fly fishers.

published *In the Ring of the Rise*, which included a section called "What the Fish Sees and Does Not See." Marinaro's book depicted the use of slant tanks as tools for underwater visualization of bugs and flies on the surface. Other than an article later posted by his protégé Jim Birkholm (aka J. Castwell) on the website Fly Anglers Online, slant tanks seem to have been little noticed—a surprising situation in light of their utility and ease of use. A few years after publication of *In the Ring of the Rise*, Brian Clarke and John Goddard added substantial insights on fish vision in their excellent book *The Trout and the Fly*. Their studies employed submerged cameras within real streams.

As a result of his investigations, Marinaro developed some novel flies, most notably the "thorax" patterns, which were intended to incorporate the key characteristics of surface-floating insects as viewed from underwater. Clarke and Goddard followed up with several patterns of their own, the USD Paraduns and Poly-Spinners, designed specifically with the trout's view in mind. None of those flies has really caught on in a big way with the fly-fishing public. Moreover, consideration of how a fly or the bug it aims to imitate may appear to fish is rarely more than a superficial part of fly discussions at streamside or in print. But it seems too important an issue to neglect.

THE TROUT'S EYE

A good place to start in discussing the differences between how a bug looks to us and to a trout is to consider the construction and mechanics of the trout eye relative to our own. They both work on the same basic principle, similar to the one employed by a camera: light rays reflected from an object enter the eye through an opening in a clear cornea, pass through a hole (the pupil) in a pigmented, shielding curtain (the iris), and are focused by refraction through a lens onto a screen (the retina). The retina is composed of light-sensitive receptor cells that in principle are like the sensors or pixels in a digital camera. The focused light forms an image of the object on the screen, and the more receptors in the retina (or pixels in the sensor), the higher the resolution of details in the image. The image pattern is transmitted to the brain—or to the camera's computer—for interpretation.

The key factor necessitating differences in construction of a trout's eye compared with our own is the medium in which it must operate: water. In order to focus light on the retina, a human eye makes good use of the laws of refraction governing light rays that cross a boundary between two media of different densities: the less dense air outside the eye, and the denser aqueous medium within it. Light slows down in the denser medium, causing it to bend when it crosses the boundary at any angle other than exactly perpendicular. The degree of bending or refraction depends on the relative speed of light in the two media, as denoted by

their refractive indices, and the angle at which the light beam strikes the boundary. Air has a refractive index of about 1, while the refractive index of water is about 1.333. Thus light travels in air at virtually the same speed as it does in a vacuum, whereas in water its speed relative to a vacuum is $1/1.333$, or about 75 percent as fast.

The outer surface of the human cornea is curved in a way that causes light rays striking it and passing into the aqueous interior to bend toward the center, the first step in achieving focus. The partially focused light then goes through a thin, flattened crystalline lens—with a refractive index greater than water—to complete the focusing process. When everything works correctly, a fully focused image falls on the light-sensing receptors in the retina.

A fish's eye, on the other hand, cannot make use of the difference between refractive indices of the media outside and inside the eye, because they are essentially the same substance: water. Light remains unfocused after passing through the cornea, and the entire burden of focusing the image falls on the lens. The bigger job requires a thicker, rounder, and more powerful lens, with a higher refractive index, than the lens of the mammalian eye.

The difference in lens architecture between human and trout eyes also necessitates a change in the focusing mechanism. In both cases, provision must be made for the fact that light reflecting from near objects will focus at a different point than light from distant objects, unless some accommodations are made. Our eyes handle the situation by changing the shape of the lens using muscles attached to it. The human lens is curved but relatively flat. Muscles stretch and further flatten the lens to focus light from distant objects, and pull in a different direction to curve and thicken it for focusing on closer objects.

The thick, relatively inflexible round lens of a trout's eye is not easily amenable to shape shifting. Instead, the whole lens is pulled backward toward the retina to focus on distant objects, by a muscle attached to its bottom edge. Close focus is achieved by relaxing the muscle to allow the lens to return to its resting position farther from the retina.

This design means that trout are shortsighted. When relaxed, their eyes are focused on near objects, and they can focus very closely indeed—on objects only one or two inches from their noses. It is more of an effort for them to see distant scenes clearly. It also means that trout eyes have a tremendous "depth of field," so that when focused on an object about two feet away, everything from two feet to infinity is simultaneously in focus. Of course, in a fish's watery world, infinity is usually not very far away. Visibility never exceeds one or two hundred feet, even in the clearest midocean water. Fresh water contains more particulates, including sediments and microorganisms, so visibility in typical trout habitat is seldom more than twenty feet, and often much less. Thus environmental conditions are more of

The eye of a trout is tailored for operation in an aqueous medium, necessitating differences in design from a human eye.

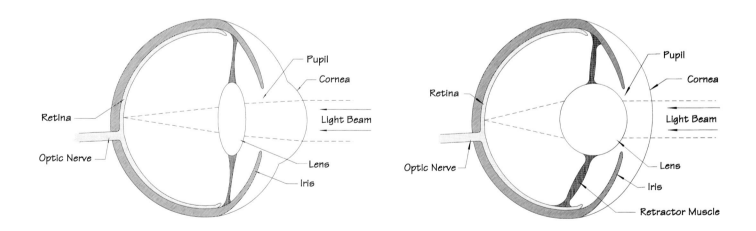

Human (left) **and Trout** (right) **Eyes** share the same basic components of cornea, iris, pupil, lens, and retina. But whereas the human eye relies on the cornea for initial light refraction and partial focusing, that job falls entirely to the large spherical lens in a trout's eye. Focusing of near and far objects is also accomplished by different mechanisms. In humans, the lens is flattened or thickened; in trout, the lens is moved closer to or farther from the retina by a retractor muscle.

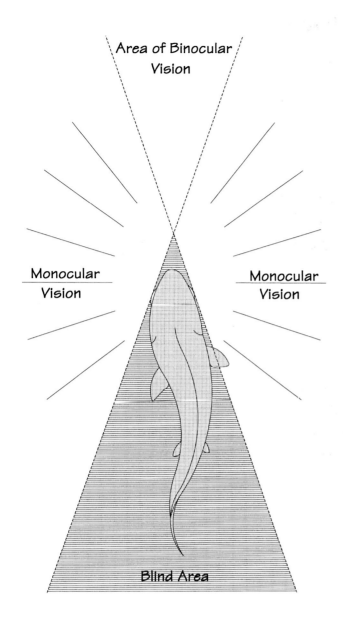

Area of Binocular Vision

Monocular Vision

Monocular Vision

Blind Area

Placement of a Trout's Eyes on the side of its head, slightly forward of center, gives it a very wide field of view. Lateral objects are observed with just one eye, objects in front can be seen stereoscopically, and anything directly behind the trout is not visible.

a limitation than eye design when it comes to viewing distant underwater objects.

Not only do the shortcomings of the aqueous medium restrict clear vision, but studies indicate that trout eyes are also inherently less able than ours to distinguish details. That may come as a surprise to any angler who has marveled over the ability of a picky trout to consistently discriminate between mayflies in a complex hatch, not to mention the small differences between the counterfeits we proffer. Yet the receptor density—a limiting determinant of detail resolution—in the retina of a trout is severalfold lower than in the human eye. Reduced receptor density and lens size, together with studies on the ability of juvenile trout to distinguish details of objects at various distances, are consistent with a maximum visual acuity that is four to fourteen times inferior to humans. While it is known that receptor density increases a bit in older trout, the gain would still leave even a large fish with vision less sharp than our own.

Somewhat offsetting a trout's reduced visual acuity is its close-focusing ability. Just as we can make out details and read even very small type if we bring it close to our eyes (at least until we grow older and lose our near-focusing ability), so can a trout employ the same maneuver—in spades. A bug that is just a fuzzy blur at a distance should show up in much more detail when it's two inches away.

Taken together, the known facts of trout vision suggest that when feeding, a fish in normal underwater conditions is unable to spot a small bug until it is within several feet of the trout's position. At that distance, the potential prey is indistinct and must display some generalized characteristics to alert the fish to the possibility of its being a genuine menu item. In fast-flowing water, a trout has to react quickly or the prey will pass by and escape. If the reaction time available is very small, as in riffles, runs, and rapids, swift action and prey capture is more important than unerring identification. But in slower, smoother water, where there is more time to study the object, the initial clues induce the fish to move in for a closer look. At a distance of one to three inches, even a shortsighted trout is much more capable of making an informed decision about prey identity.

Another important difference between human and trout vision results from altered placement of the eyes on the head. Our eyes are both situated anteriorly, providing excellent binocular forward vision but leaving us blind in all other directions. The eyes of a trout, in contrast, are set farther back on the sides of the head. This gives it a very wide field of view, though only a portion of the field is seen in stereo. Each eye can see about 180 degrees laterally, and somewhat less in the vertical plane. Most of the visual field is covered by only one eye, but slightly forward placement enables binocular vision in a 45-degree cone extending in front of and above the fish. Higher concentrations of receptors in the regions of the retina responsible for forward and upward views enhance visual capability in those directions. The penalty for forward eye positioning is a complete lack of coverage directly behind the fish, yielding a narrow blind area in the rear. Thus unless detected by one of its other senses, a trout is unaware of predators or prey approaching from directly astern. On the other hand, its binocular forward vision provides excellent depth perception, a key capability for any predator.

Can trout see in color? That used to be a matter of some debate, but is now long settled by irrefutable scientific research—and the answer is yes. In fact, there are reasons to suspect they have better, or at least more extended, color vision than we do. Behavioral studies show that trout can discriminate not only between objects of different colors, but also between many shades of any one color. What's more, there is evidence that trout at some stages of their lives can perceive ultraviolet (UV), infrared (IR), and polarized light, at wavelengths that escape detection by our own eyes.

Color is a fascinating subject on its own if you stop and ponder it for a while. We know quite a bit about the physiology of color perception, and the basis for discriminating between light of different wavelengths; but color itself is a mental construct. Light isn't colored; it merely generates the sensation of color in our brains. There is no way of knowing whether the way you perceive the color red is anywhere close to the way I perceive it; much less what red looks like to a trout. But that's a discussion for another day. The relevant point here is that trout can distinguish between light of different wavelengths, and they use that capability to help make decisions about whether to accept objects in their realm as desirable prey, or to reject them as irrelevant.

The eyes of rainbow trout contain three types of receptors for light within the wavelength range that our eyes can see, and the absorption properties of the receptors suggest they have comparable capabilities within the familiar red-green-blue (RGB) spectrum. These receptors respond maximally to light at about 580 nm (red), 530 nm (green), or 440 nm (blue). For comparison, human retinal receptors absorb maximally at about 565 nm, 545 nm, and 440 nm. But in both cases the three receptor types are activated by a range of wavelengths on either side of their maxima, and there is considerable overlap. Thus light at a wavelength of 470 nm stimulates the blue receptor most strongly, but it also stimulates the green and red receptors to lesser extents. This overlap in receptor sensitivity is critical to perceiving the full spectrum of colors in the visible range. By comparing how much each receptor type is stimulated, the brain can interpret a wavelength of 470 nm as neither blue nor green, but as some hue in between.

Color perception is influenced by a variety of factors, known and unknown. The absorption spectrum of each receptor—that is, the degree to which it responds to light of different wavelengths—and the amount of overlap between the spectra are very important. Numbers of receptors of each type can also be expected to have a major effect. Beyond the initial light absorption, there is considerable processing of the signal from the receptors in the eye itself, and then in the brain.

When comparing a trout's perception of color with ours, there are a couple of extra variables added to the mix. During at least the early and late (sexually mature) phases of their lives, trout have significant numbers of a fourth type of light receptor that is responsive to UV and polarized light. Those are receptors and sensitivities that we don't have at all. It is virtually impossible to know what color a trout perceives when it looks at an object bathed in the full wavelength spectrum of sunlight, including UV, and maybe with a dose of polarized light as well.

What is the bottom line of all this semitechnical discussion of color vision? Mainly, it's that while we can expect some similarities between the colors that trout and we perceive in an object, it's probably useless to get too wrapped up in trying to exactly duplicate a natural insect's colors in our synthetic flies. The whole enterprise could be undone, for instance, by a marked absorption of UV light in the body of a natural bug, which a trout can see but we cannot. The synthetic materials we use to build the fly are unlikely to absorb similarly; therefore, we have no clue that the color a trout sees in the natural and the imitation are very different.

Trout and human eyes also differ in their ability to control the amount of light impacting the retina. Trout have no eyelids, and their pupils are fixed at a single size: wide open. Thus they have no quick and easy way to adjust for changes in light levels. With eyes that are naturally more sensitive to light than ours, that inability creates difficulties in dealing with bright light. It's probably similar to what we experience when coming out of a dark theater into sunlight, before our pupils have had a chance to adjust. Or even more aptly, to those occasions when an optometrist puts dilating drops in our eyes to prevent contraction of the pupils. So trout are essentially photophobic, and tend to be more active during the times when light levels are moderate, such as early morning, evening, and cloudy days.

Though trout can't make quick adjustments to light intensities, their eyes do undergo slower, dramatic transitions to handle the different levels of night and day. Like us, trout have two categories of light receptors, cones and rods. The cones are fewer in number but respond to variations in wavelength, enabling color vision. Rods aren't responsive to color differences but are more sensitive to low light levels. In trout, cones are at the surface of the

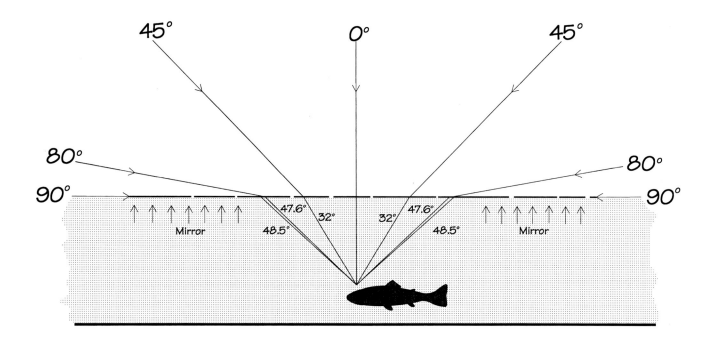

The Trout's Window into the world above the water surface. Light from the atmosphere above the surface, comprising 180 degrees (in cross section) from one horizon to the other, is bent and compressed into about 97 degrees (48.5 degrees on each side of vertical) upon penetrating the water. Compression is greatest near the edges, where the 10 degrees of light nearest the horizon are compressed into about 1 degree underwater. However, most of the light in that region doesn't penetrate the water at all, and is instead reflected. In consequence, there isn't enough light for a trout to see anything from the horizon to about 10 degrees above it. The net result is a cone of useful light with an apex at the trout's eye, and extending about 47.6 degrees around the vertical axis. Within the cone, a trout can see into the space above the surface, though with increasing distortion toward the margins. Outside of the cone, the surface appears as a mirror to the fish, reflecting the bottom of the stream or lake.

retina during the day, while rods are buried within it under a layer of pigment, to protect them from bright conditions. As night approaches, the cones migrate into the retina while the sensitive rods move to its surface. Scientists estimate that trout can see two to four times better in the dark than we can. The whole migration process is reversed a little before dawn. Conversion in each direction takes one to several hours to complete; while it's in progress, color vision is impaired.

It therefore seems likely that color is a less important factor in fly pattern choice during the twilight hours.

UNDERWATER VISION

The medium in which a trout's eye must operate imposes peculiarities of its own, some of them easily apparent to the casual observer, but others not so intuitive. Water is, of course, much more dense than air and interacts with light in its own special ways. First on the list of notable effects is the rapid attenuation of light intensity as it penetrates deeper into the water column, and some of the light is absorbed and converted to heat. Even in very clear water like Oregon's Crater Lake, only about 1 percent of the sur-

face light remains at a depth of one hundred feet. Light reduction is far greater as turbidity increases. Much of the light is scattered in all directions, a phenomenon that is magnified by the presence of suspended particles, from tiny bacteria up to larger sediment plainly visible to our unaided eyes. Light scattering causes a marked reduction in the light's directionality, enveloping everything in a diffuse dim glow. It also results in a profound decrease in contrast so that objects in even the clearest water appear as if in a fog that increases the farther the object is from the observer. Add in small amounts of fine suspended sediment and algae and, from a submerged position, the water can quickly take on the appearance of a cloudy soup; even though it may look remarkably clear to an above-water observer peering down into relatively shallow water.

The attenuation of light intensity with increasing water depth and turbidity is not uniform across all wavelengths. In pure water, blue light (about 460 nm) is the least affected, with attenuation increasing for both longer and shorter wavelengths. Red light drops off quickly, being absorbed within the first few meters. But in water with significant amounts of organic material, particularly algae, the

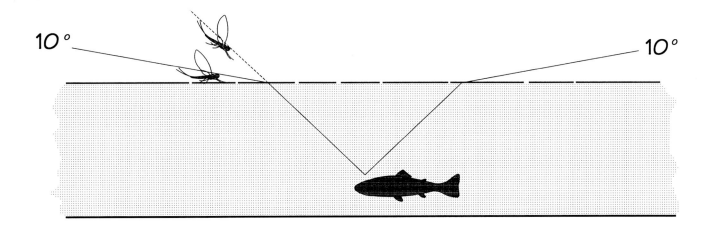

Seeing Around Corners. The vast majority of the light striking the water from the horizon to 10 degrees above it is reflected, so any object (such as an insect on the surface) in that region is invisible to a trout below. As a bug approaches Snell's window, its upper parts (like raised wings) intersect the 10-degree line and start to appear in the edge of the window. The light reflected from the wing tips is bent as it goes underwater, allowing the trout to "see around the corner." The fish perceives the observed wing to be directly along its line of sight, as depicted by the dotted line above the surface.

overall color frequently appears green. That's because chlorophyll efficiently absorbs blue but not green wavelengths. Thus depending on water depth and the quantity and nature of suspended particles, the color of objects—including bugs and flies—may be quite different than they appear to us in the air above.

The Window

Many fly fishers have heard of the "window" at the water surface, through which a fish can see objects above—including floating insects, predatory birds, and approaching anglers. It's often referred to as "Snell's window," after the scientist who formulated the laws governing the phenomena responsible for its existence. The surface window and the mirrorlike area surrounding it are probably the most important, and underappreciated, aspects of underwater vision impacting our sport. So let's take a look at their nature and the implications for the way trout see prey and the flies that imitate them.

When light from the atmosphere strikes the water surface, part of it is reflected, part is absorbed, and part is transmitted. The portion that is transmitted into the water is greatest when the angle of incidence is 90 degrees to the surface (referred to as the normal angle)—in other words, straight down. As the angle of incidence increases, more and more of the light is reflected and correspondingly less enters the water. At about 80 degrees or more from the normal (that is, about 10 degrees or less above the horizon), virtually all of the light is reflected and none is transmitted below the surface. Light rays that do penetrate the water are bent according to Snell's Law, which states that light passing from a less dense medium to a denser one will slow down, and that at any incident angle other than the normal (perpendicular), it will change direction. The greater the angle, relative to the normal that the light strikes the surface, the greater will be the amount of bending in the denser medium.

What this means on a lake or stream is that when light strikes the water from directly above, it goes straight through and remains on the same path. As the angle increases, the light is bent more and more until, at slightly less than 90 degrees from normal (i.e., almost parallel to the surface), light striking the water is bent to 48.5 degrees from normal. Another way of putting it is that 90 degrees of atmospheric light is compacted into 48.5 degrees when it arrives at the trout's eye underwater. Examination of The Trout's Window diagram on page 188 should help make this concept clear.

Physics thus dictates that all of the light striking a trout's (or any other organism's) eye from above the surface is contained within a 97-degree cone, with the eye at its apex. The cone moves with the trout wherever it goes. The angles never change, but as the fish goes deeper, the circle inscribed by the cone on the surface gets larger; and conversely, as it approaches the surface, the circle gets smaller. That circle is the trout's window into the world above. Within it, objects (like insects and flies) on the surface are visible, as well as anything beyond the surface, such as ospreys and fly fishers. Outside the window, nothing above the water can be seen. That part of the surface appears as a mirror to the fish.

Now that I've laid out the basic principle, let me do a little fine-tuning. First, while the theoretical angle of the underwater cone is about 97 degrees, covering 180 degrees of view above the water, in reality the edges of the cone contain very little light. Look again at The Trout's Window diagram. Light originating near the horizon, at almost 90 degrees from the normal angle, strikes the water surface so obliquely that most of it is reflected and very little enters the water. In fact, from the horizon to about 10 degrees above it, the amount of light penetrating the water is too little to be visually useful. To the fish, that part of the field appears as a fuzzy dark area on the edge of the window. So for practical, visual purposes, the dimensions are somewhat different: 160 degrees of above-water light (subtracting 10 degrees above the horizon on each side) is squeezed into an underwater cone of slightly more than 95 degrees. I'm not just nitpicking here; the 10-degree "blind" area above the horizon, into which a trout cannot see, has important implications as you'll see below.

Second, squeezing 160 degrees of the above-water visual field into 95 degrees underwater inevitably leads to some distortion in the surface window. Since most of the squeezing goes on at edges, that is where most of the distortion occurs. A bug on the surface exactly in the middle of the window is hardly distorted at all, assuming flat conditions without ripples. As the bug moves toward the perimeter of the window, it appears progressively shorter and wider, until at the very edge it looks to the trout below like a very squashed bug indeed.

Lastly, objects at the edge of the window appear from below as if tilted forward and much higher above the horizon than they really are. That is because light reflected from the surface object is literally bending around corners. As a result, light from the front of a fly, rather than its bottom, is directed down into the trout's visual path. But the trout doesn't realize that it is seeing around a corner; it perceives the fly to be along the direction it is looking.

The Mirror

Let's turn our attention now from the clear window in the roof of the underwater world to the reflective area surrounding it. No light that a trout can see from its position penetrates this region from above; all incident light in that area of the air-water interface is reflected back up into the atmosphere. The same phenomenon takes place in reverse on the trout's side of the boundary: all light (visible from the trout's position) in that section of the surface is reflected back down toward the bottom. Thus the surface area outside of the window acts as a perfect mirror if the water surface is smooth, and a distorted mirror if it is riffled.

The way that a trout might utilize that mirror is something that most fly fishers probably haven't given much thought. For instance, everyone knows that the hooks on their dry flies hang beneath the surface (except for infrequently employed inverted patterns). But how many realize that when those flies are approaching on the current from upstream, the trout sees two hooks—one real, the other reflected—before the fly enters Snell's window? Similarly, when an insect like a big salmonfly is struggling in the surface film, with its legs dangling underwater, a trout may see twelve legs instead of six while the bug is outside the window. And as we saw in chapter 11 for some of the still-water bugs, an insect like an aquatic beetle or backswimmer that hangs just beneath the surface will appear as twins to the trout, until it moves out of the mirror region and into the window.

Another way that a trout may use the mirror is to look behind objects on the bottom. For instance, a rock might block a trout's view of a predator or prey hiding on the other side. But glancing up at the mirror, the lurker's presence is revealed. In this way a trout can avoid dangers and find a meal that it might otherwise have missed.

Brian Clarke and John Goddard pointed out in *The Trout and the Fly* that if a wet fly has a light-colored back, it might increase its chances of exciting a fish's interest. It seems probable that fish in still or calm water use the mirror to watch for prey that might be skulking on the bottom. If it has a light back, a wet fly will stand out in the mirror against the reflection of the dark lake bottom. Coupling a light dorsal side with a dark ventral side might offer the best of both worlds: a fish below the fly will see a dark silhouette against a light sky, and a fish above it may see the light back of the fly itself or its reflection in the mirror. Maybe that is one of the secrets to the success of the popular Prince Nymph: dark brown on the bottom, with white wings on its back. The red thread often incorporated into the head can't be bad for visibility, either.

While in the mirror area of the surface, from underwater the bend of a dry-fly hook appears twice—the actual hook below, and its reflection above.

An insect, like this backswimmer resting just under the water surface, is reflected in the mirror area and appears to be twins from below. A swarm of them could be even more confusing.

When viewed directly, a rock on the bottom blocks from view anything behind it.

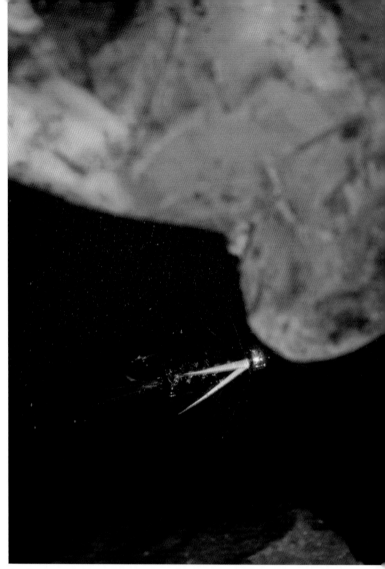

A glance at the surface reveals objects lurking behind the rock: predators, prey, or, in this case, a Prince Nymph.

MODELING THE STREAM SURFACE

As air-breathing anglers, we seldom get the chance to view the world from underwater—from our quarry's point of view. And even if we don mask and snorkel to venture into the chilly depths, the opportunity for leisurely examination of bugs and flies floating naturally on the currents is limited. Short of joining the fishes, is there a way to get something approaching a trout's-eye view of our flies, and the bugs they represent? Can we just put a fly or an insect into a glass of water and take a look?

While the glass-of-water ploy is better than nothing—we can at least see how the color of a fly changes when wet—it leaves a lot to be desired if the goal is to come as close as possible to seeing things like a fish would. Because of the way light bends when it enters water, the view that a trout has of the surface is impossible to see through the side, or even the bottom, of a drinking glass.

So how about an aquarium? We're getting closer now. A good quality rectangular aquarium offers less distortion and improved clarity compared with a drinking glass. It's a great way to view objects that are completely underwater. But if you kneel down and try to look through the side of a standard rectangular aquarium up toward the surface, you'll experience some difficulties. The surface appears to slant upward at an extremely steep angle, and assuming the aquarium is not extraordinarily wide, what little you can see of the surface is mostly a reflection of the rear wall of the aquarium. It's all "mirror," with only a tiny slice of the far edge of Snell's window right up against your side of the glass. Surely this is not the way a trout sees it. What's going on here?

The problem with viewing the water surface through an ordinary aquarium is that the side of the tank through which you are looking presents a second light-bending interface.

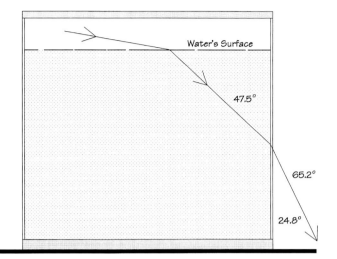

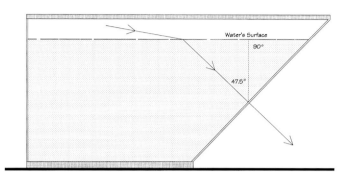

Rectangular Aquarium. From an observer's position just outside the bottom right of the tank, light entering the water from above is first bent downward at the water surface near the edge of Snell's window, and then bent downward again as it leaves the side of the aquarium. Thus to see even the far edge of Snell's window, an observer's eye must be very low and close to the side of the tank. Light rays entering more centrally in Snell's window emerge from the tank at even more oblique angles, making it virtually impossible to see them from the side.

Slant Tank. Light enters the tank in the same way it would in a rectangular aquarium. But because the viewing side is slanted by 47.5 degrees, light from the edge of Snell's window passes through it perpendicularly and is not bent, permitting observation without interference from the tank walls. Note that as an observer looks more vertically into Snell's window, the light from the surface hits the wall at an increasing angle and is bent again; so the observer must move toward the tank to see those areas.

Snell's Law applies here just like it does at the water surface. After having been bent once when it entered the water through the surface, to reach your eye the light leaves the dense water, crosses even denser glass, and then passes into the much less dense air. The net result is that light rays from the surface are bent sharply downward when they come out the side of the aquarium. No matter how close you get to the side of the tank while looking upward, you can't get a good view of the water's surface. The Rectangular Aquarium diagram shows how the light path in a regular aquarium makes surface-viewing impractical.

What we need is something like an aquarium, but with a viewing side that won't bend the light rays (much) as they leave the tank. The only way to achieve that is to arrange for the light to exit the aquarium at 90 degrees (or very nearly so) to its side; Snell's Law stipulates that light passing through a density boundary will stay on the same path only when at a right angle to it.

The solution is simple enough: just build a tank with a slanted side so that light coming from the part of the surface of most interest hits it at 90 degrees. In other words, a "slant tank." In our case the part of the surface of particular interest is the edge of Snell's window as perceived by a trout. The edge of Snell's window is about 47.5 degrees from vertical. So if our slant tank has a viewing side inclined forward by that same amount (47.5 degrees), light from the edge of the window will pass straight through to our eyes; just like it would if a fish were in our position. The Slant Tank diagram demonstrates the principle. With a slant tank constructed according to this design, we can see anything at the edge of Snell's window without artifacts introduced by the tank walls.

Side view of an acrylic slant tank. Note the tan paper-covered piece of plastic on the bottom, which will be reflected in the water surface at some viewing angles. A red rock provides scale and orientation.

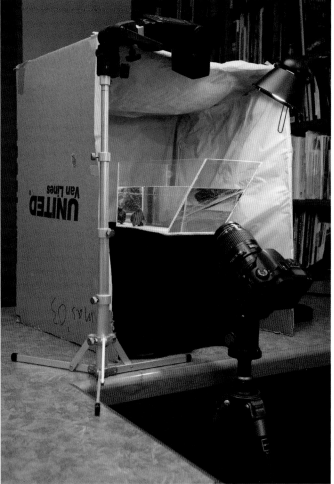

Slant tank setup for photography. A box with a blue-painted interior above the tank simulates the blue sky. An electronic flash provides photographic lighting and is positioned to simulate the sun. A lamp at the right provides working and focusing illumination. The approximate position of the camera is illustrated, but in practice no tripod is used. Living bugs move around, so the camera has to move to follow them.

Now that the principle of the slant tank is clear, let's move on to using it. I built a slant tank of clear $^1/8$-inch acrylic plastic, 6 inches wide by 6 inches high, and with a bottom $8^1/2$ inches long slanting up to a top that is $13^3/4$ inches. When observed through the slanted side of the tank, anything on the surface above Snell's window will be visible. Beyond the edge of the window, the surface acts as a mirror, reflecting whatever is in the bottom of the tank. For the purposes of visibility and contrast, I covered the

The view of the water surface through a slant tank. The camera was positioned in front of the slanted side of the tank so that the boundary between Snell's window (blue area, top) and the mirror region (tan area, bottom) of the surface was near the middle of the frame. A red rock on the bottom is reflected in the surface mirror. Two identical, hackled dry flies were placed on the water surface—one within Snell's window, the other in the mirror region. For the latter fly, only the portions that extend below the surface are visible from our position.

bottom of the tank with tan-colored paper, which shows up in the mirror area of the surface. In some cases I placed a cutaway cardboard box, with a painted blue interior, above the tank to simulate the blue sky. Above and to one side of the tank was an electronic flash, pointed down into the water and simulating the sun. On the other side of the tank was a lamp so that I could see what I was doing.

I know that after all this buildup, you must be eager to see the view through the side of this tank. In the photo-

graph of the water surface through the slant tank, the part of the surface in Snell's window is the blue area at the top, and the tan area below is a reflection of the tan-colored bottom of the tank. I placed a red rock on the tank bottom to help with orientation. One fly is floating on the surface in the window; another identical one is floating in the mirror area. This photo clearly shows the boundary between the two regions, and the dramatic difference in appearance of an object floating inside or outside Snell's window.

Slant tank photo of a *Cinygmula* mayfly dun on the mirror area of the water surface. In this frame, we are looking up at the surface at an angle greater than 47.5 degrees, so the predominant view is of the tan bottom of the tank reflected in the surface mirror. Snell's window is outside of the frame. At center bottom we can see the disturbances of the surface created by the dun's feet as it stands on the water, as well as by a portion of its abdomen that is dragging a bit. The bug itself—legs, body, wings—above the surface is shielded from view.

In this frame, the dun is standing half in, half out of Snell's window. Its body is now visible, and the wings have merged with it. It's now a recognizable, if distorted, bug.

The bug is now fully in the window and the details are getting clearer.

Let's move on now to the heart of the exercise—to see how real bugs and flies look on the surface of the water from a trout's position. The accompanying photo series shows a *Cinygmula* mayfly dun, initially on the mirror region of the surface, then entering the edge of the window, and finally fully within it. This is the sequence that a trout would see while watching the dun drift toward it on the current.

I've photographed several different species of mayfly duns in the slant tank, and though a few details vary, they all look essentially like the shots of the *Cinygmula*. Many newly hatched duns will pull their abdomen and tails up off the water as soon as they can, standing on their tiptoes as if straining to reach the sky. So the dimples of their footprints would be the only clues of their presence in the mirror region of a trout's view.

The *Cinygmula* dun moved very little during the photo session, so the varying positions relative to the window were primarily due to my moving the camera forward, thereby changing the position of the window. Exactly the same thing would occur if a trout were swimming forward in the direction of a bug on the surface. The principle is identical for a stationary trout watching an insect drifting toward it.

In the second frame of the series, the dun is still standing in the mirror area, but the edge of the (blue) Snell's window area has come into view at the top. Note that the tips of the dun's upright wings are becoming visible in the window, but appear separated from the impression of the feet on the mirror's surface.

5

As the dun moves deeper into the window, details of the abdomen start to show up.

6

The dun rotates as it reaches a point well within the window, and the clarity of the view is notable.

Trout in flowing water usually take up a position on the bottom, shielded from the direct current and facing upstream. From this station they watch for food coming down the conveyor belt. In order to intercept a bug drifting along on the surface currents, a trout has to look well upstream to anticipate the target's arrival at the critical area of attack. So the first place a trout sees a surface insect is in the mirror area, outside Snell's window. The only parts of a bug that can be seen there are those that penetrate below the surface, or distort the surface film. As the bug enters the window, body parts above the surface start to material-ize, but with lots of distortion. Finally, when the bug is well into the window, everything becomes clear.

Studies show that most trout holding in a significant current initiate their rise to surface prey before the target enters the window of clear vision. For a lightweight insect like a mayfly dun, which stands on the surface film rather than floating within it, the fish must therefore recognize and respond to the tiny indentations where the film is bent. Most of the time trout rise at about a 45-degree angle to meet the approaching meal, keeping it right at the edge of Snell's window.

In fast water, a trout probably gets just a quick, distorted look at its target as the bug moves into the edge of the window, just before it disappears into the trout's mouth. If the fish lets the target move overhead into the clear portion of the window, the current will sweep the bug behind it and downstream. So the trout has to make a quick decision based on little footprints in the mirror and a quick blurry glimpse at the edge of the window.

The situation is different in slow or still water. A trout can let the potential meal move overhead, then drift back underneath it with the current, or hang motionless beneath it in a lake or pond. The fish gets the chance for a long, clear examination. The last photo of the *Cinygmula* dun demonstrates what good prospects fish in that situation have for making the correct call. It's no wonder that trout in slow, flat water are often hard to fool. Not only do they get the opportunity to closely inspect the fly, but leaders and fly lines cutting across the mirror and the window stand out like sore thumbs if there is no surface chop to break up their outlines.

Are we any closer to understanding the factors involved with inducing a trout to rise and accept our dry flies? I think we can answer with at least a strong "maybe." It's clear that a stream-dwelling trout usually spots its quarry well ahead of it, when the only things visible are those dimples in the surface caused by tiny little feet. The indentations act like small prisms, allowing the light from above to leak through. Against the background of the dark reflected bottom, those little points of light must stand out like stars in the night sky. So it's a pretty safe bet that trout look for stars, and that is the first cue for them to begin to rise. If the insect on which they've been selectively feeding—during a heavy hatch—has a star pattern of approximately six points arranged in an oval shape about 8mm long, then they continue to watch for that pattern.

That is not to say trout count stars or consciously measure dimensions. But they must develop a mental picture of the pattern they're looking for. Small stars in a compact group represent a small, light bug; larger stars, in deeper indentations and farther apart mean a bigger, heavier insect is standing on the other side of the mirror. So the first key to imitation must be in getting a fly's stars to align correctly, or at least satisfactorily.

Once the trout is on the move, it is half committed. Some energy is already being wasted if the rise has to be called off. The fish gets one last chance to abort as it approaches the edge of the window, where it anticipates some confirming evidence. What is the first thing it expects to see there? Take another look at the second photo in the *Cinygmula* sequence. For a mayfly dun, the tops of the upraised wings enter the trout's window before any other part of the insect. It is the first solid confirmation that there

is really a bug up there; up to that point the trout has seen only dents in the water.

It was a very similar photograph of a mayfly entering Snell's window that led Vince Marinaro to what he believed was the key to a trout closing the deal: the wing. He said that when feeding on mayfly duns, a trout looks first for the star pattern of the feet, then a natural-looking wing tipping over the edge of the window. So to paraphrase one of the experts: feet and wings—get those right, and you're probably most of the way there in fooling trout in moving water.

Slant tank photos dispel some common notions about what is and is not important in a fly. For instance, a lot of us have been concerned about whether the underside of our flies matches the color of the real bug. At the same time, many anglers think that the topside of a fly is out of sight, out of mind, as far as trout are concerned. So if you incorporate some gaudy bright color in the wing, to more easily see the fly on the water, it won't make any difference to a fish below the fly. And maybe to some trout, it won't. But it's not because they can't see the color in the wing—they can. And there is no doubt that sometimes it matters. On the other hand, trout in fast water probably never see the underside of a bug, or of an angler's fly, because they take it before it gets far enough into their window to show up.

For an illustration of which parts of a dry fly are visible in the water, let's take a look at the well-known Royal Wulff in a slant tank. The first frame in the photo series of the Royal Wulff shows the fly in side view, where we can see all of its appealing features, including the red floss body and white calftail wings. Those attributes are completely invisible to a trout looking upstream into the mirror area of the surface, where only hackle, tail fibers, and the hook can be seen (second frame of the series). As the fly nears the window, a trout sees the tips of the white wings and brown hackle appearing at the edge (third and fourth frames). Not until it is fully within the window can the entire fly and the red body be observed (fifth and sixth frames of the series).

Let me quickly add that the above comments about surface visibility apply primarily to mayfly duns, which hold themselves above the surface. Mayfly emergers and cripples, which are at least partially submerged, will be largely visible from underwater. And low-floating bugs like big stoneflies and terrestrials ride in the film rather than on it, and will be easily seen by trout whether they are in the mirror area or inside Snell's window. So accurate representation of various body parts will likely be more important in those situations.

For instance, a big golden stonefly is anything but light on its feet when it's unlucky enough to find itself in the water. From below, even in the mirror area, it appears in full silhouette with antennae waving and legs kicking.

1

When viewed in profile as it rests on the water surface near the front of a slant tank, all the features of a Royal Wulff dry fly are visible.

2

In the first look at the Royal Wulff that a trout on the bottom of a stream would get, in the mirror area of the surface, only the bend of the hook (and its reflection), as well as some hackle and tail fibers can be seen.

3

As the fly approaches Snell's window, the white calftail wing and some reddish brown hackle above the surface begin to show up at the edge, disconnected from the parts of the fly's underside visible in the mirror area.

4

Further movement of the fly toward the window brings the two parts of the image almost together.

5

With the fly fully into the window, it is now clearly recognizable as a Royal Wulff.

6

As the fly rotates, from below the water, we can make out even the red floss in the body. Note that the body color was not visible while the fly was in the mirror area, even as the wing color became visible in the edge of the window.

The golden stonefly is fully visible from below water even when it's in the mirror area just outside of Snell's window. Reflections give the impression that it has more than the six legs typical of an insect.

Some bugs have a hard time riding high regardless of size. A much smaller stonefly like a yellow sally (Chloroperlidae) often loses the battle with gravity and slips into the film, showing buggy details to any trout lurking below.

Terrestrials generally fall into the same category as stoneflies; unable to perch on top of the surface film, they usually wind up struggling within it. Even the smaller ants seem ill equipped to avoid becoming waterlogged. One interesting thing that I've noticed about ants is that when dropped from the air, they usually land on the water upside down. They struggle mightily to turn over, with legs waving uselessly in the air. Eventually some of them manage to right themselves. But many become waterlogged and sink into the depths, unless a fish eats them first. Beetles float low in the water and do a lot of flailing about without making much progress in any direction. Grasshoppers can sometimes navigate to shore, but their mostly useless kicking generates a lot of commotion. Commotion is not what a bug wants if it's in trout water.

Large caddisflies like *Arctopsyche grandis* (chapter 6) also have trouble standing on the surface film without falling through, but the smaller ones are as good at it as mayfly duns. Many caddisflies don't hang around on the surface very long once they've hatched, but sometimes a dry caddisfly is just what the fish seem to want. Grannom caddisflies (chapter 4) frequently hatch in such massive numbers that there are bound to be lots of adults on the water for a while.

A yellow sally (Chloroperlidae) stonefly may be much smaller than a golden, but it still has trouble walking on water. In this underwater view within the mirror area of the surface, much of the bug rides low enough to be visible.

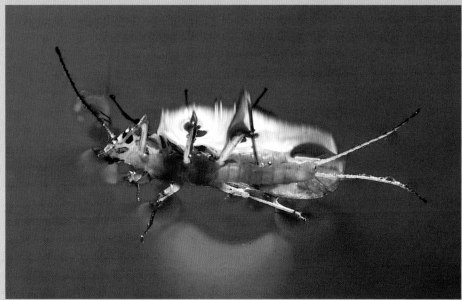

At the edge of Snell's window, all parts of the yellow sally can easily be seen, though a little distorted.

When fully within the window, virtually every detail of the yellow sally stonefly is clear.

When an ant falls into the water, it often lands upside down, as can be seen in this slant tank photo of an ant in the mirror area of the surface.

When an ant does manage to right itself, it has to struggle mightily to keep its head above water. Slant tank photo taken through the nonslanted side.

A low-floating ground beetle shows up in perfect profile in the mirror area of the slant tank.

A grasshopper generates attention-getting waves as it struggles in the mirror area of the slant tank.

A grannom caddisfly standing on the surface creates foot impressions and distortions in the film, allowing some of the blue "sky" above to be seen within the mirror area of the slant tank.

As it moves into the edge of the window, we (or a trout) get a blurry view of the parts of the bug above water.

When well within Snell's window, the grannom caddisfly is fully visible from below.

The wings of a spent spinner create dazzling patterns on the surface, even when viewed in the mirror area of the slant tank.

Mayfly spinners present an interesting case—they are usually easier to see from underwater than above it, particularly those in the spent-wing position. Lying flat in the surface film, often in the low light of dawn or dusk, spinners can be virtually invisible to us. We may see trout noses popping up here and there but have no idea what they're eating. At those times of day, it's a good bet that spinners are generating the activity. Their clear, fluted wings trap air beneath them and act like little prisms. From below, whether in the mirror or the window areas of a trout's vision, they can appear to glow and shimmer with color.

COMPLICATING FACTORS

Examination of insects and flies in slant tanks is a good first step towards visualizing how they must look to trout. Slant tanks do a good job of illustrating the basic principles of underwater vision, and anyone who uses them is likely to come away with new thoughts on the imitation of surface bugs. But like any model, they are simplifications of the real world. The trout's situation in any stream or lake will certainly vary from the ideal conditions of the slant tanks set up in our basement, and the trout's eye will no doubt perceive them differently than our own. You can probably think of a number of factors that will have complicating effects. Here are some that occur to me.

1. **Surface disturbances.** The surface of water in a slant tank is perfectly smooth (assuming you don't shake the supporting table). A lake or slow section of a river may be like that at times, but most often there will be wind ripples or waves or currents or even churning whitewater. Disturbances in the window will cause distortion, hindering clear vision. Waves on the surface in the mirror area will alter the reflection of the bottom and the "starbursts" associated with bug feet. Moreover, there will be small areas in the waves where the plane of the water surface temporarily varies from exactly horizontal. Light from above will penetrate those areas, giving fleeting glimpses of the upper world all the way down to the horizon—briefly eliminating the 10-degree blind region. Rippling water will present moving bits of scenes not unlike the frames in a movie, except more distorted.

2. **Light intensity and direction.** In a natural body of water, all the light comes from above. Its intensity varies with season, time of day, and weather conditions. During the day the direction of the light source goes from low on one horizon, to nearly overhead, to back down on the other horizon. It is

Spent spinners are an equally impressive sight when viewed inside Snell's window.

difficult to reproduce all those variables in a slant tank.

3. **Reflected light.** Light enters a lake or stream through the surface, hits the bottom, and is reflected back up. The nature of the reflected light affects the appearance of objects on the surface. If the water is deep, less reflected light makes it back to the top. A light bottom will reflect more light than a dark one. Clear water will return more light than will murky. All of those variables affect how well the underside of a bug or fly will be illuminated, and how dark the mirror around Snell's window will be. Some of them are difficult to replicate experimentally. For instance, the depth of a slant tank is very shallow by comparison with a river and the water is always clear (if you want to see much of anything). Other variables, like the reflectance of the bottom, are fairly easy to manipulate.

4. **The eye's sensitivity to light.** When we make observations in a slant tank, we are of course using human eyes. Studies indicate that a trout's eyes are more sensitive in low light than ours, so when the light is too dim for us to make out much detail, a trout may still see quite well. Conversely, trout have no eyelids or pupils, so in bright light they may be partially blinded. For a period prior to dawn and dusk, trout eyes undergo a migratory switch between receptor types (rods and cones) differing in sensitivity to light—a phenomenon with unpredictable effects on vision. Slant tank observations don't take such differences into account.

5. **Color perception.** Color is a mental interpretation of data received from retinal receptors sensitive to various wavelengths. Trout eyes have three primary receptors with peak responses to wavelengths not so different from ours. So we can infer that trout color perception in the visual range is similar to human. But the range of responses of the three red, blue, and green receptors is not identical; thus colors perceived by the two species in that range are likely to differ somewhat. Moreover, at least during some portions of their lives, trout can detect wavelengths in the ultraviolet range, as well as polarized light, that we can't see at all. Slant tanks are no help in visualizing the colors that only a trout can see.

6. **Visual acuity.** The average trout eye has significantly fewer retinal receptors than the typical human eye. So its resolution of detail, or acuity, should be correspondingly lower than ours—with visual differences akin to looking at an old-style television

The author's simple bug net, a gift from his then-eight-year-old son, became his primary tool in the studies leading to this book.

versus a new high definition TV. We can see things in a slant tank only through our HDTV eyes.

7. **Contrast detection.** Resolution—the ability to distinguish two closely spaced points—is not the only factor involved in recognizing an object. Contrast also plays a big role. Contrast is the ratio of "lightness" between two adjacent spaces. If the letters on this page were to be printed with progressively lighter ink, at some point the contrast with the white paper would become so low that you wouldn't be able to make out the words, no matter how good the resolution of your eyes. There is evidence that trout eyes are particularly adept at picking out contrasts. Maybe that's how they can spot those bug footprints on the surface—they clearly see the contrasts. Slant tanks don't assist us in understanding how a trout perceives contrast.

8. **Mental abilities.** Most visual processing takes place after the light-responding signals of the retina leave the eye. Almost half of a trout's brain is devoted to sight. Surely some amazing computations and transformation of data into capabilities goes on there, not all of which are the same as in humans. Modeling that process is, of course, completely out of the slant tank's league.

Don't let the above list dampen your enthusiasm for playing with slant tanks. No tool is perfect. The goal is to get meaningfully closer to understanding nature. Slant tanks accomplish that much. After we've learned whatever they can teach us, there will always be more to be concerned about. We'll have to worry about perceptual abilities, behaviors, and who knows what else. It's always something, isn't it? But that's what keeps it challenging and fun. I wouldn't have it any other way.

Index